AREA OF LEGAL JEWISH SETTLEMENT IN RUSSIA IN 1825

W9-DAK-776

ARCHANGEL

VOLOGDA

PERM

VIATKA

ROMA

KAZAN

UFA

NI OROD

ORENBURG

SIMBIRSK

NZA

SAMARA

RATOV

ASTRAKHAN

KAZ

Caspian Sea

RSIA

Provinces within which Jewish settlement was permitted

Provinces where residence rights were withdrawn in 1825

Kurland Province (and the city of Riga) where new Jewish settlement was forbidden

Zone 50 versts from the western frontiers within which new Jewish settlement was forbidden (about 25 miles)

0   100   200   300
Miles

Russia Gathers her Jews

12/25/86

Russia Gathers her Jews

THE ORIGINS OF THE "JEWISH QUESTION" IN RUSSIA, 1772–1825

John Doyle Klier

NORTHERN ILLINOIS UNIVERSITY PRESS

DEKALB, ILLINOIS 1986

Copyright © 1986 by
Northern Illinois University Press
Published by the
Northern Illinois University Press,
DeKalb, Illinois 60115
Manufactured in the
United States of America
All Rights Reserved

Designed by Jo Aerne

Library of Congress
Cataloging-in-Publication Data

Klier, John.
Russia gathers her Jews.

Bibliography: p.
Includes index.
1. Jews—Soviet Union—
History—18th century. 2. Jews—Soviet Union—
History—19th century. 3. Antisemitism—Soviet Union.
4. Soviet Union—Ethnic relations.
I. Title.   DS135.R9K53   1986
947'.004924   86-2473
ISBN 0-87580-117-X

For my parents,
Eugene and Frances Klier,
with love and gratitude

Contents

Illustrations

Maps

PREFACE

espite the physical liquidation and emigration of a great part of East European Jewry, vestiges of the Jewish Question still can be found in the region. Controversy surrounds the treatment of Jews in the Soviet Union, while the Soviet government, for its part, conducts an active policy of "Anti-Zionism," characterized by many affinities to prerevolutionary rhetoric toward the Jews. Neither has the Jewish Question entirely vanished from contemporary Polish politics. Placing these relevant considerations to the side, the history of the Jews in Eastern Europe is also of interest simply on its own terms.

Unfortunately, serious obstacles block the study of East European Jewry in the latter day. Two world wars, the Holocaust, and various cultural purges have removed much of the physical evidence of Jewish life. More important, they also claimed the lives of an entire generation of scholars.

This is not to say that there is any shortage of literature devoted to East European, and especially Russian, Jewry. There exists an impressive corpus of pioneering studies, based on sound methodology and close familiarity with official sources and socioeconomic evidence. Yet this scholarship exists in a curious intellectual vacuum. It dates to the prerevolutionary period and is largely the creation of Russian Jewish historians. They were, for the most part, men of action as well as scholarship, and their research was a weapon in their struggle for human and political rights for Russian Jewry. Their work is a necessary starting point for the study of the Jews, and in a less tragic age would have given rise to reassessments and qualifications. This normal progression failed to occur in the discipline of Russian Jewish history, for the reasons listed above. Consequently, the judgments of these early pioneers and partisans have become securely established in the secondary literature. Even as the study of other areas of Russian and Soviet history has become more sophisticated and diverse, bibliographies devoted to Russian Jewry are dominated by the names of men who wrote their most important works almost a century ago: I. G. Orshanskii, S. M. Dubnow, Iu. I. Gessen, and N. N. Golitsyn, as well as a host of lesser-known adepts.

I. G. Orshanskii, virtually the first significant historian of Russian Jewry, was as renowned for his journalistic polemics on the Jewish Question as for his scholarly studies. Indeed, the two works upon which his reputation as an historian is based, *The Jews in Russia* (St. Petersburg, 1872) and *Russian Legislation on the Jews* (St. Petersburg, 1877), are compilations of articles from Jewish newspapers and scholarly journals. The two foremost professional historians of Russian Jewry, S. M. Dubnow and Iu. I. Gessen, were both influential activists in the struggle for civil rights for Jews in the early twentieth century. The work of the leading anti-Jewish historian, N. N. Golitsyn, *Russian Legislation on the Jews*, was prepared in the 1880s for a government commission charged with reforming the legal position of the Jews. None of these scholars was remote from the political context of the day, and neither were their works.

While the practice of history is seldom enhanced by an attendant political agenda, neither is it invariably invalidated by such preoccupations. Indeed, the very passion with which these polemicist-historians approached their subject makes their biases easy to detect and to filter out. More dangerous, because less obvious, was their collective tendency to rely upon simplified systems of historical causality. Russian Jewish historians especially, writing in the late nineteenth and early twentieth centuries, had no doubts about the political hostility of the Russian state toward the Jews or the level of anti-Jewish popular hatred. They were contemporaries of the physical pogroms of 1881–1882 and 1903–1906, as well as the legislative pogrom which lasted until the revolutions of 1917. Looking back on the nineteenth century, they argued plausibly that the political, economic, and social condition of Russian Jewry as a whole had deteriorated significantly. From their perspective, there was an atmosphere of historical inevitability about this process. The task which historians, Jewish and non-Jewish alike, set for themselves was the identification of the principles which spawned the apparently implacable Russian hatred of the Jews.

All of these scholars were living in a nation with an established religion, the Russian Orthodox Church, which was visible, vigorous, and jealous of its prerogatives. As late as 1911 they witnessed the bizarre incident of a ritual murder accusation—the Beilis Affair—being used to advance the political interests of the state. Small wonder that contemporary scholars therefore pointed to "the tradition of Russian religious intolerance" and "Muscovite xenophobia" as the key factors in the evolution of Russian Judeophobia in the nineteenth and twentieth centuries.

An emphasis on the religious factor dominated the work of Orshanskii, who portrayed Russian legislation concerning the Jews as arising from a historical struggle between native Russian religious hostility, obsessed with the menace of Jewish proselytism among Christians, and a more pragmatic desire to harness the economic resources and energy of the Jewish community for the interests of the state. In this unequal struggle, the greater weight was always on the side of religious interests, which accounted for the overwhelmingly negative character of legislation. Orshanskii was also aware of broader political factors, such as the Russian-Polish struggle in the borderlands, and of economic and social concerns, but he believed these to be shaped by the overarching religious-pragmatic dichotomy.

The strongest and most articulate arguments for a religious foundation for Russian policy are to be found in the numerous works of S. M. Dubnow (Dubnov), one of the founders of the discipline of Jewish history in Russia. The breadth of his scholarship ensured that his opinions would dominate secondary literature on the Jewish Question in Russia. This is particularly so in English; a three-volume translation of his *History of the Jews in Russia and Poland* (Philadelphia, 1916–1920) remains the universally cited work and colors all secondary accounts of Russian Jewry and of Russian policies toward the Jews.

Dubnow emphasized a long tradition of religious antipathy toward the Jews in Russia, originating in Kievan Rus' and developed to horrendous extremes in Muscovy. It was important for Dubnow to argue that this tradition survived into the imperial period because he portrayed resurgent religious intolerance, reinforced occasionally by economic factors, as the motive force in the development of Russian attitudes and legislation. Sudden turns of policy, and indeed any turn of policy which Dubnow perceived as harmful to the Jews, were explained with reference to this tradition. The good intentions of enlightened rulers like Catherine II or Alexander I might dilute or divert this unpleasant reality, Dubnow conceded, but they could never totally suppress it. Dubnow discerned a "Muscovite face" behind the "European mask" of St. Petersburg.

A fundamental flaw in the work of all historians who emphasized the religious theme is a failure to explain what impact Muscovite traditions might have in lands which represented a different cultural and religious tradition, such as Lithuania, Belorussia, and the Ukraine, for this is where "Russian" Jews actually lived. Moreover, the Russian officials charged with dealing with the Jews were not medieval Muscovites, but the offspring of Peter the Great's bureaucratic system, with a different ethos and contrasting values. Nor, in the complex world of the partitioned Polish state, was religious prejudice, however real, an adequate guide for workable policies. Neither Orshanskii nor Dubnow effectively demonstrated how or why religiously motivated anti-Jewish sentiments were the decisive element in Russia's Jewish policies.

Dubnow's only rival as the principal historian of Russian Jewry was Iu.
I. Gessen, whose *History of the Jewish People in Russia* (Leningrad, 1925–
1927) was the last great synthetic history of tsarist legislation toward the
Jews and the motives which underlay it. Whereas Dubnow's great
strength was his familiarity with the internal workings of the Jewish
community, based on a thorough command of Hebrew and Yiddish
sources, Gessen was a master of work in the tsarist archives, both before
and after the 1917 revolutions. As a consequence, his analyses of the
attitudes and assumptions of Russian policymakers are more judicious and
balanced. Gessen saw the motive force of legislation to lie in a mistaken
belief that the Jews posed a serious economic threat, through their exploitive activities, to the native, Christian population. (This was a theme
which had also been struck in N. N. Golitsyn's detailed *Russian Legislation
on the Jews*, with the difference that Golitsyn believed that Jews really did
pose a genuine menace to the economic well-being of the areas where they
lived.) Gessen argued that time and again the Russian administration
made the Jews a scapegoat for the economic activities of the Polish nobility
and the deficiencies of the peasant economy. This misguided decision to
hold the Jews responsible for all economic disorders was complicated by
the attempts of well-intentioned bureaucrats to legislate the problem
away. What resulted were sudden, hasty, and invariably unsuccessful
attempts to change the very character of Jewish life.

After Gessen's last published works in the 1920s, there were a few
efforts by Soviet scholars, largely unsuccessful, to interpret Jewish history
in Russia through a Marxist prism. A few veteran scholars, such as Saul
M. Ginsburg, emigrated to continue a more traditional approach in exile.
The Soviet Great Purge, the Second World War, and the Holocaust put
an end to any remaining efforts. Today, important research into the history of Polish Jewry is continued by the Jewish Historical Institute in
Warsaw, and by such scholars as Artur Eisenbach. Only a few surviving
archives, such as those of the YIVO Institute for Jewish Research in New
York and the Ginsburg Archives in Jerusalem, are open to researchers.
The massive archives of tsarist Russia in the Soviet Union are apparently
closed to foreign and domestic investigators of the Jewish Question. For-
tunately, sufficient archival material has been published to permit charac-
terizations of Russian bureaucratic attitudes toward the Jews. (The archives of the Jewish Committee of 1802–1804, which would be the most
important for the study of the post-partition period, were apparently
destroyed by fire in the early 1860s.)

Except for the translation of Dubnow's work, there is little scholarship
available in English devoted to Russian-Jewish history. The most compe-
tent secondary accounts, Louis Greenberg, *The Jews in Russia* (New
Haven, 1944–1951), and Salo W. Baron, *The Russian Jew under Tsars and
Soviets* (New York and London, 2d rev. ed. 1976), devote little attention to

the subject of this book and seldom go beyond the standard interpretations. Isaac Levitats, *The Jewish Community in Russia, 1772–1844* (New York, 1943), is important and informative, though it is restricted to the internal life of Russian Jewry.

The study of the origins of the Jewish Question in Russia has failed to keep pace with recent scholarship devoted to society and bureaucracy in Russia in general, or the later period of Jewish life in Russia in particular. Isabel de Madariaga, for example, has published a magisterial work, *Russia in the Age of Catherine the Great* (New Haven and London, 1981), which illumines the context in which Russian policies on the Jews developed. Our understanding of the nature and activity of the Russian bureaucratic organs has been expanded by Daniel T. Orlovsky, *The Limits of Reform: The Ministry of Internal Affairs in Imperial Russia, 1802–1881* (Cambridge, Mass., 1981), S. Frederick Starr, *Decentralization and Self-Government in Russia, 1830–1870* (Princeton, 1972), and George Yaney, *The Systemization of Russian Government* (Urbana, Chicago, and London, 1973). Sophisticated studies of the "cadres" of the Russian bureaucracy include W. Bruce Lincoln, *In the Vanguard of Reform* (DeKalb, Ill., 1982), Marc Raeff, *The Origin of the Russian Intelligentsia* (New York, 1966), Richard Wortman, *The Development of the Russian Legal Consciousness* (Chicago, 1976), and P. A. Zaionchkovskii, *The Governmental Apparatus of Autocratic Russia in the Nineteenth Century* (Moscow, 1978). It was this body of often faceless bureaucrats who fashioned the corpus of Russian law on the Jews, and it is crucial to understand their training and value systems as a way of appreciating the motivations underlying their treatment of the Jews.

Important new work has appeared on the modern history of the Jews in Russia, often challenging the traditional interpretations. Michael Stanislawski, *Tsar Nicholas I and the Jews: The Transformation of Jewish Society in Russia, 1825–1855* (Philadelphia, 1983), has detailed the extent to which the theoretical formulations of earlier reigns found practical application under Nicholas I. The consequences of these policies included the virtual destruction of the values of the traditional Jewish community and the massive dislocation and reorientation of Russian Jewish society. Offering a thesis which may be tested by the following study, he has argued that Russian treatment of the Jews was not anomalous and did not differ from the pattern and framework of overall governmental activity. In a series of articles, listed in the bibliography, Hans Rogger has explored the attitude of Russian officialdom toward the Jews at the end of the nineteenth century and has shown the tenuousness of some common assumptions regarding the motivations of Russian legislation. Rogger has questioned the strength of the religious element in Russian Judeophobia and has challenged the belief that later governments cynically manipulated it as a means of deflecting opposition from the government. Perhaps most important, he has demonstrated the widespread sense among Russian bu-

reaucrats that the Jews were a genuine menace to the agricultural population, which had to be protected from them. The circulation of such ideas
in the provinces has been further studied in I. Michael Aronson, "The
Attitudes of Russian Officials in the 1880s toward Jewish Assimilation
and Emigration," (*Slavic Review* 34 [March 1975]), which examines the
provincial committees appointed by the government to make recommendations in the aftermath of the anti-Jewish pogroms of 1881.

   This critical approach to the policies of late tsarism must be brought to
bear on the earlier period, especially because the assumptions developed at
that time endured and influenced policy into the twentieth century. The
concerns of high tsarist officials investigated by Rogger and Aronson have
a familiar ring to anyone acquainted with the views of their predecessors a
century earlier. They were the creators of the twin myths of Jewish
exploitation and the defenselessness of the peasantry.

   A start has already been made on the reinterpretation of the initial
period of Jewish settlement in the Russian Empire. Matthias Rest has
explored the legal aspect of Russian Jewish relations in *Die Russische Judengesetzgebung von der Ersten Polnischen Teilung bis zum "Položenie dlja Evreev"
(1804)* (Wiesbaden, 1975). Arnold Springer, in "Enlightened Absolutism
and Jewish Reform: Prussia, Austria, and Russia," (*California Slavic Studies*
11 [1980]), and "Gavriil Derzhavin's Jewish Reform Project of 1800,"
(*Canadian-American Slavic Studies* 10 [Spring 1976]), has investigated the
attitudes of the representatives of Enlightened Absolutism toward the
Jews in general and toward Russian Jewry in particular. In a series of
articles, cited in the bibliography, Shemu'el Ettinger has explored Russian
attitudes toward the Jews over time and has reevaluated the activities and
assumptions of the Russian bureaucrats who first revealed an awareness of
a Jewish Question in the Russian state.

   The purpose of the present study is to provide a survey of Russia's
acquisition and administration of her Jewish population, which was
gradually gathered under Russian control. It seeks to incorporate the
fresh perspectives which have been brought to bear on Russian, and
especially Russian Jewish, history. It concentrates on the Russian side of
the Russian-Jewish relationship, focusing on three basic questions:
What, for Russians, was the Jewish Question? How did they become
aware of it? How did they propose to deal with it?

   Special attention is given to two subsidiary themes. In the course of the
period under review, Russian Judeophobia was largely transformed from
a simple, primitive religious hatred based on a view of the Jews as deicides
into a set of more sophisticated, modern myths, encompassing a view of
the Jews as participants in a conspiracy directed against the very basis of
Christian civilization. This view predominated in the second half of the
nineteenth century, but its foundation was laid in the period from 1772 to
1825. As will be seen, these concepts largely came from the West. Marc

Raeff, in his article "Seventeenth-Century Europe in Eighteenth-Century Russia?" (*Slavic Review* 41 [Winter 1982]), has noted that "much work is still needed before we can confidently ascertain and assess the process by which Western norms, values, ideas and practices were transferred to Russia in the eighteenth century, or at any other time" (p. 619). This book is a contribution to that ongoing work. It will also serve as a reminder, if one be needed, that contributions of the West to Russian culture could have a darker, malevolent side. Finally, this work traces the survival of these new, imported attitudes and assumptions beyond the period of their initial gestation, emphasizing those elements which became an integral part of Russian Judeophobia as it continued to flourish in the nineteenth century and beyond.

Note on Spelling and Dates

The transliteration system used in this work is that of the Library of Congress, with a few modifications. Names commonly encountered in English are retained: thus, Alexander I rather than Aleksandr I, and Simon Dubnow rather than Shimon Dubnov. Jewish names, with a few exceptions, are transliterated from their Russian forms, as are Hebrew and Yiddish forms used by Russian officials.

This study ranges over five hundred years of Eastern European history and deals with the crossroads of three or four distinct cultures. I have decided to utilize the nomenclature of cities and territories according to the usage of the community politically dominant at that time. (For example, Wilno under Polish rule, and Vilna under Russian rule.) This system is sometimes strained when dealing with the Russian-Polish borderlands and requires the use of two or three variant forms, but has the virtue of avoiding glaring anachronisms. Any confusion will, I hope, be minimized by the accompanying maps.

Dates pertaining to specifically Russian events (e.g., the promulgation of the Statute of 1804) are given according to the Julian Calendar (Old Style), in use in Russia during the period under consideration; this system was twelve days behind the western Gregorian Calendar (New Style). Events of a European character (e.g., the Battle of Austerlitz) are given according to the Gregorian Calendar. Where there is the possibility of confusion, dates are marked O.S. or N.S.

Acknowledgments

When I began a study of the Jewish Question in Russia over a decade ago, I had no idea how much assistance I would require from individuals and institutions. Now, looking back, I am all the more grateful for the bountiful help I have received. Professor Benjamin Uroff, at the University of Illinois, supervised the first incarnation of this book, and I would like to thank him not only for his initial direction but for the training that enabled me to complete the present version. I acknowledge too the continuous support of Ralph T. Fisher and the Russian and East European Center at the University of Illinois.

The final version of this work was much improved by sympathetic readings by John T. Alexander, Hans Rogger, and Robert B. Luehrs. Bibliographical assistance was provided by Gregory Freeze, Carol Nash, Lindsay Hughes, Dianne Farrell, Jean Mingay, David Griffiths, and Pia Pera. I relied heavily upon the swift and invaluable editorial assistance of the entire staff of the Northern Illinois University Press. Special thanks go to my wife, Helen, who was a patient and long-suffering earlier editor, and to Gloria Pfannenstiel, who typed more than one revision.

For the past fifteen years I have been located at Fort Hays State University, the geographical center of the United States. Research on the high plains of Kansas would have been impossible without the generous assistance of Kate Turner Michelson, the staff of the University of Illinois Library Slavic Division, and three inter-library loan librarians at Fort Hays: Mac Reed, Roman Kuchar, and Marc Campbell. I must thank a multitude of libraries, including those of the universities of Helsinki, Harvard, Yale, California at Berkeley, Hebrew Union College, the Jewish Theological Seminary, as well as the New York Public Library, the Library of Congress, and the YIVO Institute of New York City.

I am pleased to acknowledge the financial assistance of the International Research and Exchanges Board, the Fulbright-Hays fellowship program, the Kennan Institute, the University of Illinois Summer Research Laboratory, and numerous grants from the Graduate Research Committee at Fort Hays State University.

A large number of Soviet officials made my research trips to the Soviet Union especially fruitful. I appreciate the excellent working conditions at Leningrad State University, the Library of the Soviet Academy of Sciences in Leningrad, the Leningrad Saltykov-Shchedrin Public Library, and the Lenin Library in Moscow. Special thanks to every Soviet official who signed a *zaiavlenie* the first time a request was made.

Photographs in this work are courtesy of the School of Slavonic and East European Studies of the University of London, the British Museum, and the Polish State Historical Institute. The maps are the work of William L. Nelson.

My family—Helen, Sebastian, and Sophia—have been a loving distraction from the world of kahals and law codes. Finally, this book is dedicated to my parents.

Russia Gathers Her Jews

I

POLANÔ-LITHUANIA: "PARAÔISE FOR JEWS"

T he irony of the Jewish Question in prerevolutionary Russia was that in substance and origin, it was not really "Russian" at all. Russia's miniscule Jewish population was expelled from the country in 1742, and thereafter individual Jews were denied either admission or temporary residence. This situation changed as a consequence of the three partitions of Poland, which gradually introduced the largest Jewish community in the world into the Russian Empire. As a direct result, Russian officials were forced to acquaint themselves with the socioeconomic and political situation of Polish Jewry. They also embarked upon a search for a formula to fit the Jews somehow into the Russian legal system.

While the post-partition period was crucial for the development of Russian-Jewish relations, it had little immediate effect upon Jewish society itself. Life within the autonomous Jewish community went on much as before, a perfect illustration of the Russian proverb "God is in heaven, and the tsar is far away." Outside interference, in the shape of reform or restriction, continually threatened the Jews, but invariably came to naught. The Russian state failed to fulfill its promise of legal equality made under Catherine II or its threats of wholesale transformation made under Alexander I. Both approaches failed equally to destroy the existing system of Jewish autonomous self-government. For their first fifty years as Russian subjects the Jews largely attained their fond wish that the government "not impose any innovations upon us."[1]

But the absence of immediate, practical accomplishments is deceiving. It was during this same period that the most important Russian assumptions about the Jews were formulated. To be sure, the Jewish Question carried a low priority for the Russian administration, but bureaucratic awareness of its existence began to gestate and take shape. For the century after 1825, it is virtually impossible to find attitudes toward the Jews among Russian officials or the educated public that do not have antecedents in this period. Enduring prescriptions for the resolution of the Jewish Question likewise have their genesis before 1825.

Simultaneously, there evolved the legal framework within which the Russian government operated during the nineteenth century. Russian legislation inclined to place the Jews in separate and distinct social and legal categories with their own body of legislation, thus belying an initial willingness to integrate Jews into Russian economic life. Born of pragmatism, this tendency became enshrined in the Russian legal tradition. Originally neutral toward the Jews, legislation was gradually linked with unflattering assumptions about the impact of the Jews on peasant life. These assumptions gave rise to a body of discriminatory legislation, best exemplified by the occupational and residential restrictions known as the Pale of Jewish Settlement. A significant part of this legislation, originating between 1772 and 1825, was still in force in the waning years of the monarchy's existence. A knowledge of the genesis of Russian assumptions about the Jews and the legislation to which they gave rise is indispensable for a clear understanding of the fate of the Jews in the Russian Empire prior to 1917.

Before turning to the "Russian" Jewish Question, however, it is necessary to consider the "Polish" Jewish Question. As noted above, when Russians came first to deal with the Jews, they encountered institutions, practices, laws, customs, and prejudices which had been developed during the centuries-long sojourn of Jews in the Polish state.

Jewish settlement in Kievan Rus' long antedated Jewish colonization in Poland. But while the Jewish population disappeared in most of the successor states of Kiev, it grew to enormous size in Poland. The origin of the Jews of Poland remains controversial; it is shrouded in mystery, legend, and fantasy. Identifiable Jewish settlements cannot be found in Poland earlier than the mid-twelfth century. Two "German migrations" of Jews can be dated to the late thirteenth century and to the fifteenth century. These two influxes were in response to a complex mixture of mercantile opportunities in Poland and religious persecution in Western Europe. Polish sovereigns received all settlers in their eager desire to populate the country's empty marches. "Germans" were especially welcomed because they frequently helped to constitute a commercial class which native Poles had not developed. In this case, the economic activity of a Jew from Germany was fully as welcome as that of a Christian. The Christian Church displayed some antipathy to the Jews here as elsewhere, but this was not as yet a popular phenomenon.[2]

Migrating Jews, like migrating German burghers, brought with them the same relationships that bound them to Western rulers. In the West,

Jews who could perform services or provide goods were given a form of royal protection whereby they were seen as the prince's servants, subject to his will and disposition, a legal status defined as *Kammerknechte*. This concept was imperfectly transplanted to Poland: while the Jews of Poland never acquired the legal status of Chamber Serfs *(servi Camerae)*, they did enter into an analogous relationship with the kings of Poland.[3] This relationship was mutually advantageous. The kings protected the Jews from various antagonistic forces, and in their turn the Jews provided special duties, services, and revenues. The latter differed from place to place but were often an important source of royal revenue.

This spirit of royal toleration was rooted firmly in the idea of financial advantage gained from the Jews, and it was obvious that a decline either in the power of the king or of the revenue production of the Jews could have disastrous consequences for the latter. The Jewish communities of Poland were well aware of this implied threat and were usually diligent in paying, or making at least a *pro forma* attempt to pay, the financial obligations which they owed the crown. The actions of the Polish kings provide ample proof that their interests were pragmatic and financial. In Germany even Jews living on nonroyal estates were subject to the jurisdiction of the ruler. In Poland the kings were uninterested in those who had been forced for various reasons to reside on the domains of noble landowners. The Sejm Constitution of 1539 and the Directive of Sigismund Augustus (28 January 1549) both made clear that such Jews were the concern of the landowner. By the end of the sixteenth century the Jews were under the protection of the king *only* if they dwelt on crown lands.[4]

As wards of the Polish crown the Jews received all their rights and privileges in Poland in the form of special grants from the kings, this being another reflection of the Polish adoption of German-Jewish practices. In fact the first Polish privileges emanating from the court were verbatim imitations of Western models. The most famous Polish charter for the Jews, that of Boleslaw the Pious (16 August 1264), which granted special concessions to some Polish-Jewish communities, was copied from a grant of Ottokar of Bohemia (29 March 1254).[5] This charter of Boleslaw was a mutually advantageous agreement. It granted the Jews inviolability of person and property, guaranteed protection of their public and private religious practices, and placed litigation between Christians and Jews under the jurisdiction of the king himself or his representative, the *wojewoda* (palatine), who served as royal administrator in the Polish provinces.[6]

There is no doubt that the Jews recognized the importance of these grants. Any privileges granted by a particular king had to be confirmed by his successors in order to retain their validity. There was no guarantee that a new ruler would confirm past privileges or would not retract those he had already given. (Such an instance occurred in 1454 when King Casimir IV yielded to clerical pressure and for a brief time rescinded the privileges he had granted the year before.) Typical of medieval practice, there was no uniformity of application: privileges were often granted only to a certain area or to a specific community, the collection of such privileges thus giving the appearance of a legal patchwork quilt. While it was improbable that a king would ever allow the general collection of nationwide privileges to lapse, failure to confirm a particular grant, especially one relating to a trade concession, could have ruinous repercussions. Each community therefore carefully guarded copies of general and particular grants and diligently applied for reconfirmation at each royal coronation.[7] It was vital for the Jews not only to gain confirmation of desired privileges but to preserve original copies of those granted in the past as added proof of their existence. Damage to communal archives was invariably followed by a request from the community concerned that the king issue another royal patent.

The grant of privilege charters to the Jews of Poland accompanied and encouraged the rise of the autonomous Jewish community, an institution that was to play an important part in Jewish life in Poland before and after the partitions. The mingling of the secular and the religious in the life of Polish Jewry made necessary the rise of such communities wherever the national government would permit it. The need for cemeteries, ritual baths, dietary supervision, organized worship, and schooling, as well as the human desire to dwell among cultural compatriots, all played a role in this growth. In addition, the financial demands placed upon Polish Jewry were best met through such organizations. Salo Baron's general synopsis of Jewish communal growth is certainly applicable to Poland:

> There is little doubt that much of Jewish communal evolution can be explained only by the state's self-interest in the effective fiscal and ecclesiastical organization of Jewish subjects; the influence of political and economic struggles between the organized Jewish group and similar groups among their neighbors, especially the burghers; the evolution of corporate bodies in a particular society; the forces of imitation of institutional and legal patterns developed by the non-Jewish nations; and, generally, by that subtle and often indiscernible interplay of social and cultural influences between the Jews and their environment.[8]

For their part, the Jews of Poland formed special communal structures in response to communal needs and to specific external pressures placed upon them by the state. The community organization was well suited to lobby for the confirmation of privileges. For instance, the confirmation patent of Sigismund Augustus in 1549 came in response to requests by the elders of the Jews of Great Poland.[9] This need for an effective means of reconfirmation undoubtedly strengthened the growing communal structure, a structure that could easily be utilized to lobby for royal grants and even to negotiate with royal officials on the sum of taxes due.[10]

The Polish crown, to which most Jews were at first directly subordinated, cared little about the problems of the internal administration of Polish Jewry. This lack of interest lasted as long as duties and services were rendered promptly. Moreover, the crown was quite willing to acquiesce in the growth of a wide-ranging communal autonomy which corresponded to that enjoyed by many corporate bodies within the decentralized Polish state. As early as the 1367 privilege of Casimir the Great (reconfirmed in 1453), it was made clear that judgment in cases involving only Jewish litigants was the responsibility of the Jewish community elders. A court case would be moved to the jurisdiction of the wojewoda court only if the communal leaders refused to accept it, and this was a very rare occurrence. The elders' decisions were to have the force of law.[11] Having granted these concessions, the privileges said nothing regarding the selection of these oft-referred-to elders, this being tacitly left to the discretion of the wojewoda.[12] A typical arrangement was that granted to the Kraków Jews by the wojewoda Tescyński on 9 April 1527. This generous grant provided that litigation between Jews and Christians be decided by the wojewoda, assisted by Jewish elders whom he would appoint. Differences between the Jews themselves were to be resolved by their rabbis, as determined by the appropriate dictates of the Mosaic Law. Lastly, the Jews could be judged only in their own section of the city and could be imprisoned only in their own prisons.[13] In a subsequent decree of 1532 the king even more forcibly recognized the responsibilities of the rabbis by giving them "power to administer and direct the synagogue, and to punish, rectify and chastise the Jews regarding their excesses and crimes in their rite and transgression of their faith, and to assume judgment in all other things, with the counsel of the elders, to the extreme of life itself, according to Mosaic law."[14]

Under Sigismund Augustus in 1551 the community began to crystallize into its final form. The community, or *kehillah* (*kahal* in its Polish form), was made more powerful on the local level, and its autonomy was recognized.[15] The king himself surrendered the right to appoint rabbis, a right which he had enjoyed and exercised almost from the beginning of Polish-Jewish relations, and the local Jews themselves now received the prerogative. The community often reflected a certain tension between the religious and the secular power (i.e., between the rabbi and the elders), and the rabbi was soon displaced as the actual head of the community by the elected elders. A Poznán decree of 1571 indicates the new functions of the elders:

Firstly, if there be some truant [*discolos*] Jews and sinners in Jewish law, the Jews themselves, through their elders, shall proceed to reprove, to chastise, and to punish according to their custom in all transgressions, or even to expel and extirpate [them] from the city, or to deprive [them of] life, that in [such cases] no difficulty or impediment be imposed on the palatine.[16]

As the autonomy of the kahals grew there was a theoretical diminution in the jurisdiction of the wojewoda. However, the wojewoda was actually deprived of few prerogatives of real importance in the Jewish community's relations with the Gentile world. An example of such lost powers, for instance, was the surrender of the wojewoda's right to make Jews appear in court on the Sabbath or on Jewish holidays. In fact, as the power of the kings declined the wojewoda came more and more to stand as the sole administrative defender of the Jews against the attacks of hostile neighbors.

Jewish communal institutions grew more complex and sophisticated in the seventeenth century, culminating in the great Jewish Congress, or Va'ad. This council of representatives of all the kahals of Poland and Lithuania had its origin in the crown's despair at trying to tax the Jews individually. Instead, it was realized that they might be successfully assessed as a community for a negotiated amount, just as the crown did with the cities. The resultant Council of the Four Lands (Va'ad Arba Arazot) provided an opportunity for the Jewish Leadership to meet and consult on matters of common interest.[17] Reflecting the conflict of interests that remained between Polish and Lithuanian Jews as well as Gentiles after the Union of Lublin of 1569, the Jews of Lithuania withdrew from the Council of the Four Lands to establish an independent organization, the Council of the Lituanian Land (Va'ad Medinat Lita), in 1623.[18] These bodies enjoyed a distinguished existence until their abolition by the Polish state in 1764.[19] The sixteenth century can be seen in retrospect as the apogee of the autonomous Jewish community in Poland, and their status gave rise to the popular saying that Poland was *rajem dla żydów*—"paradise for Jews."[20] The following century was to be dominated by "the Catastrophe"—the Cossack uprising of 1648, followed by widespread foreign intervention in Poland, all of which tended to cripple the economic well-being of most kahals. Economic decline was followed by growing social tensions within the community, which took the form of class antagonisms and religious warfare.

The economic decline of the Jews in Poland-Lithuania was variously preceded by or accompanied by a decline in their social standing. Medieval Poland had been quite remarkable for its religious toleration—not only of Jews, but also of Muslims and a variety of heterodox believers—and this toleration was reflected in the relative security enjoyed by the Jews.[21] The charges of ritual murder and host desecration, which were staples of Western European violence against the Jews, occasionally prompted violence against Polish Jewry, but always on an abbreviated scale. Bernard Weinryb estimates that in the fourteenth and fifteenth centuries there were only two or three outbreaks of violence or persecution of Jews each generation.[22] While Poland's tolerant traditions weathered the outbreak of the Protestant Reformation, they began to wane in the course of the Catholic Counter-Reformation. The Jesuit leaders of the Counter-Reformation imported the traditional anti-Jewish feelings of the Christian West. The Jews were also threatened by association with the most radical teachings of Protestantism, Anti-Trinitarianism.[23] The rising level of religious antipathy could be witnessed in the growing determination of the Catholic clergy to enshrine in legislation an inferior status for the Jews. The clergy advocated distinctive and insulting dress for the Jews, culminating in the clerically motivated demand by the Diet of Piotrków in 1538 that the Jews wear a distinctive yellow headband. This was one of many unsuccessful attempts to encumber the Jews with insulting marks and symbols. In 1566 and 1588 Lithuanian statutes forbade "ostentatious" dress by Jews.[24] The Church also called for the physical separation of Christians and Jews.

The prestige of the Jews in the eyes of the native population suffered because of these attacks. Teimanas notes that before the seventeenth century, legal documents had utilized standardized phrases of a positive connotation to refer to the Jews: *providus, honestus, generosus*, or, in short, terms characteristically applied to members of the urban commercial classes. From that earlier era too had come the folk legend of Abraham Prochównik, a wise Jew who was elected king of Poland, but who sagely stepped aside after one day in favor of a Christian candidate. By the mid-sixteenth century, however, law codes and documents almost invariably referred to the Jews in pejorative terms: *infidus, perfidus, incredulus*.[25] Poland was also the scene of a number of ritual-murder accusations. Even in the face of a papal prohibition against such charges, the clergy continued to foment them and to invent "pious frauds" that led to the torment and murder of individual Jews. In contrast to the relative security of earlier ages, incidents of persecution and violence averaged two every three years in the sixteenth and seventeenth centuries.[26] In the past the Jews had frequently been compared to the Turks—who had also found a measure of toleration in Poland—but such an association took on especially sinister connotations during the Turkish wars.[27]

As significant as the religious hatred of the Church, however, were the tensions generated by the economic rivalry of the Jews, concentrated in the commercial classes, and their Gentile competitors. (It should be noted that the bulk of attacks on Jews discussed above were by students and city people.) Certainly there was nothing new in this rivalry: the economic struggle between Gentiles and Jews, the latter often aided by the wojewoda, is an unending theme in the history of the urban development of Poland. Nor were such struggles restricted to Christians and Jews: Armenians and Scots were equally notorious for their clashes with vested urban interests.[28] Still, the struggle with the Jews took on a special sharpness in the century before the partitions. The economic functions of the Jews in previous centuries had tended to be "complementary," i.e., functions which the indigenous population was not able to fulfill. With the growth of cities and the evolution of the national economy some of these complementary functions changed their character and became areas of competition.[29] The native population endeavored to revive old prohibitions on the Jews or devise new ones.

The most desirable privilege a city could obtain was a complete prohibition of Jewish trade or residence (*de non tolerandis Judaeis*). Warsaw, for one, obtained such a grant from Sigismund I in 1525.[30] Even those cities that possessed such prerogatives had to guard against infractions, especially in the form of collusion between the Jews and the wealthy magnates who rented them housing within the city limits. Jews who were unable to dwell in the city often reached agreements with the local *szlachta*, or petty nobility, which enabled them to take up residence on lands free from repressive urban legislation.[31]

The example of Warsaw is not really typical, since the Jews were diligent in securing the right of residence in most urban centers. The Jews were customarily required to secure a permit to dwell in a specific area. Such permits carefully set forth the details of Jewish life in a given location. Arrangements for the construction of synagogues and ritual baths, the trades to be permitted to Jews, and their duties to the king and the city were enumerated. In certain cities such as Lwów and Kraków, special streets were set aside for the Jews. This was not a discriminatory measure but a true privilege. The Jewish quarter had its own special prerogatives within the city, and on occasion steps had to be taken to keep Christians out. Only later did these areas become ghettos based on discrimination and lack of privilege, and everywhere this process took place very slowly.[32]

The Jews enjoyed notable success in competition with Christian merchants and tradesmen. For example, in those towns where production was controlled by guilds, the Jews frequently founded competitive guilds of their own, as in Kraków, where the furrier dealers organized in 1613 and the barber-surgeons in 1639. But it was not in guilds that the Jews were to operate most successfully. The guilds themselves, Christian or Jewish, were never as strong in Poland as in Western Europe, especially since important elements in Christian society were opposed to guild restrictiveness, particularly the large landowners. In private towns there were often no guilds at all, and in crown cities both the nobility and the clergy took full advantage of their exemption from guild control.[33]

The guilds ultimately represented economic retrogression in Poland, and Jewish guildsmen were always in a minority. The Jewish commercial triumph in the cities can more readily be observed in nonguild, artisan production or in middleman activities. Bewildered Gentile contemporaries resorted to a variety of accusations to explain the obvious Jewish superiority in these fields. Almost without exception one encounters the charge that the Jews were dishonest, crafty, unscrupulous, and immoral and that consequently no honest Christian could hope to defeat them in economic competition. These charges by contemporaries were less proof positive of innate Jewish commercial immorality than a cameo picture of the evolving practices of capitalism. Jews undersold competitors, they hawked their wares openly and aggressively, they attempted to lure customers into their shops, they sold in volume and cornered the market.[34] To the medieval Polish mind, such tactics represented a spiteful attempt to harm and ruin Christians. Gentile businessmen at a loss to understand how a Jew could sell cheaply and still survive in the market sought the answer in religious antipathy strong enough to induce Jews to commit economic suicide in order to harm Christians. As late as 1788 one angry tradesman summed up such resentment:

> Not suprisingly, the Jews ruin the merchant class; in this way they also ruin themselves, for it can't be denied that the Jews are poor in spite of their turnover of goods. This can be explained by the fact that the Jew, maliciously wishing to ruin the merchant class, ruins himself, selling goods for next to nothing and thus drawing the wrath of competitors down on himself; but the consumer supports them and their creditors protect them.[35]

There were other factors involved as well. At times government trade restrictions accentuated any Jewish proclivity to undersell by forcing the Jews to sell at a price lower than their Gentile competition. Within the Jewish community itself there was practiced a system of price fixing and trade monopoly which controlled internal competition between potential Jewish rivals for contracts with Christians.[36] In the final analysis it was a combination of advanced marketing techniques and a superior product, as in branches of the clothing industry where the Polish Jews introduced a quality product employing methods of mass production, that created hostility between the Christian and the Jew in the Polish marketplace.[37]

The resulting Jewish-Christian rivalry led to harassments and lawsuits against the Jews by the burghers and corresponding attempts by Jews to circumvent restrictions imposed on their trade and residence. The cities maintained constant pressure aimed at the expulsion of Jews into the countryside, and these efforts did occasionally meet with success. In their turn the Jews frequently allied themselves economically with the magnates or szlachta against the burgher class.

These tensions outside the Jewish community were a continuing impetus to further consolidation and growth of the kahal leadership, which gained enormous power in pre-partition Poland. Not only did this leadership control the internal life of the community in both secular and religious spheres, but it also served as an intermediary between community and government, especially in the area of tax payments. This was an important prerogative because it allowed the leadership to apportion the rate of tax payment among the individual members of the community.[38] There was little recourse for the individual so assessed; he could protest in the local Jewish court, controlled by the elders, but this was the final court of appeal. Moreover, the government supported the local community when it excommunicated that rare protester who refused to pay his allotment. It has already been noted that the elders had replaced the rabbi as the head of the community. Abuses began to appear in the exercise of authority by this powerful group.

Originally the Jewish community had probably been primitively democratic, governed through a plenary assembly of all adult males. As the kahals grew larger, such meetings became a practical impossibility and rule passed into the hands of representative bodies and permanent officials. At the same time, democratic controls became largely ineffective.[39] The kahal elders tended to belong to the wealthier elements of the community, since these were usually the individuals with the time and inclination for such duties as well as the financial resources, as kahal elders were generally personally responsible for the payment of communal debts incurred under their aegis. It is not surprising that the kahal leadership began to circumvent restrictions against nepotism or multiple terms, or that the leadership gradually emerged as a firmly established oligarchy. Complaints to the wojewoda concerning rigged elections were sometimes effective, more often not.[40] The leadership, once firmly established in a community, manifested a reluctance to tax itself stringently and often passed the burden of taxation onto those least able to pay and therefore politically impotent. The kahal elders undoubtedly did take risks for the community, and their position as mediator between the greed of the government and the natural reluctance of the population to pay its taxes was not always comfortable. Nonetheless, by the time of the partitions the system of tax assessment seems to have been most unfair. Both Prussian and Russian investigators specifically asserted that the Polish-Jewish masses were on the verge of exhaustion, burdened by abject poverty while the communal rich lived in unbecoming luxury. These charges were at times exaggerated, but by the eighteenth century there was considerable truth in them.[41]

It is necessary to draw a balanced picture of the role of the kahal leadership. To Russian commentators of the eighteenth and nineteenth centuries their exploitative role was indefensible, the more so because they held the masses fast by bonds of religious superstition and fear. Yet the kahal administrators did serve to maintain with real success the cultural unity of the Jews of Central Europe as well as the unique features of their religious-secular life. The elders must be credited with maintaining a semblance of community integrity when legal, social, and religious forces acted to tear it down. Ultimately, these pressures overwhelmed the traditional community. In the period of disintegration, the rearguard resistance of the communal leadership, which in Russia was frequently directed against "enlightened" Jews within the community, served to further discredit the leaders in the eyes of unsympathetic observers.

Allusions have already been made to the other destructive forces working on Polish Jewry, causing its position to decline noticeably in the eighteenth century. The Church and the burghers continued their dual attack on the Jews, but as long as the king, through his lieutenant the wojewoda, remained a strong guardian of the Jews, their position was secure. Just as the decline of the monarchy meant increasing anarchy in the commonwealth, so too did the Jews lose their traditional supporter. The magnates and szlachta (the great and petty landowning nobility) came more and more to substitute for the king in this function. This relationship was reinforced by the tendency, already enunciated in royal decrees of 1556 and 1569, for local members of the szlachta to occupy the post of wojewoda.[42] The interests of the noble landowner and the Jews gradually became linked by bonds of economic collaboration.

The eclipse of the financial well-being of the Jewish communities accompanied the domestic turmoil of seventeenth-century Poland. The uprising of Hetman Bogdan Chmielnicki in the Ukraine in 1648 had disastrous consequences for Jews, who were favorite victims of murder and pillage because of their role as middlemen in the oppressive feudal system of the Polish borderlands. The northern communities that had been spared this social upheaval fell victim to the military operations attending the First Northern War (1655–1660) and the Russo-Polish War (1654–1667).[43] The Polish Jewish communities, in the past generous contributors to appeals from needy Jews elsewhere, were now themselves the subject of appeals and collections throughout the communities of Europe.[44]

The physical destruction during these conflicts accentuated financial problems that had been taking shape even before 1648. Under increased financial pressure from the crown and from bribe-hungry members of the bureaucracy, the individual communities had begun of necessity to contract debts. The institution most eager to grant such loans was the Catholic Church. Monastic orders especially considered such loans a good investment for surplus capital. These lenders preferred that the loan never be paid off, since the interest on the principal provided a steady and generally reliable yearly income. Numerous examples of such transactions exist. For instance, the Jews of Łuck contracted a debt in 1676 with a local monastery for the sum of six hundred Polish złoty, the interest on which was forty-eight złoty per annum. Both the movable and immovable property of the community was pledged on bond, the synagogue included. All resident Jews were forbidden to move elsewhere until the debt was repaid. The pledge of the synagogue as collateral is sufficient proof of the grievous state in which such communities found themselves.[45] In 1773 the Wilno community was forced to pawn the synagogue's furnishings in order to keep the Piarist monks from seizing the Great Synagogue for arrears.[46] The central kahal of Witebsk was plagued by an inability to force its subordinate communities to pay their taxes, and in support the Va'ad Medinat Lita was forced to threaten the recalcitrant communities with excommunication and to warn that all religious services would be suspended outside a six-mile radius from the city. In 1711 the Witebsk community voiced its sorrows in an entry in the community minute book:

> It has been quite some time that great misfortunes have come down upon us. We suffered greatly at the hands of the Polish and Russian soldiers and in addition the wojewoda levied on us various taxes, thus the payment of a tithe was imposed upon all inhabitants. And even this was to no avail. Our misery is very great. Trouble follows upon trouble, as it is written: "In the morning thou shalt say: 'Would it were even!' and at even thou shalt say: 'Would it were morning!' . . . " There is no alternative but the imposition of the meat tax, which is an onerous burden to which no community in our province was ever subjected before.[47]

So serious did these debts become that the Polish Sejm of 1764 appointed a Liquidation Commission to restore some order to Jewish financial affairs. This committee discovered that the Community of Wilno (3,206 persons) owed 832,000 gulden, Grodno (2,418) owed 448,500 gulden, Pińsk (1,277) owed 310,000 gulden, and Brześć-Litewski (3,175) owed 119,700 gulden. The bulk of the Wilno debt was owed to the Jesuit order, although the Dominicans, Friars of St. Bernard, Augustinians, Carmelites, Basilians, and the Penitents of the Wilno monastery also had claims, as did individual laymen and priests. The Liquidation Commission, in setting up a rate for repayment, accepted a sworn statement from the Wilno Community that its annual income from taxes and collections was 34,000 gulden, although interest alone on debts outstanding came to 36,224 gulden. The attempt of the Polish government to facilitate debt repayment by the Jews was ultimately a failure, the more so when it rescinded the prohibition made in 1766 forbidding the contraction of further debts. In actuality, the only concrete accomplishment of the commission was to add to the financial burden of the Jews by assessing them 20,000 gulden for its expenses.[48]

Reference has already been made to the intensification of economic ties between the Jews and the native Polish landowners. Jews, owing to the variety of financial functions they were able to perform, were welcome on the large estates which often became a refuge during the periodic expulsions of the Jews from the urban centers. The szlachta eventually replaced the kings as the Jews' protectors. Ultimately this placed many Jews in an uncomfortable position. The Polish landowner of the eighteenth century—like his Russian counterpart—often had no real desire to manage his own serf estate. The Jews, on the other hand, excelled as middlemen and estate managers, the so-called *arendarz* (arendator). They thus became the agents standing between lord and peasant. On the eve of the partitions it is estimated that a third of Poland's Jews were engaged in some form of arendator activity.[49] The Jews were especially energetic in leasing the numerous prerogatives and monopolies that the landowner enjoyed. On the estates the Jews often controlled the sale of salt and fish and ran the grain mills as well. The most important of these leases was usually the right of propination, a permit to distill and market alcoholic beverages that had been granted to noble landowners in 1496. This was a convenient process for utilizing surplus grain (although some observers complained that it often utilized nonsurplus grain as well) at a time when no extensive market economy existed in Poland. The grain mash made excellent fodder for farm animals over the winter, and the alcohol itself could be sold to the peasantry. As in the case of the notorious salt *gabelle* in prerevolutionary France, the Polish peasant was often forced to buy the liquor whether he wanted it or not. As the economic position of the Jewish communities worsened, individual Jews in the countryside came more and more to monopolize product leases, services, and alcohol production and sale. To the first Russian commentators it seemed that almost every Jewish house served as a tavern. Nor were leases exclusively concerned with economic activities. Catholic Polish nobles in the Ukraine with a clear conscience leased to Jews the right to collect dues on Orthodox churches. The figure of the Jewish arendator forcing the peasants to pay for the use of the church keys became rooted in popular folklore and added a bitter religious note to Christian-Jewish relations.[50] This middleman role of the Jews reinforced the frequently heard accusations of "Jewish exploitation." While there were indeed some isolated Jews who grew rich on the profits of the manor trade, the bulk of Polish Jewry were fully as oppressed as their Christian counterparts. The money that they secured from the peasants slipped through their own fingers and into the pockets of the landlord. As the power of the landowner over the Jew increased, the economic relationship became increasingly one-sided. Small wonder that the petty szlachta emerged as the force most determined to protect the Jews from reform, be it Polish or Russian.[51]

By the time of the partitions even the internal solidarity of the kahal had begun to decay. Internal disputes were nothing new, but seldom in the past had communities violated the self-protective code that all disputes be

A Polish view of a Jewish *arendarz* from the second half of the nineteenth century.

settled internally and no occasion ever be given for the central authorities to intervene. The most prominent example of the breakdown in internal discipline was the struggle of the Wilno kahal in 1785 to depose its distinguished rabbi, Samuel ben Avigdor. Before the dispute was settled, the entire community had been split into two camps and the Wilno wojewoda Radziwiłł and the Catholic bishop Massalski had been brought in on different sides. Although the kahal (or more properly the elders) eventually had its way, "it had damaged itself irretrievably in the struggle; and the prestige of both rabbinate and Kahal in all other communities in the country [Lithuania] had likewise suffered."[52] Even earlier, in 1749, an economic dispute between two communities, Shklov and Kopys, was appealed to the Lithuanian Exchequer, an unheard-of breaking of ranks.[53]

The integrity of the community was further undermined by the rise of Hasidism. The movement was inspired by Israel Baal Shem Tov (c. 1700–1760), a charismatic leader whose career soon became overgrown with legend. On one level, Hasidism was a reform of certain Jewish traditions, especially deemphasizing Torah learning and study, while preferring the "Oral Torah" to Scripture. The movement tended to be more mystical—it had Kabbalistic ties—and revivalistic than institutional Judaism.[54] But Hasidism has often been seen as an antiauthoritarian movement as well, directed against the traditional leadership of the community. The Hasidic leader, or *tzaddik*, for example, served as an intermediary between the community and God, and for the faithful his authority superseded that of the rabbi. Institutional Judaism quickly recognized the threat, and the movement was put under a ban by 1772. Effective in Lithuania, the ban failed to stem the rapid growth of the movement in Poland and the Ukraine. The bitterness of the struggle grew so sharp that a form of religious civil war broke out in many communities between the Hasidim and their tradition-minded foes, known as the *Mitnaggedim*. In the course of this conflict both sides broke the elemental code of Jewish survival of the past and denounced opponents to the secular authorities.[55]

As the era of the partitions approached, therefore, the Jews were an integral part of the Polish socioeconomic system and possessed a significant measure of political autonomy. Yet theirs was an unhappy role: in the cities they were the objects of commercial and religious hatred; in the countryside they were squeezed by the landlords and were victims of the religious and class hatred of the peasantry. Simultaneously, the community itself was increasingly threatened by economic and religious stresses.

The destruction of Poland, and the transferral of Jewish communities to new governments, occurred in three stages. The first partition of Poland (1772) was designed to give compensation to Austria and Prussia for the great Russian gains that came about as a result of the Russo-Turkish War of 1768–1772. Poland lost almost one-third of her territory and slightly more than one-third of her population. Russia received the poor and underpopulated provinces of Polotsk (Połock), Vitebsk (Witebsk), and Mogilev (Mohylew). Austria received rich and fertile lands in Galicia. Prussia took Warmia and West Prussia, effectively cutting Poland off from the sea.

The second partition (1793) was designed to prevent the possible emergence of a strong, reformed, and anti-Russian Poland in the aftermath of the reform Constitution of 3 May 1791. Russia received the territories east of the line Druja-Pińsk-Choczim, which included much of the Ukraine, and the remainder of Belorussia. Prussia received the territory Częstochowa-Rawa-Działdowo (Soldau), which comprised all of Great Poland

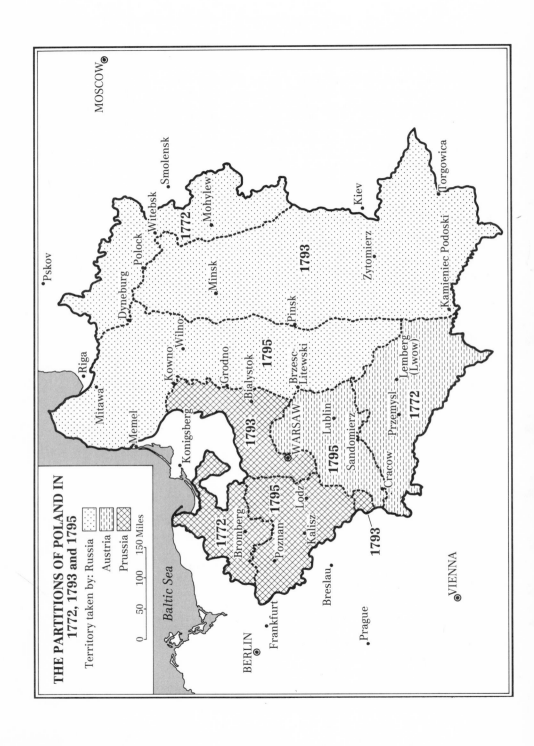

THE PARTITIONS OF POLAND IN
1772, 1793 and 1795

Territory taken by: Russia
Austria
Prussia

0   50   100   150 Miles

and included the cities of Dantzic, Thorn, Posen, Gniezno (Gnesen), Kalisz, and Sieradz. Russia gained more than three million new subjects, Prussia just over a million.

The third partition, which ended the national uprising led by Tadeusz Kościuszko, sought to destroy the very name "Kingdom of Poland." The remnants of the Polish state were divided by Russia, Austria, and Prussia. Russia received Kurlandia, parts of Lithuania including the cities of Wilno and Grodno, and the remains of the provinces of Podlasie and Wołyn. Prussia gained Kraków and the balance of the provinces of Kraków and Sandomierz (renamed New East Prussia and New Silesia). Austria acquired the lands bordered by the Russian and Prussian territories ("Western Galicia"), which included the cities of Lwów (Lemberg), Tarnopol, and Halicz.[56]

Estimates of the total number of Jews transferred to each partitioning party differ wildly. An Austrian census of dubious accuracy registered 224,981 Jews of both sexes in 1773 in the newly acquired territories of Galicia. (A census of 1774 reduced the count to 171,851.)[57] By 1795 the total number of Austria's Polish Jews may have been as high as 260,000.[58] Prussia received 65,000 Jews in 1772, and added a total of more than 100,000 in the partitions of 1793 and 1795.[59] There were hardly more than 45,000 Jews in the lands annexed by Russia in 1772, but in 1793 and 1795 she acquired lands which had a Jewish population of 289,022, according to the Polish census of 1765.[60] The results of Russian censuses conducted between 1797 and 1800 recorded 151,277 male Jews enrolled in the urban estates.[61] However inexact these figures might be, their overall import is unavoidable: only the Austrian Empire acquired a sizable Jewish population in 1772; Prussia and Russia had to wait until 1793 and 1795 to acquire equally large Jewish settlements.

The Jews who now fell under Russian imperium were not uniform in culture or tradition. The areas annexed in 1772, which became the Russian provinces of Mogilev and Polotsk, had once been part of the territory of the Grand Duchy of Lithuania. Jews here maintained a sense of identity derived from a development slightly different from that of Polish Jewry. Indeed, the Lithuanian Va'ad had withdrawn from the common Council of the Four Lands in 1623 in part to affirm the unique features of Lithuanian Jewry. Russian Jews displayed a reluctance, born of the Lithuanian tradition, toward the establishment of a central authority in the period of the autonomous kahal in Russia from 1772 to 1844, in sharp contrast to Jewish practice in the Polish Commonwealth. Russian Jews never created a central authority to deal with problems of general concern, leaving such initiatives to outstanding individuals or to an energetic kahal leadership, usually coming from the community in the most immediate danger. This lack of unity was especially evident in the uncoordinated struggle against the Hasidic movement.

Despite a dislike for centralized authority, Belorussian Jewry was remarkably homogeneous, a feature that would not mark the communities annexed after 1793. By and large, the rabbinical authorities had successfully arrested, if not reversed, the rapid spread of Hasidism. While individual kahals might still be shattered by the debates between the partisans of both sides, the Jews of the new Russian territory generally remained faithful to the older traditions. At one time there had been yet another sect, the Karaites, centered in Troki, located near Wilno. Originating in Egypt and the Middle East, the Karaites claimed to follow written law and the scriptures, to the exclusion of rabbinical traditions and laws, represented especially in the Talmud. By the eighteenth century their center had shifted to Łuck in Wołyn and Halicz in Galicia, and the former entered the Russian Empire only with the later partitions.

The bulk of Russian Jewry was Ashkenazic, taking its traditions and culture from the great medieval communities of Germany. There were no important Sephardic communities, those whose original home and culture were Hispanic. Yiddish was utilized in daily affairs, while Hebrew was maintained for ritual. Jewish youth was carefully educated by the individual community, with the stress placed on Torah and Talmud studies. In education and tradition, Russian-Polish Jews were and would continue to be conservative, and, as such, both the despair and the rival of the future Jewish enlightenment movement centered in Germany and best represented by the Berlin school of the Jewish philosopher Moses Mendelssohn.

In appearance as well as in language, the Jews were a cultural anachronism as contrasted with their Polish Gentile neighbors. Uncut beards and earlocks were still ritually respected among Polish Jews, and while Jews had never consciously separated themselves from Christian Poles by dress, as Catholic ecclesiastics had sometimes advocated, they had retained medieval Polish dress while the Poles themselves adopted German fashions. Thus, these new Russian subjects were differentiated from the more or less hostile Christian population by religion, speech, and dress, and segregated from them politically as well. As such they presented an obvious, though not necessarily pressing, challenge to the Russian state administration.

2

RUSSIA'S AMBIGUOUS
JEWISH LEGACY

When Russian journalists in the late nineteenth century sought an appropriate catchword to describe the Jews, the expression they most frequently used was *terra incognita*, emphasizing the ignorance of most Russians about the nature of Jewish society. If the Jews constituted an unknown quantity after a hundred years of Russian rule, how much more mysterious they were to the first Russian officials charged with governing them after the initial partition of Poland in 1772. Precedents and guidelines from Russian administrative experience were lacking, except for expulsion decrees earlier in the century.

Officials who wished to do more than maintain a status quo which they did not understand or who had to deal with unexpected problems in a vacuum were not left entirely to their own devices. Three broad traditions, religious, pragmatic, and reformist, existed to give them guidance. These traditions were the outgrowth of centuries of interaction between Jews and Gentiles in Western and Eastern Europe. They were seldom precise, self-contained, or mutually exclusive, and bureaucrats could pick and choose among their disparate strands as they saw fit. It is necessary to review the nature of these three traditions in order to appreciate the options available and the choices made by Russians after 1772.

THE RELIGIOUS TRADITION

In A.D. 986, so the Russian chronicle *The Tale of Bygone Years* asserts, Jewish Khazars endeavored to convert the pagan ruler of Kiev, Vladimir, to Judaism.[1] This episode was neither the beginning nor the end of the intertwined history of the Russian and Jewish peoples, but these long-standing contacts, like the apocryphal Vladimir tale itself, have often been obscured by legend and invention. Despite the ambivalence that usually characterized the early relations of the Eastern Slavs and the Jews, it is the motif of rejection, first encountered in the chronicles, that has come to dominate the secondary literature. A historical tradition, beginning with Orshanskii and elaborated by Dubnow, portrays Russian attitudes as a seamless web, a tradition uniformly hostile to the Jews.

It would be more accurate to recognize the Eastern European legacy to eighteenth- and nineteenth-century Russia as a mixed and ambiguous one. Episodes of fierce and brutal religious persecution are striking, but there were extensive periods of accommodation as well. The evidence suggests that the population of Kievan Rus' was not invariably hostile to the Jews, the most salient proof being that Jews were able to live peacefully within its borders. The attitudes of successor states of Kiev, such as Muscovy, should not be read back to the earlier period.

A major difficulty in assessing Kievan attitudes toward the Jews is the anecdotal and imprecise nature of the sources. Bernard Weinryb, at one extreme, argues that "most of the sources and hypotheses concerning the beginnings of east-European Jewry are no more than fiction. . . . Conjectures and speculations about the early existence of Jews and their continued existence into later centuries find no independent support in source material."[2]

It is true that the first Jewish settlement in Eastern Europe—colonization of the north shore of the Black Sea dating to classical times—long antedated the period of Slavic hegemony in the area and did not necessarily survive. Nonetheless, Slavic settlements and the subsequent Kievan state were contemporaneous and contiguous with the Khazar state that controlled the lower Volga and the Crimea. About A.D. 740, the Khazar ruler Bulan converted to Judaism and was joined by the upper strata of the community, and perhaps influenced the lower orders as well. It has long been conjectured that Kiev itself was founded by the Khazars, and there is newly discovered evidence of the existence of a community of Khazars, practicing rabbinical Judaism, in Kiev in the tenth century.[3] The "Jewish Gate" was a recognized landmark of the old city, and while not decisive evidence of a permanent Jewish quarter, its name at least implies trade with the Jews. Indeed, it is in the guise of a commercial element that the Jews invariably appear both in Old Russian and other sources. The Khazar Jews in Kiev in the tenth century, for example, were obviously engaged in trade.[4] A number of chronicle accounts describe the social revolution which broke out in Kiev in 1113 upon the death of the unpopular prince Sviatopolk II. Both well-to-do officials and Jews were the victims of the mob's fury.[5] These disorders have been anachronistically called a "pogrom" by some scholars. In fact, they were only indirectly aimed against Jews, and even then only at their economic functions, in all probability their role as agents of Prince Sviatopolk's hated salt monopoly.[6]

While princes and commoners coexisted tolerably well with the few Jews resident in their midst, the newly established Orthodox Church took a more negative perspective. Russia's conversion was accomplished through the agency of Byzantium, which had a long tradition of anti-Jewish ideology.[7] Following this lead, it was Russian Byzantinists (i.e., native Russians under the cultural influence of Byzantium), like Hilarion of Kiev in the middle of the eleventh century and Cyril of Turov in the middle of the twelfth century, who most articulately propounded anti-Jewish themes. Their sermons emphasized the opposition of the Old and New Testament, of Law and Grace, of the Jewish synagogue and the Gentile Church.[8]

An anti-Jewish clerical bias can also be detected in the saints' lives included in the Kievan Crypt Paterikon, dating to the early thirteenth century but continuously expanded throughout the second half of the fifteenth century. Several stories, especially the *vita* of the abbot Theodosius, were at one time considered decisive evidence of a Kievan Jewish community. Theodosius allegedly sought out Jews in the city for theological disputations in the (disappointed) hope that they would martyr him. This detail of the *vita* may well be a later interpolation. A similar criticism has been made of the *vita* of the Kievan monk Eustathius, who was crucified by a Jewish slave trader in the Crimea because he refused to follow the law of Moses.[9] The account, which suggests a non-Russian, Byzantine provenance, is a genre tale with little direct applicability to conditions in contemporary Kiev.[10] Yet these *vitae* have a utility beyond any light that they might shed on the presence of Jews in Kiev: they display a sharp religious hatred directed against the Jews by the Kievan clergy. Far from depicting Russian reality, they indicate the spread of Byzantine Judeophobia into the clerical intelligentsia of the Eastern Slavs. Additional evidence is found in an East Russian recension of the ecclesiastic charter of Iaroslav the Wise, which dates at least to the thirteenth century.[11] Its prohibition against sexual relations between Christians and Jews displays affinities with previous Byzantine codes, without necessarily indicating direct influence.

The very fact that the Christian Church was so newly established, and still battling against pagan survivals in the form of the "dual faith," added a special urgency to attacks on rival religions. Still, these anti-Jewish enthusiasms apparently had little effect upon the general population. The sophisticated biblical exegesis of such representatives of the clerical elite as Hilarion or Cyril was neither suited nor intended for mass consumption by an imperfectly Christianized people. In the words of George Fedotov: "The [anti-Jewish] theme is missing in the sermons of those simple and popular preachers who spoke to the half-converted masses, to whom the warning against unchristian propaganda would be more befitting."[12]

A comparison with contemporary Europe is revealing. The murderous frenzy of the Crusades never communicated itself to Kievan Rus'. There was no Russian equivalent to the Western European and Polish charge that the Jews poisoned wells and spread the plague. The story of the martyred Eustathius in the Kiev Paterikon lacked the essential elements of a ritual murder tale, and such stories never gained much popularity in Russia. The English cult of St. Hugh of Lincoln—the model for the Prioress's Tale in Chaucer's *Canterbury Tales*—spread all over Western Europe in the thirteenth century but bypassed Russia.[13] (As Dmitri Obolensky indicates, the Russians were not averse to picking up the cults of other "Latin" saints.)[14] Russia lacked the popular identification of the Jews with the Devil, which became a significant cultural phenomenon in the West.[15] There were no Russian equivalents of the anti-Jewish stereotypes which appeared in the medieval miracle plays, or in Church art and architecture. Despite the recurrent Byzantinist theme of the opposition of the Old and New Testaments, Russian churches did not carry the Western motifs of "Ecclesia" and "Synagoga" common in medieval cathedrals in the West.[16]

This argument from silence cannot prove any positive claim about Kievan attitudes toward the Jews, but in the absence of tangible evidence of the type found in Western Europe only a tenuous case can be made for the argument that anti-Jewish feeling was a vital ingredient of Kievan culture, or that the concerns of the clerical elite were communicated to a wider popular audience. Finally, it should be noted that a few popular stories treated Jews with a measure of respect. Amid the characters in the heroic folk epics, or *byliny*, was the *Zhidovin* or "Jew," a fierce warrior who did battle with the knightly Russian defenders of the Christian faith.[17] The average Jew was not an epic figure but a common tradesman, of course, and was probably viewed only in this guise by the general population.

Whatever the ultimate attitudes of Kievan Rus', those of her successor states were not uniformly hostile. The commercial functions performed by the Jews made them welcome in various locales. The great town builder of southwestern Russia, Daniil of Volynia-Podolia (1221–1264), included Jews within the ranks of the townspeople whom he settled in newly formed urban centers, a practice continued by his successors.[18] Jews were an important component of the Grand Duchy of Lithuania even before its union with Poland and its own large, tolerated Jewish population.[19]

The attitude of Muscovite Russia, on the other hand, presents a striking contrast. Muscovy produced the strident Judeophobia which many commentators have in mind when they speak of the "tradition of Russian anti-Semitism." It is therefore important to identify carefully the nature of Muscovite Judeophobia in order to consider its potential influence on post-partition Russian policymakers and to appreciate its subsequent role in Russian history.

Jews rarely figure in contemporary accounts of appanage Russia, the term given to the post-Kievan period of external domination by the Mongol Golden Horde and the internal political disintegration-reintegration which characterized the "gathering of the Russian land" under Muscovite hegemony. By the sixteenth century, however, the situation had changed dramatically. There are numerous domestic and foreign accounts, running into the seventeenth century, which emphasize the particular animus directed against Jewish settlement in the Russian land.[20] Muscovite armies which captured Polish-Lithuanian cities in the course of the Livonian War offered Jewish communities they found there the simple choice of conversion to Christianity or massacre. The most celebrated example of such tactics occurred in 1563 when the city of Polotsk was captured by Ivan IV.[21] Not even economic advantage could overcome this hostility. In 1550 Ivan IV responded to a request of the Polish king Sigismund Augustus that Polish Jewish merchants be allowed to trade in Russia as in the past (*kak po starine*). Ivan petulantly refused, noting, "It is not appropriate to allow Jews to come to Russia with their goods, since many evils result from them. For they import poisonous herbs into our realm and lead Russians astray from Christianity. . . . "[22] The latter concern was to predominate in Muscovite attitudes toward the Jews, compounded from fears for the integrity of the Orthodox faith and growing xenophobia in the face of strong forces which threatened its national life.

Most commentators have connected the rise of articulate and forceful anti-Jewish religious feeling in Muscovy with the movement of the so-called Judaizers (*Zhidovstvuiushchie*) which arose in Novgorod in the 1480s and spread to Moscow before it was forcibly repressed by the clerical authorities.[23] Scholars still debate the true nature of this heresy and the extent of actual Jewish influence.[24] At least some of the opponents of the "Judaizers" earnestly believed that they were resisting Jewish influence. Dmitrii Gerasimov, the agent for Archbishop Gennadius of Novgorod abroad, sought Western polemical works attacking orthodox Judaism, with the intention of using them against the Novgorod heretics.[25] Whatever the reality of the charge of conversionary activities by the Jews, the movement resulted in an influx of foreign and homegrown anti-Jewish propaganda, such as the famous *Enlightener* (*Prosvetitel'*) attributed to the abbot Iosif of Volokolamsk. Iosif, the spokesman for the "Possessors," or advocates of monastic landholding in the Orthodox Church (against which the heretics also apparently agitated), specifically accused the heretics of converting to Judaism and of propounding the Mosaic Law, animal sacrifice, and circumcision.[26] Iosif's more general accusations, of anti-Trinitarianism, iconoclasm, and the denial of the divinity and resurrection of Christ, could also be attributed to the influence of Judaism.[27] The secular motives that entered into the heresy merely sharpened the antagonism of the Orthodox authorities against it.[28]

As to the question of why the Jewish element in the heresy, real or imagined, would be emphasized, it should be noted that the charge of apostasy (i.e., the rejection of the Christian faith) was a more serious and less forgivable crime than heresy (i.e., errors in Christian doctrine). This became a matter of real concern when the movement was suppressed and the proper punishment of the heretics—some of whom had recanted—was being debated. The clerical leadership sought the maximum punishment as a means of destroying the movement, root and branch. This was in fact the fate of the leadership of the heresy; some were executed and the rest were imprisoned for life.[29] The fear of conversionary activity became firmly rooted in the Russian mind in any event, and concern with Jewish proselytism reappeared again and again in Russian history, constituting a tangible legacy of the Judaizer affair.

Concern with religious proselytism, Jewish or non-Jewish, should be placed in wider context. The sixteenth century, from which dates Ivan's rejoinder to the Polish king, witnessed the international religious crisis of the Reformation, which brought questions of religious orthodoxy to the fore and generated a concern for the integrity of religious teaching and a concomitant antipathy to everything heterodox. This was particularly the case in Poland-Lithuania, Muscovy's immediate western neighbor. Poland's traditional toleration, which had made it a haven for all manner of heterodoxy, declined when confronted with the vigor of the Catholic Counter-Reformation and the Church Militant.[30] Elements of medieval European hatred of the Jews began to spread to Poland. Charges of sacrilege and host desecration—"pious frauds"—were made by preachers as an expedient way of spurring religious enthusiasm among the masses. Upon occasion such accusations led to riots and the judicial murder of Jews. The Catholic Church in Poland began to discover its own child martyrs, done to death at Jewish hands. There were echoes in Poland of medieval and Renaissance hostility toward the Talmud.[31] In 1648, the uprising of Bogdan Chmielnicki in the Ukraine triggered anti-Jewish violence of catastrophic proportions and destroyed the last vestiges of prosperity for many Jewish communities in the Ukraine.[32]

In the atmosphere of general alarm and religious tension, heterodoxy and heresy drew an immediate response. Faced with new and unfamiliar dogmas, the authorities permitted the sharp demarcation between Christianity and Judaism to blur. Anti-Trinitarian heresies, which had a long tradition in Poland as "Socinianism," could and sometimes were seen as "Judaizing," since Judaism was also a well-known, if discreet, foe of the doctrine of the Trinity. An outbreak of "conversions to Judaism" caused widespread concern, culminating in the arrest and execution of Katherine Weigle, the widow of a prominent Kraków burgher, in 1539. These events, which were notorious in their day, were followed by a rash of rumors that the Jews were converting Poles and secreting them in Turkey or Palestine for safekeeping. This was a charge of double force, because it also linked the Jews with the Ottoman enemy of the Polish state. The rumors of these conversions were taken so seriously that a special royal commissioner was appointed to scour the Jewish communities of Lithuania in search of these "converts."[33]

Events in Poland at times carried at least an indirect connection to Russia. The runaway serf and peasant ideologue Teodius Kosoi escaped from Russia to Lithuania in 1540, where he propounded radical theological theories which some have professed to see as "Judaizing" doctrines.[34] There was ample reason, therefore, for theologically unsophisticated Muscovy to feel itself under siege and to vent some of its resultant rage on a religious rival more familiar, at least in scriptural terms, than vague and shadowy Protestantism. This point may be seen in the theological arguments which Ivan IV made against Protestantism. In a religious debate in 1570 with Jan Rokyta, a representative of the Protestant Polish Brethren, Ivan polemicized:

> Concerning the other words of Deuteronomy, if there is need to follow them, there is need to be circumcised and comply with all the laws of Moses. For that reason you are Judaizers, as true Christians ought not to be, for Christ nullified it (the Old Law) through the mystery of His divine and human appearance, and instituted the New Law.[35]

It is noteworthy that Muscovites came more and more to identify the Jews with Poland, home not only of Jews but of Judaizing heresies as well. This connection was made decisively during the Time of Troubles, Muscovy's doleful social and dynastic crisis. As fearful as Muscovites were of very real Catholic, "Latin," influences spreading into the land from Poland at this time, they showed equal concern with Judaism. When negotiations were undertaken by some boyars to place Prince Wladislaw of Poland on the Muscovite throne, it was stipulated that Jews from Poland were not to be permitted to enter the Russian state.[36] Attempts were made by Muscovite publicists to discredit the Second False Dmitrii by describing him as a "Jew by birth" (*rodom zhidovin*) who was surrounded by heretics and "deicidal Jews" (*bogoubiits zhidov*).[37] There was a tangible basis for these anti-Jewish preoccupations. Jews served as auxiliaries in the Polish armies which intervened in Muscovy after the election of the Romanov dynasty to the throne.[38] The number of Polish-Jewish prisoners of war was sufficient for their fate to be considered in the treaties of the period.[39] Thus, at a time when the religious and political integrity of the Russian state was under attack, Jews, however few, were to be found in the enemy camp. The defense of the Russian land came to include its defense against the "deicidal Jews."

The Muscovite fear of foreign political or religious domination was assuaged somewhat when the military balance began to tip against Poland, a state of affairs graphically confirmed by Peter the Great's meddling in the elections of Poland's kings, and by the Russian triumphs in the Great Northern War. The issue of the Jews, with its religious connotations, was not an important one at the time; nor should it have been, given Peter's rather cavalier attitude toward religion in general. Despite a sizable fund of apocryphal stories professing to show Peter's antipathy or sympathy toward the Jews[40]—virtually all of them involving economic and not religious considerations—no formal laws were forthcoming during his reign. This was despite the fact that in the seventeenth century Russia acquired portions of the Polish Ukraine where Jews were settled. Peter's immediate successors displayed ambivalence and intolerance in equal measure. Occasional concern was voiced over the activities of Jewish tavern keepers and revenue farmers, and recurrent attempts were made to expel the Jews living in the Ukraine, beginning in 1727.[41] Nonetheless, Jews were still invited into Russia for the fairs, and the very repetition of the expulsion decrees suggested that they were being indifferently enforced.

When the Russian state bestirred itself to act vigorously against the Jews once more, it was again the fear of proselytism that provided the goad. In 1738 the government investigated the case of a retired Russian naval captain, Aleksandr Voznitsyn, who had converted to Judaism under the influence of a Jew from Smolensk district, Borokh Leibov. The investigation culminated in the public burning of both Voznitsyn and Leibov before a large crowd in St. Petersburg on 15 July 1738. The mechanics of the investigation reveal the single-mindedness of the authorities. Leibov was also accused of the ritual torture of a Christian serving girl in order to obtain her blood, and the murder of an Orthodox priest. The Senate informed Empress Anna that these charges could not be effectively investigated if Leibov was executed too promptly. His execution took place expeditiously nonetheless.[42] It was under the influence of this episode that Anna reaffirmed the expulsion decree issued by Empress Catherine I in 1727, expelling all Jews from the Ukraine.[43]

Such leniency disappeared once and for all with the ascension to the throne of Peter I's daughter Elizabeth in 1741. Devoutly Orthodox and fiercely intolerant, she pursued a crude campaign of forced conversion against the non-Orthodox, especially Muslims and Jews. On 2 December 1742, invoking the decrees of her predecessors, she announced the expulsion of "these haters of the name of Christ, the Savior," warning that their activities could only harm devout Christians.[44] Not all of Elizabeth's subjects agreed, and a petition came to the Senate from the merchants of Riga, who feared the economic consequences of the loss of their Jewish middlemen in trade with Poland. Elizabeth scornfully rejected the recommendation of the Senate that some Jews be permitted to reside in Riga with her famous retort "I desire no mercenary profit from the enemies of

ELISABETA   PRIMA,
Imperatrix et   Autocratrix
      Omnium   *Rossiarum*.

Empress Elizabeth Petrovna

Christ."[45] To close the last loopholes in her ban, the empress also withdrew, in 1744, the provision permitting temporary visits to Russia by
Jews attending fairs.[46] "Muscovite" intolerance had triumphed.

There was an additional, unintended effect of Muscovy's *cordon sanitaire*
against the Jews. While Russia remained free of Poland's Jews, her reli-

gious culture was uncontaminated by Poland's anti-Jewish stereotypes. Before the acquisition of Polish territory, Russia proper lacked trials for sacrilege or ritual murder. Even after the partitions, the Orthodox Church in Russia was slow to accept the cults of ritual murder victims included in the church calendar of the Orthodox Church in Polish territories.[47] As for the Talmud, it is doubtful that many Russian churchmen were even aware of its existence. For the Russian Orthodox clergy, and for their congregations, the crimes of the Jews were the crucifixion and their continuing rejection of Christ, and these crimes alone were sufficient to exclude them from the realm. The more creative and fanciful aspects of Judeophobia in Poland and the West were simply not needed.

This situation found reflection in Russian popular culture, which totally ignored the Jews as subject matter. The energetic search of nineteenth-century investigators failed to discover popular sayings or songs in Russian which dealt with the Jews in either positive or negative terms.[48] (Only gradually, after the partitions, did the first timid borrowings take place from the rich storehouse of Ukrainian Judeophobic lore. Such sayings were often as anti-Polish as they were anti-Jewish.) In his magisterial study of the Russian *lubok*, or popular print, D. A. Ravinskii neatly summarized the situation: "The Jew in Moscow in past times was quite unheard of; therefore there are no humorous pictures of them." The sole exception which he could find in the eighteenth century was a woodcut published in Kiev by Adam Goszemski—in Polish.[49]

The religious tradition inherited by Russian statesmen after 1772 was a variegated one. The indigenous traditions of Muscovy treated the Jews as an abstraction in the form of a vague threat to the integrity of the Christian faith. The methods which this perspective offered for dealing with the Jews were crude and unsophisticated: forced conversion, wholesale expulsion, massacre. The regime of Catherine II was aware of this hostility—it provided a motive for Catherine's rejection of a proposal to admit the Jews into the empire for trade purposes in 1763. But there was little practical guidance for her servitors after 1772 (despite the assumptions of scholars like Dubnow and Orshanskii that religious intolerance was a major factor underlying Russian treatment of the Jews under the empire). The most obvious "Muscovite" approach to the Jews after the partitions would have been to expel them from those areas in which they lived, as the Russian state had done in the past. Practical logistics, European opinion, and, most of all, the bureaucrats' own views of the interests of a well-ordered state militated against this.

At the same time, Russian officialdom had to be aware of religious hostility of a different sort: the collective attitudes of the population of the newly annexed areas. This hostility was more practical because it grew not out of abstractions like the Russian variant but out of the daily intercourse of

"The Jew Leiba," printed in Kiev in the second half of the eighteenth century. In the background, Poles are beating a protesting Jew. In an accompanying Polish and Latin text, Leiba laments the loss of Palestine and complains that the lack of radishes and garlic in Poland may force the Jews to eat pork.

Christian and Jew. A further complication was that religious considerations frequently served to mask some economic complaint. These views also contained a more imaginative view of the Jews as an active, anti-Christian force, armed with the precepts of the Talmud and with the ritual slaughter-er's knife, seeking to harm the body as well as the soul of the devout Christian. Finally, these prejudices coexisted with a pragmatic acceptance of the presence and role of the Jews amid the local Gentile community.

This religious tradition, which in no way can be considered "Muscovite religious intolerance," had a dual effect on the Russian administrators who encountered it. It placed limitations on how they could treat the Jews under the law if they wished to maintain public order and the loyalty of new subjects. In addition, some of the prejudices of this tradition began to percolate into the bureaucratic consciousness, helping to shape the emerging Russian conceptions of the Jewish Question.

THE PRAGMATIC TRADITION

In counterpoint to the religious tradition was a coexisting tradition of pragmatic acceptance of the Jews throughout Europe. Banned from landownership and from agriculture in general, the Jews of necessity had become an urban, mercantile people in the midst of societies which were overwhelmingly rural and agricultural. As such, they were called upon to perform a variety of services within the medieval economy. The inevitable consequence was a measure of toleration, albeit inconsistent and transitory.

The most striking exemplar of the pragmatic tradition was Poland, where, as noted above, the Jews developed a distinctive cultural and political life. A Jewish presence was to be found in Kievan Rus' and, despite the ferocity of Muscovite religious attitudes, even in Moscow itself, although in minute numbers. (There are rather more examples of Jewish converts to Christianity in Muscovy, but they need not be considered here, since conversion immediately removed their "Jewishness" in the eyes of the state.) Muscovite rulers, such as Grand Prince Ivan III, occasionally utilized Jews as diplomatic agents and as medical personnel.[50] In his letter to Ivan IV of 1550, King Sigismund Augustus asked that his Jewish subjects be admitted into Muscovy "as of old" (*kak po starine*). This phrase may have been merely a diplomatic usage, or it may have implied a recent economic relationship between Polish Jews and Muscovy.

The seventeenth century was dominated by a series of wars between Muscovy and Poland, and the inevitable consequence was the arrival of Polish-Jewish refugees, hostages, and prisoners of war in Muscovy. While policy still prevented Jews from coming to Muscovy from Poland—a Russo-Polish trade treaty of 1678 denied them entry—peace treaties concluding hostilities between the two rivals were more permissive. Prisoners taken in the Smolensk War of 1632–1634 were permitted to remain in Muscovy after the end of the war, and this provision included unbaptized Jews.[51] In 1655 special sections of Moscow and Nizhnii Novgorod were reserved for Jewish prisoners of war—the Russo-Polish war over the Ukraine having begun—in order to hinder their contact with the Orthodox citizenry. Subsequently, Jews who refused to convert to Orthodoxy were exiled to settlement in Siberia.[52] The Treaty of Andrusovo of 1667, which ended the war, specifically gave freedom to Jewish prisoners of war and permitted them to remain in Russia. The leaders of the two opposing sides in the church schism both reportedly had contacts with Jews. The Old Believer priest Avvakum participated in discussions at the home of F. M. Rtishchev together with a converted Jew, Backa, who was later accused of Judaizing propaganda. While the former patriarch Nikon was under detention in the Voskresenskii monastery, he was visited by "foreigners, Poles, Circassians, Belorussians, and baptized Germans and Jews," with the permission of the Russian government.[53] A small Jewish community also sprang up illegally in Moscow itself, clustered around Daniel von Gaden (Fungadanov), a Jewish convert to Lutheranism who served as a medical doctor in Russian service. The position of these Jews was always irregular and precarious, as demonstrated by the fate of their protector von Gaden— murdered in the *strel'tsy* (musketeer) mutiny of 1682.[54]

Jews continued to reside, de facto if not de jure, in those areas of the Ukraine ceded to Russia by Poland. Jews were also to be found among the merchants who attended the annual fairs in Kiev, Nezhin, and elsewhere. On the basis of evidence assembled for a ritual murder trial in Chernigov in April of 1702, it is apparent that Jews owned private property, hired Christian servants, and met together from time to time for ritual purposes.[55] This settlement was far from the Russian heartland and was of no special concern to the central government. Indeed, when the Chernigov ritual murder case was reported to Peter the Great, he evidenced more skepticism than concern.[56]

Such was not the case with Peter's more devout successors, who set about expelling Jews even from the borderlands. The town of Smolensk was an important center for the entry of Polish trade goods into Russia, and a small group of Jews resided there in the capacity of farmers of excise taxes and customs duties. One of them, Borokh Leibov—the same Borokh Leibov who was burned at the stake for conversionary activity in 1738— built a synagogue for the Jews in the local village of Zverovich. Protests from the local Orthodox clergy led to the exiling of Borokh from Smolensk to Poland, and then to the formal expulsion of all Jews from the Ukraine.[57]

Such decisive measures soon provoked a reaction. The hetman of Little Russia, Daniel Apostol, petitioned the crown to permit the admission of Jews in order to attend the region's annual fairs. The response of the government, in the guise of the Supreme Privy Council, is revealing, and demonstrated that pragmatic considerations could temper even Russian intolerance. In 1728 the council allowed the Jews to visit the Ukrainian fairs for wholesale trade.[58] In 1731, Smolensk province was included as permitted territory, and in 1734, in response to petitions from Khar'kov, that district was included as well. Jews were permitted to engage in retail as well as wholesale trade in Khar'kov and this right was soon extended to the entire Ukraine.[59]

Pragmatism had its limits as far as the integrity of the Christian faith was concerned, however. In the aftermath of the trial and execution of Borokh Leibov, the government issued another expulsion order directed against Jews who had entered the Ukraine, ostensibly to trade at the fairs, but who had then found permanent residence on the estates of local land-owners. The expulsion was delayed by war for a year, but was carried out in 1740. In all, 573 Jews were expelled from the Ukraine, where they had been residing on 130 private estates.[60]

The collusion of the local gentry ensured that the expulsion decree of 1740 was ineffective. Within the year the failure of the authorities to remove the Jews completely came to the attention of Empress Elizabeth Petrovna, newly arrived on the throne through a palace coup. The em-press was a fanatic on the subject of the religious uniformity of her realm. The heterdox were to be forced into the fold of Russian Orthodoxy or pay the consequences. She embarked upon a program of persecution of Mus-lims in the South, to the detriment of Russian interests in the area. Under-standably, she was not slow to reaffirm the Jewish expulsion decree of 1727, making an exception only for those Jews who were willing to con-vert to Orthodoxy.

Again there was opposition within the empire to such absolute mea-sures, accompanied by warnings of harm to the local economy. The Gen-eral Military Chancellery of Little Russia, for example, petitioned the Senate, on behalf of local Greek merchants, at least to permit Jews to enter the state temporarily for the fairs, since they were the principal intermedi-aries for trade with Poland. A similar warning and request came from the administration of Lifland province, advising the Senate that the expulsion of all Jews from Riga would seriously disrupt trade connections. These were complaints from areas somewhat removed from the centers of Rus-sian politics, but the arguments that they presented were convincing to the Russian membership of the Governing Senate. This body reminded the empress that past expulsion orders had exempted Jews who wished to visit Russia briefly for the fairs. The Senate asked the empress to consider whether, in this regard, it might not be worthwhile to grant a small measure of toleration to the Jews. The Senate petition occasioned Eliza-beth's famous rejoinder, mentioned earlier: "I desire no mercenary profit from the enemies of Christ."[61] The following year a new expulsion order specified that even temporary entry of the Jews into Russia was strictly forbidden. The Senate further announced that it would no longer even accept petitions requesting the admission of Jews into Russia.[62] Although this episode is an obvious demonstration of the triumph of religious intolerance, it simultaneously shows that centers of pragmatism were to be found not only in the Ukraine or Riga, where the economic consequences of intolerance would most obviously be felt, but in the midst of the Governing Senate itself.

In an autocracy the will of the autocrat is decisive, and when the supreme authority, Elizabeth, was a religious fanatic, economic arguments would always prove ineffective. The ascendance to the throne of a less intolerant ruler might have been expected to produce a rapid reversal of Elizabeth's anti-Jewish policies. Such a reversal did not immediately occur for reasons that were, ironically enough, pragmatic.

On 28 June 1762, Catherine, the wife of the emperor Peter III, deposed her husband in a coup d'état and came to the throne as Empress Catherine II. A former German Lutheran, a patron of Philosophes, a sponsor of reformist legislation, and the proclaimer of religious toleration within the empire, she was hardly the exemplar of Muscovite Judeophobia, and still less of the religious enthusiasms of the late Empress Elizabeth. Yet the lot of the Jews did not initially improve under her rule, although she had a specific opportunity to reverse the policy of her predecessor. A Dutch Jewish merchant, one Kalmar from The Hague, had approached the Russian government with a proposal to sponsor a Jewish colonization scheme in Russia.[63] The project, which was sympathetically received, was placed on the agenda of the Senate for consideration. In a fragment from her third-person memoirs, Catherine described the episode:

> On the fifth or sixth day after Catherine II's accession to the throne, she was in the Senate, which had been ordered moved to the Summer Palace so that all its affairs might go more quickly. . . . Every matter in the Senate was carried according to a schedule, with the exception of matters of extreme urgency, and as luck would have it, at this session a project to permit the Jews into Russia was first on the agenda. Catherine was in a difficult position if she should give her approval to such a proposal, even though it was universally recognized as beneficial, and was rescued from this dilemma by the senator Prince Odoevskii, who rose and said to her: "Would it not please your majesty to see before this is decided what the Empress Elizabeth inscribed in the margin of a similar proposal in her own hand?" Catherine ordered them to bring her the files and found that Elizabeth had written, out of devotion, in the margin: "I desire no profit from the enemies of Jesus Christ." It was not yet a week since Catherine had come to the throne, raised to it in order in protect the Orthodox faith; she had to deal with a devout people, with a clergy

who had not recovered their estates [secularized by Tsar Peter III] and who were in difficult circumstances as a result of this unfortunate measure; minds were in great agitation, as is always the case after so many important events; to begin with, such a project would have had an unsettling effect, yet it could not possibly be seen as evil. Catherine simply answered the procurator-general, when he approached her after the vote for her decision: "I desire that this matter be postponed to another time." Thus, it is often not enough to be enlightened, to have the best of intentions and the means of carrying them out, however often [people] might express bold decisions about wise conduct.[64]

This outcome is revealing, since it demonstrates that pragmatism could work against the Jews as well as in their favor. While the project might be "universally recognized as beneficial," the need for a usurper, new to the throne, to retain public confidence was paramount. Incidentally, there is little doubt that Catherine, while recognizing the existence of anti-Jewish feeling among churchmen and the general population, did not approve of it. In her French-language account, Catherine noted that Elizabeth acted "from devotion" (*par dévotion*), while she herself recognized the need to placate "the devout" (*un peuple dévot*). In the eighteenth century, *dévotion* had several connotations, indicating both religious piety and also religious devotion carried to extremes, the immediate stage before universally despised "fanaticism." The latter connotation was the one habitually implied by Catherine in her French writings.[65]

Although aloof from anti-Jewish religious practices, Catherine displayed other concerns regarding a Jewish presence in Russia, which discouraged an immediate reversal of policy. Writing to Diderot in 1773, Catherine noted that Belorussia "swarmed" (*fourmille*) with Jews, a rather striking usage given the relative numerical insignificance of Belorussian Jewry. In the same letter she observed, apropos of the admission of Jews into Russia, that "their entry into Russia can cause great harm to our petty tradesmen, since these people draw everything to themselves, and it could happen that their return would be more of a hurt than a help."[66]

In any event, at first Catherine maintained the Russian quarantine against Jews, just as she retained Elizabeth's policy, slightly muted, of forced conversion and petty persecution of Muslims in the South. Thus when Catherine issued an ukase inviting foreigners to settle in the Russian empire, she specifically excluded Jews, again out of deference to public opinion. Yet Catherine soon came to realize that she had other constituencies to placate. In 1764 the empress received a petition dealing with the rights of Little Russia from the szlachta, elders, and hetman of the Ukraine, which included a request that Jews be permitted at least short-term admission to the area. In March of that same year, the Riga city council echoed the Ukrainian request, emphasizing the economic hardship the city had undergone since the expulsion of the Jews.[67] At the same time, the government embarked upon a program of active recruitment to bring foreign settlers into New Russia, as Russia consolidated its hold on the Black Sea littoral. Russian agents were soon scouring Europe for would-be settlers. The appropriate officials were not particular as to the nationality of these pioneers. As Prince Potemkin was later to say, he would colonize the area, "even with Jews."[68] In fact, the governor of New Russia in 1764, A. P. Mel'gunov, employed French emissaries to recruit Jewish settlers from Prussia and Poland.[69]

These various elements came together in a scheme, sponsored by the empress herself, to accomplish by stealth what she dared not do openly. A secret agreement was struck whereby selected Jewish merchants were granted permission to live and carry on business in Riga in return for sponsoring a project designed to resettle groups of their coreligionists in New Russia. Apparently both sides kept their side of the bargain.[70] To expedite these clandestine activities, the Chancellery for the Guardianship of Foreigners, charged with promotion of foreign colonization in Russia, sent an order to the authorities in New Russia: "People of any nationality and [religious] observance crossing the border with the intention of entering service or settling in the New Russian province shall immediately be admitted into the aforesaid province. They shall not be asked their nationality or observance, or required to produce passports."[71] Catherine thus developed a unique device for circumventing the laws of the empire which she ruled—border officials simply stopped looking at passports!

With the taboo on Jewish settlement thus violated, Catherine's government gradually became less circumspect. In 1768 war broke out between the Russian Empire and the multinational Ottoman Empire. Prisoners of war, as was customary, were permitted to settle in Russia. The law now specifically included Jews, while noting that they were to settle only in New Russia. Jews were nonetheless to be found scattered throughout the empire, at times in the most unexpected places. In her correspondence with Diderot noted above, Catherine mentioned that a number of Jews had been residing in the capital itself for almost a decade—in the house of her religious confessor.

The pragmatic tradition was the one the Russian state was most inclined to follow in the period immediately after the Polish partition of 1772. The Jews were still very much an unknown entity to Russian policymakers, and the initial concern of Catherine's government was the maintenance of order, a goal best achieved, it was believed, by the retention of the status quo. As Russia came to know her Jews, however, she became aware of another aspect of this Polish inheritance, a reformist tradition.

THE REFORMIST TRADITION

A careful distinction should be made between the pragmatic and the reformist traditions. The pragmatic tradition, as noted above, prompted attempts to derive what benefits one could from the Jews within the framework of existing systems and institutions. The reformist tradition aimed at the fundamental transformation of the Jewish-Gentile relationship within states and societies. There were many variations on the broad reformist theme. While prescriptions for change came from the European-wide Enlightenment movement, policies were shaped by the numerous phases and strands of the Enlightenment, of which the French Lumière and the Germanic Aufklärung were merely the most prominent examples. Consequently, the reformist tradition was considerably more varied and diverse than the pragmatic tradition.

The Enlightenment movement ignored religious prejudices toward the Jews or, more accurately, transferred them to a secular plane. Enlightenment thinkers as a whole did not see Jewish flaws and shortcomings as innate, to be held in check by persecution and discrimination, but as transient and conditional, to be remedied by "rational" reforms. These reforms were to make Jews good citizens, harmless to their neighbors and useful to the state.

A relaxation of religious antipathy toward the Jews was inherent in the Enlightenment from its earliest antecedents. As John Locke declared in his *A Letter Concerning Toleration:* "Nay, if we may openly speak the truth . . . neither pagan nor Mahometan nor Jew ought to be excluded from the civil rights of the commonwealth because of his religion. The Church commands no such thing."[72]

By 1781 the climate of European opinion had matured to the extent that an attempt was made to translate these abstract sentiments into the world of political and social realities. In that year a Prussian court official named Christian Wilhelm Dohm published *On the Civil Betterment of the Jews* (*Über die bürgerliche Verbesserung der Juden*), which stands as the definitive Enlightenment statement on the Jews, a seminal work from which many reformers were to draw inspiration. (The extent to which Dohm was expressing ideas which were "in the air," moreover, can be seen in the fact that the famous Edict of Toleration of Joseph II was promulgated on the eve of the publication of Dohm's book.)[73]

In his treatise Dohm stressed the cardinal principle that the apparent corruption and degeneration of the Jewish race were not innate qualities, but rather a product of centuries of mistreatment and oppression.[74] Dohm posed a paradox: why did all the states of Europe desire to increase their population while at the same time consistently seek to rid themselves of Jews? He asserted that such discrimination was based on the mistaken belief by Gentiles that Jews hate Christians, compounded by the assumption that the Jewish race was morally corrupt. The first charge was refuted by contemporary Judaism's demonstrative rejection of any hatred of Christians.[75] Dohm claimed that commentators had mistaken the effect for the cause: the irregularities and perversities of Jewish life derived not from within, but in response to centuries of continuous persecution.[76] More important, this was a reversible process: "if the state of oppression into which he [the Jew] has come during the centuries has corrupted his spirit and his morals, a more equitable treatment will correct them."[77]

With these principles in mind, Dohm suggested a course of reform for the Jews, the provisions of which merit attention because they typify the assumptions that underlay reform throughout Westen Europe. First and foremost the Jews were to enjoy the same rights as all other citizens. This meant the removal of discrimination against the Jews in agriculture, trade, and the professions, which alone would suffice to work a major transformation in their economic status. Dohm reflected the physiocratic belief that many of the negative, "depraved" features of Jewish life derived from their concentration in petty trade, a pursuit looked upon as economically retrograde since it supposedly made no positive contribution to the national economy. Dohm assumed that once opportunities were opened to them the Jews would flock to other pursuits, especially agriculture. The Jews were to be encouraged to engage in agriculture by tax rebates and grants. To eliminate the possibility of fraud by the unreconstructed few who remained in trade, merchant Jews were henceforth to keep their account books in the national language of their native country. This led Dohm to a logical emphasis on the importance of public instruction being opened to the Jews, which he buttressed by a solemn promise that Judaism would not be attacked or threatened in such schools.

Dohm's reform also dealt with the knotty problem of the Jewish kehillah or religious community (the Polish kahal). He correctly recognized that its amalgam of religious and secular functions made it a difficult institution for the central government to supplant. Dohm therefore was willing to allow wide latitude to the kehillah. The community was to endure as an autonomous unit, and Jews were to retain their own law and traditions, much as towns and communities traditionally retained their own local prerogatives. Jewish judges were to provide the court of first resort whenever possible, although appeals were to be permitted to Christian courts. Dohm encouraged the retention of extensive community authority by the rabbinate, extending even to the rabbi's right to excommunicate Jewish malefactors.[78]

Dohm's prescriptions grew out of the Germanic Enlightenment tradition (the Aufklärung) encompassing what Marc Raeff has called "the well-ordered police state," in which the state is the expression of "society's conscious desire to maximize all its resources and to use this new potential dynamically for the enlargement and improvement of its way of life."[79] In pursuit of this goal, where traditional institutions had broken down they were recreated, and where they survived and appeared to function for the use of society, as in the case of the Jewish kehillah, they were retained. Dohm's project further followed the German tradition by stressing freedom for the Jews as a whole, in contrast to the French Lumière tradition, which gave priority to the pursuit of private material interest over the general welfare of the community.[80] The intellectual pedigree of Dohm's ideas eased the path by which the model of Jewish reform could be transferred to societies with a narrower conception of Enlightenment ideals.

Another observation on the nature of the Enlightenment is pertinent here. The role of Enlightenment rationalism as a driving force in the gradual emancipation of Europe's Jews seemed so obvious to historians that there has been a tendency to overlook the negative elements that it also contained. For example, the attacks which the Philosophes rained upon the heads of credulous Christian ecclesiastics could be directed against Judaism as well. While antireligious considerations provided a starting point for negative judgments of the Jews by the Philosophes, the style and manner of Jewish economic and communal life reinforced them. The degrading occupations of the Jews, the effects of persecution, the closed world of Jewish society, the alleged intellectual ossification created by the Talmud and tradition—all made the Jews suspect in the eyes of the enlightened.

The Enlightenment thus produced two distinct views of the Jews. On the one hand, the individual Jew was adjudged a human being, capable of improvement and perfection like all other men. On the other, the collective Jew was seen as the corrupted product of persecution, degraded by centuries of isolation in the petty trades, leaseholding, and usury.[81] These two trends were found combined in the policies of "enlightened despots" such as Joseph II and in those of the French revolutionaries. They merged together to produce a belief that the Jews could be reformed, but only by coercion, directed against the economically retrograde activities of the Jews. It was hoped that economic transformation would result in civic improvement or at least in increased utility for the state. All such thought tended to be abstract and removed from social realities. Further, the first attempts at reform throughout Europe generally took place where the Jews were present only in limited numbers or where they were unrepresentative of Jewry as a whole. The initial attempts at reforms by European governments were thus directed toward the Jews of Bordeaux, Berlin, or Vienna. When reform was extended to larger settlements it invariably lost much of its ideal character and took on a more pragmatic cast. Still, given the spread of Enlightenment views, reform of the Jews was virtually inevitable, especially when triggered by political upheavals like the partitions of Poland or the French Revolution. While reform was a common goal, however, the specific measures taken reflected the national conditions and peculiarities of the states which carried them out.[82]

Joseph II of Austria, for example, was willing to overlook the cultural or religious deficiencies of people who could be useful to the state in other ways. Joseph's reign was typified by the twin desires to make the Jews "useful" to the state and "harmless" for the population at large. His famous Edict of Toleration (*Toleranzpatent*) of 1782 for the Jews of Austria and Moravia entirely favored the rich or prosperous Jewish businessman. Joseph was not ready to extend similar toleration to the Jewish peddler, usurer, or leaseholder. These occupations were viewed as unproductive or exploitive, especially as pursued by the large Jewish minority in Galicia. This aspect of Joseph's reform recalled the *Polizeistaaten* of the previous century, many of which placed restrictions on Jewish peddlers and petty tradesmen.[83] In 1784 the Jews of Galicia were forbidden to lease public houses, inns, or taverns, or to distill spirits for the noble landowners. The government also considered the expulsion of Jews from private estates as a means of removing these competitors from the equally impoverished classes of Gentile artisans and craftsmen. In 1785, letters patent for the Jews of Galicia forbade them to engage in any leaseholding activities such as leasing estates, establishing mill monopolies, or making toll collections. The inertia of the Galician administration, as well as the opposition of the landowners themselves, largely robbed these measures of their efficacy.[84] The attempt to restructure Jewish economic life is of special interest, however, because it closely paralleled measures undertaken at the same time by the Russian government.

The Austrian government did not confine itself to negative actions alone, and some attempts were ultimately made to shift the economic focus of Jewish society. Joseph toyed with the idea of agricultural settlements for the Jews of Galicia as early as 1781, and by 1785, with the abolition of many of the traditional occupations of the Jews, a plan was put into effect. In a directive of 16 July 1785 the emperor ordered the Galician authorities to begin a program of agricultural resettlement. This was not an expedient time for such a program, since the government was already encountering difficulties with German colonists in the same area. By 1786, however, the first settlement came into existence in the village of Dabrówka, near the town of Nowy Sacz. The successful establishment of a colony inspired many Jewish communities to request assistance in settlement. Much as Joseph desired the continuation of this program it ultimately failed from a lack of cooperation from the local authorities, who were harassed enough by the strains imposed upon them by German colonization.[85] Nonetheless, the Austrian experience was a precedent for a similar Russian scheme attempted between 1806 and 1812, which encountered an identical lack of success.

Joseph was determined to reorder the political and social lives of his subjects no less than the economic, and the Jews were no exception. Joseph could not tolerate the traditional autonomy the Jewish community had enjoyed under Polish rule, since it ran counter to his conception of good state order. His mother, Maria Theresa, had viewed the Jews as little more than a source of income, which could best be extracted through the unrestricted internal workings of the kehillah. The Toleration Patent which Joseph proclaimed for Galician Jewry in 1789 changed much of this. Rabbis were deprived of their judicial power and of their right to ban or excommunicate members of their community. Jewish litigants were hereafter expected to bring their disputes into government courts. The power of the kehillah elders (now to be elected under the supervision of the government) was rigidly circumscribed. In the course of equalizing the Jews before the law, the kehillah was thus largely stripped of its former prerogatives.[86]

Of special concern to the Jewish masses were Joseph's attempts to assimilate or Germanize the Jews. This goal was approached in two ways. First, attempts were made to assimilate the Jews by restricting Jewish language, education, dress, and customs. The Galician Patent demanded the establishment of special schools within each community to teach the German language. (Austrian officials were quite concerned that Yiddish was a "shield for wrongdoing.")[87] Decrees of 1785 and 1787 were directed at other types of Jewish exclusiveness. For instance, all Jews were ordered to choose a German surname. Additionally, in return for their new equality, the Jews were expected to bear the same responsibilities as all other residents of the Empire. In a decree of 18 February 1788, Joseph made clear that this included military service.

Galician Jews did not respond to this decree with enthusiasm. Recruitment was not seen as a potential step toward emancipation and patriotic involvement but as a threat to important Judaic taboos surrounding food, dress, and the Sabbath. Recruits deserted in droves, and the huge bounties offered for recruits went unclaimed.[88] The whole episode served to reinforce contemporary claims that the Jews were unfit for military service. (Russian reformers certainly drew this conclusion.) These, like so many of Joseph's well-intentioned reforms, were bitterly resented by their intended beneficiaries.

Prussian administrators lacked even Joseph's good intentions toward the Jews: reform for them was a classic case of making a virtue of necessity. Before 1772 the Jewish population of the Kingdom of Prussia was minimal, restricted in the main to a few tolerated *Schutzjuden* residing in urban centers like Berlin. Yet the Prussian realm also served as a kind of workshop for reforms related to Jewish life. The great proponent of Jewish enlightenment, Moses Mendelssohn, was a resident of Berlin. Throughout the late eighteenth and early nineteenth centuries, Berlin was a center of the Jewish enlightenment movement and was associated with the names of reformers such as Hartwig Wessely and David Friedländer.

The *Schutzjuden* were always insignificant in number, and their lives rigidly controlled by the government. With the first partition of Poland in 1772 the Prussian state annexed the Netze district of Greater Poland, which included some ten thousand Jews. Frederick II attempted to implement the same residence criteria for these Jews as for those of Prussia proper. In 1772 the King's Chamber ordered the expulsion of all Jews with assets of under a thousand thalers. With the acquisition of Polish territory in 1793 and 1795, which contained a Jewish population approaching 200,000, such primitive measures were no longer realistic. There remained, after all, no rump Polish state into which Jews could be deported as had been the case in 1772. On 17 April 1797, therefore, Prussia made a significant attempt to regularize the position of her new Jewish subjects, the last such reform in Prussia before the Napoleonic Wars and the Jewish emancipation that accompanied them in 1812. This regulation was the *General-Juden-Reglement für Sud-und Neu-Ost-Preussen.*

The *Juden-Reglement* initiated a process that Raphael Mahler described as *Reglementiererei*—regulation mania—but which was squarely within the tradition of the well-ordered police state.[89] The autonomy of the kehillah was stripped away, and regulation of all aspects of the individual Jew's life passed under the purview of the Prussian bureaucracy. Regulations were laid down to govern residence, occupation, and even marriage. A permit was required for each of these aspects of daily life. The government clearly aimed at directing Jews for the maximum benefit of the state. Occupations such as the liquor trade, which the government considered undesirable, were banished outright. Peddling was also restricted. The circumstances under which Jews could practice other trades were clearly delineated. Ultimately the *Reglement* aimed at restricting all Jews to one of four categories of occupations: commerce and trade, artisanship, agriculture and related carrying trades, and hired labor. Prosperous Jews were encouraged to build factories and staff them with Jewish workers.[90] The *Reglement*, especially in its delineation of Jewish occupations, anticipated the Jewish project of the Russian reformer I. G. Frizel, governor of the nearby Russian province of Lithuania, who may well have been acquainted with it.

It is interesting that Russians concerned with the Jewish problem never mentioned France, because it was there that the rationalistic impulse to reform was taken to its logical extreme, with the advent of complete emancipation and, in theory at least, total equality. Under the Bourbon kings France had not been in the forefront of Jewish reform, although the potentiality of the Jews for improvement had been a common topic of debate among French intellectuals. The outbreak of the Revolution and the constitution of the National Assembly were not immediately followed by the emancipation of French Jewry, however much the Jews imagined that the Declaration of the Rights of Man applied to Jew as well as Gentile. The actual emancipation took place in two stages, the rights of "active citizens" being granted to the Portuguese, Spanish, and Avignonnais Jews (the Sephardim) on 28 January 1790 and to the remaining Ashkenazim of Alsace and Lorraine on 27 September 1791. This chronology is signifi- cant. The first act emancipated Jews who were already much assimilated. They stood, in their roles as wealthy merchants and well-to-do trades- men, on almost equal terms with the French middle class in language, culture, and values. Given toleration, they could stand as the social equals of the bourgeoisie. The Ashkenazim, on the other hand, were concen- trated in Alsace and were indigent artisans, petty tradesmen, and usurers, largely segregated from Christians by culture as well as religion. This group was emancipated only after prolonged and acrimonious debate, and only over the vehement protests of the clerical bloc and the Gentile repre- sentatives from Alsace.[91]

What is noteworthy about the emancipation, the most advanced in Europe for almost a half century, is the way in which it was carried out. The various corporations, such as the guilds, which had composed the basis of the socioeconomic structure of feudal France, were abolished. This included the Jewish kehillah, although its abolition came over the protests of the Jewish communities of Alsace-Lorraine, which would have preferred the continuation of an autonomous existence. In the case of the other corporations, the government took over, along with their existing financial assets, the debts and responsibilities incurred before their disso- lution. The one exception was the Jewish community. Although the com- munity, with all its myriad functions, and the various posts and offices within it were disbanded, the individual Jews retained responsibility as individuals for the debts which had formerly been borne collectively.[92]

These expedients have merited a brief résumé, because they anticipated several measures put forward by Russian reformers, especially by the poet and senator G. R. Derzhavin. Writing in 1800, Derzhavin did not point to revolutionary France as a model for imitation, but some of his proposals for financial reform suggest French influence. For the next two decades, however, the Jewish policy of France would be increasingly subordinated to the ambitions of Napoleon Bonaparte, who disliked the Jewish masses and who partially rescinded the complete emancipations of 1790 and 1791. Some of the techniques that Napoleon utilized for controlling and ma- nipulating the Jewish population of the French Empire, such as the As- sembly of Jewish Notables and the Great Sanhedrin of 1806–1807, did not so much inspire imitation as fear in the rest of Europe that such moves would gain Napoleon the sympathy of Jews outside the borders that he controlled. In Russia, such fears actually retarded the implementation of articles of the reform Statute of 1804.

Poland, the homeland of the vast majority of Europe's Jews and a land receptive to European cultural influences, was not immune to reformist ferment. Yet the most advanced views did not gain an immediate hearing, even after the trauma of partition in 1772 had given a new urgency to schemes of internal reform. In 1778, for instance, the Polish court official and influential magnate Andrzej Zamoyski prepared a draft of a reform project for King Stanisław Poniatowski. This project is a useful benchmark against which subsequent Polish reform proposals may be judged. The reform would have done little more than maintain the status quo, although the opposition of urban mercantile classes was visible in strictures to be placed on the free exercise of Jewish trade. The reform advocated the inclusion of all Jews into a useful profession, in trade, crafts, or agriculture. This provision was to be enforced by the denial of marriage certificates to Jews who were improperly employed. The Jews were to be granted equality in that they were to be responsible for the obligations each Polish social class bore, but they were not to enjoy the corresponding rights and prerogatives. Clerical prejudice was indulged by means of regulations forbidding Jews to employ Christians as servants. There were few echoes in this reform of the sophisticated responses to the Jewish problem then being discussed in Western Europe.[93]

By 1780 a proposal for reform of Jews along Western European lines appeared in an anonymous brochure entitled "Rozmowa miedzy szlachcicem polskim, szwajcarem i Żydem w Gdańsku" ("A Conversation Between a Polish Nobleman, a Swiss, and a Jew in Gdansk") which pointed to the excesses of the szlachta regime, the irrationality of existing law, and the autonomy of the kahal as the causes of the decline of Polish Jewry. Various features of Jewish life in need of reform were enumerated.[94] Two years later, in 1782, there appeared a pamphlet which enjoyed a much wider vogue, and passed through multiple editions. The author of "Żydzi czyli konieczna potrzeba reformowania Żydów" ("The Necessity of a Reformation of the Jews") aimed at awakening Poles to the Jewish Question and at dealing with it in the new, "French" way. The Poles were urged to stop viewing the Jews as a "special phenomenon of nature" to be scoffed at and persecuted, but rather to recognize that any failings which the Jews might display were not innate, but formed by the influence of religion, law, and upbringing. "A man is born neither evil nor good, clever nor stupid; he is born rather with the potentiality to become one or the other."[95] The author characterized the Jewish religion itself as based on love of one's fellow man, a precept which only Christian persecution had kept the individual Jew from fulfilling. Since the Jews were largely outside the laws that protected the occupations of most citizens, they were forced to turn to petty trade for survival, thus further encouraging the contempt with which their Polish compatriots viewed them. The author argued that the conditions of Polish life affecting the Jews would have to be changed before moral reform was possible. For instance, he observed, the Jews had finally been granted the right to engage in agriculture since 1775, and yet only fourteen families had done so, presumably because Jews were still not permitted to own land.

> Our laws regarding the Jews are wrong. Their situation, outside a class, is wrong. It's wrong to place power over them in the hands of private individuals or special Jewish bureaucrats. It's wrong to consider them a bad nation and to offer them no fatherland. Worst of all is that we allow them to live with special laws and customs. Owing to this they appear as a new *corpus in corpore*, a state within a state; in view of the fact that Jewish laws and rites are different from ours, such a state of things gives rise to conflicts, confusion, mutual distrust, contempt, and hatred.[96]

The reforms advocated by the author were generous, but at a price. The Jews were to be admitted to the urban estates, the power of the wojewoda was to be decreased, and the Jews were to be permitted to vote for and serve in the magistracy, as well as to enjoy the other rights and responsibilities of the merchant classes. In return, the Jews must abandon their unique political and cultural autonomy. The kahal structure was to be dismantled. The Jews were to surrender their distinctive dress and "jargon" (Yiddish). While the anonymous reformer went further than most in the rights he was willing to grant the Jews, almost all of his successors shared his emphasis on the necessity of Jewish assimilation.

The problem thus broached, it became a subject for intense debate among Polish intellectuals. Theoretical considerations of Jewish reform in Poland reached their zenith during the period of the Quadrennial Diet (1788 to 1792), the last attempt at internal reform before Poland vanished from the map. Clericals and obscurantists as well as the liberals took up the cudgels for some transformation in the status of the Jews. The discussions within the Diet itself were generally associated with three men, the deputy Mateusz Butrymowicz, the publicist Hugo Kołłataj, and the chairman of the Finance Commission in the Diet, Tadeusz Czacki. Butrymowicz can be characterized as a typical representative of the cultural assimilationist view, given his willingness to allow the continuation of kahal autonomy. While he called for the elimination of distinctive Jewish language and dress and the frequent celebration of religious holidays, Butrymowicz proposed that the kahal preserve its control over religious life, taxation, and litigation. Butrymowicz apparently felt that with the removal of Jewish exclusiveness, the kahal would become less of a closed society and that the Jews themselves would become "useful."[97] Kołłataj occupied the middle ground on questions of cultural and political autonomy. He argued from the liberal position that "all men should have equal rights of person and property before the law in Poland," and he stressed that under

Tadeusz Czacki

no circumstances should religion be a disqualifying factor for any position in society. Kołłataj was less concerned than Butrymowicz with abolishing the outward signs of Jewish culture. Instead, he explored means by which the Jews might be brought closer to Christians in daily life, and yet protected from traditional Polish Judeophobia. His solution was to abolish the form and preserve the substance. He advocated the abolition of the kahal, along with undesirable aspects of Jewish communal life like the power of excommunication exercised by the leadership. In its place, he proposed new institutions to govern Jewish communal affairs. In effect, he envisioned a more open kahal structure. Such institutions would include a spiritual court whose sentences would be overseen by a wojewoda commission. The elders and leaders of these new communities were to be men of education and enlightenment; to hold office they were required to possess a certificate of graduation from a Polish school and a knowledge of "logic and natural law."[98] Ultimately these programs, as well as others more liberal and more reactionary, were lost amid the politics of the Diet, and no reform of Jewish life was ultimately voted on. This same fate befell the project developed by Czacki, but with one major difference. Following the partitions, Czacki chose to pursue his career in the Russian Empire and eventually came to the attention of Tsar Alexander I. When the tsar appointed a commission to study the reform of Russian Jews, Czacki was invited to participate as a consultant. Traces of his earlier project are thus to be found scattered throughout the Jewish Statute of 1804. A brief examination of Czacki's project, *Rozprawa o Żydach i Karaitach*, published in 1807, is therefore warranted.

Czacki began his discussion by stressing the importance of some sort of reform in the condition of the Jews. According to Czacki, (1) the Jews numbered over 900,000 and were constantly increasing in population despite an infant mortality rate higher than the rest of the population and despite the sickly, weak condition of Jewish children;[99] (2) Jewish youth were educated "in full ignorance," passing from rudimentary study directly to concentration on the Talmud, while their moral education was "next to nothing"; (3) rabbis were said to exercise despotic power over the Jewish masses; (4) Jews controlled three-fourths of the export trade and a quarter of the import trade of Poland, were usually able to undersell Gentile merchants, and dominated crafts; (5) only fourteen Jewish families were directly engaged in agriculture, while Jewish leaseholders ruined the peasantry.[100]

To remedy these conditions, Czacki argued that the Jews must become a free people, equal in every respect to the Christian population. The Jews were to be permitted entry into one of these well-defined economic classes, trade, crafts, or agriculture, with special tax benefits promised for those who chose the last occupation. To encourage the Jews to embark on this economic transformation the undesirable occupations of innkeeping and leaseholding should be forbidden for fifteen years. Jews would enjoy an active voice in the general community, with the right to participate in the election of officials as well as to serve themselves in offices appropriate to their class. Taxes, obligations, and privileges were to be the same for Christians and Jews.

Czacki dwelt at length on questions of education and enlightenment. The Jews were to be invited and encouraged to attend Christian schools with the guarantee that their faith would be respected therein. In lieu of such attendance, Jewish communities could establish their own schools. These institutions were to be strictly supervised by the government, however, and a demanding course of preparatory study was required for all instructors.

The Jews were offered, on paper, extensive benefits approaching a genuine emancipation. Czacki wished to make of them Polish citizens of the Judaic faith. Thus, while religious freedom was guaranteed, the unique features of Jewish autonomy were also attacked. Hebrew was to be permitted for religious worship, but Jews were expected to learn and utilize either Polish, German, or Russian in their everyday affairs. Legal restrictions were placed on the business activity of any Jew who could not meet this language requirement. The Jews were to abandon the use of a special garb and the Yiddish language. The kahal itself was saddled with few restrictions under Czacki's plan, evidently because the author believed that with the participation of the Jews in the general political life of the nation, autonomous institutions would wither and die. In addition, Czacki appreciated the traumatic effect of reform implemented too rapidly, and his equivocation on this point may have been an attempt to soothe Jewish sensibilities. A liberal before the term, Czacki believed that proper institutions would purify and revive the Jews of Poland.[101] This was a theme that Czacki helped to spread among Russian reformers.

The espousal of values associated with Enlightenment thought was not restricted to Christians alone. Individual representatives of the Jewish intelligentsia likewise attempted to view the ossified Jewish community through the prism of rationalism. These "enlightened" Jews drew inspiration from the European-wide movement for reform and in their turn influenced Gentile reformers by serving as living proof of the potential of the Jews for reform. The importance of such a living example helps explain in part the influence within the European intellectual community of the Berlin *Schutzjude* Moses Mendelssohn (1729–1786).

Mendelssohn can hardly be considered a radical reformer. Even his espousal of Enlightenment ideals was quite in keeping with his earlier intellectual orientation toward an already long-established rationalistic tradition within Judaism. This tradition was perhaps best represented by one of Mendelssohn's chief inspirations, Moses Maimonides, the medieval Jewish thinker who, in his *Guide to the Perplexed*, attempted to explain

Judaism by an appeal to reason. The ideals that could be drawn from this tradition were not uniform, however, and the Jewish enlightenment movement (the Haskalah) represented in Western Europe by Mendelssohn displayed marked differences in other locales. The Haskalah of Berlin was not the Haskalah of Wilno.

Mendelssohn himself never went beyond an attempt to create a rational Judaism based on the essential principles of natural religion. Mendelssohn was at heart a conservative and unwilling to surrender the ritual law of the Jews—although this was the logical development of his thought—because he wished to use it as a means of preserving Jewish identity. Mendelssohn thus differentiated between Christianity, a revealed religion, and Judaism, a "revealed law," a differentiation which allowed him to preserve, to his satisfaction, both the ideal of Judaism as a natural religion and the strictures of the Mosaic Law. Judaism was not a religion revealed to a tiny handful and buttressed by miracles of questionable authenticity as was Christianity. The revelation at Sinai was a historical fact, witnessed with certainty by the whole people. The law was thus given for God's own reasons and was subject to obedience even if its purpose was no longer understood. In return for bearing this special responsibility, the Jewish nation would receive some reward, known but to God. The revelation in Judaism, then, was in "law," not "religion," and aimed at guiding man's daily actions but not his innermost beliefs.[102] Mendelssohn's work, while ultimately superseded by more radical reformers such as Hartwig Wessely and David Friedländer, was a groundbreaking and innovative attempt to bring Judaism into conformity with Enlightenment thought while at the same time preserving its uniqueness.

In his attempt to introduce believing Jews into the mainstream of European culture, Mendelssohn was forced to make concessions. One of his chief targets, therefore, was the vast power of communal and religious leaders. In his great work *Jerusalem*, Mendelssohn strongly attacked the union of church and state, singling out the power of the rabbis to ban or excommunicate from the community as a special evil. He pleaded for the creation of a neutral society into which Jew and Gentile could come as equals.[103] In his exhortation to the "House of Jacob" to "adopt the mores and constitution of the country in which you find yourself, but be steadfast in upholding the religion of your fathers, too" can be seen clearly prefigured the famous formula "Be a Jew at home, but a man in the street."[104]

To further his aim of assimilation in external trappings, Mendelssohn began his celebrated translation of the Old Testament from Hebrew into German. Mendelssohn scorned Judeo-German "jargon" and openly admitted that his translation was designed to acquaint Jews with German and with German culture. Mendelssohn faced forceful opposition from some rabbinical foes, but this served only to enhance his position among Gentiles as a sincere reformer of his race. This view was reinforced by Mendelssohn's low opinion of the inferior economic position of the Jews and his stated wish that they choose occupations more honorable than usury and peddling. Mendelssohn's name became inextricably linked with the Berlin Haskalah, even when this movement went far beyond any concessions Mendelssohn would have made to Gentile society. The "Berliners" would continue to invoke Mendelssohn's name especially in their attempt to spread the Haskalah to Eastern Europe. A principal agent of the West European Haskalah was the monthly periodical *Me'asef* (*Collector*), which was first published in Königsberg in 1783 and transferred to Berlin in 1787. It is noteworthy that even this moderate publication had practically no readership in Eastern Europe.

There was an eastern Haskalah movement, but it differed in important respects from that of the Berlin *Maskilim*, as the proponents of Haskalah were called. The motives of the "Berliners" could often be traced to economic considerations, especially their desire to strip away restrictions on their commercial activities which were motivated by religious prejudice. To accomplish this they were willing to make numerous concessions in the direction of assimilation. In contrast to the Berliners, always suspect in the eyes of the traditionalists, the Jews of Eastern Europe maintained their economic and cultural environment. Reaction to oppression within and without the community was apparent in the rise of Hasidism, directed against the stagnant learning of rabbinical Judaism. Hasidism, quasi-mystical, contended with the rabbinical party in Poland and Russia, plunging these communities into religious civil war. There was another strain of opposition to the entrenched rabbinicalism, however, an "Eastern Haskalah." These Eastern Maskilim, in contrast to the Berliners, operated within the context of traditional culture. What they opposed, with trenchant humor and biting satire, was the ossified state of Jewish learning, typified by *pilpul*, or casuistic argumentation and haggling devoid of substance, as well as the mania for commandments governing all aspects of life (*mitzvot*). These reformers looked to Maimonides, Mendelssohn's inspiration, as a vital source of rationalism and practicality within Judaism. The attacks never extended beyond the traditional Jewish educational schema: they were completely out of sympathy with ideals of economic and cultural reform. It is important to stress how insignificant in number were these Eastern Maskilim when contrasted with the Hasidim and their opponents, the Mitnaggedim.

Even more insignificant was the isolated Berliner. Ironically, representatives of the Berlin outlook gained greatest access to the ears of Russian reformers. This is perhaps to be expected, since they were willing to tell these reformers what they wished to hear: assimilation was not only necessary, but possible, if carried out by governmental fiat. Thus, as will be seen, Jewish partisans of reform, like Dr. Il'ia Frank and Judah Leiba

Nevakhovich, played major roles as ideologists in the formulation of Russian reform. At the same time they remained in intellectual isolation from the vast majority of their coreligionists. The reforms they espoused were hostile to the established communal authorities and bitterly resisted by them. For most Eastern European Jews, reform was something done to them by the agents of the state, not a process in which they participated with enthusiasm or commitment.

3

RUSSIA AND the Jews:
FIRST IMPRESSIONS, 1772–1796

Russian administrators encountered organized Jewish communal
life as a tabula rasa, since the few Jews who lived in Russia before
1772 did so as illegal residents of St. Petersburg or as settlers of
unknown nationality in New Russia. By imperial decree, Jews, and, still
less, autonomous Jewish communities, were simply not tolerated within
the boundaries of the empire. The task of the Russian bureaucracy after
1772 was to integrate the Jews into the empire's juridically defined social
and economic systems. This task was not one restricted only to the Jews.
The Russian state was in the midst of explosive territorial growth as it
became the Russian Empire. The partitions of Poland were merely one
episode in a century of acquisition. Despite desultory governmental attempts at integration, most of these areas still constituted large undigested
entities possessing their own distinct legal traditions and inhabited by pop-
ulations that maintained their traditional social and economic relationships.

Catherine found this an intolerable state of affairs, given her pro-
nounced opinions on how a well-governed state should be organized. On
the national scale, she longed for complete institutional uniformity throughout the empire, accompanied on the local level by the abolition of existing
autonomous political rights.[1] This approach by Catherine spelled doom
for the noble privileges of the Germanic "Baltic Barons" in Livonia and
Estonia, as well as for the freedoms of the Ukrainian Cossacks.[2] Equally
vulnerable were the autonomous institutions of Polish-Lithuanian Jewry.

Catherine also had strong conceptions of the proper social structure for
her realm. Her ideal was based upon "a static model in which each legally-
defined category of the population possessed its own clearly-enunciated
and exclusive rights, privileges and obligations."[3] The diversity of the
population in newly acquired areas, and their vexing failure to correspond

Empress Catherine I at the time of the first Polish partition.

to Russian models, caused endless difficulties for those in search of clearly defined categories. The juridically enunciated Russian estates comprised a simplified structure of nobles, serfs, free peasants, townspeople, and clergy. Where was one to fit the free Cossacks of the Ukraine, the *Landsassen* of Livonia, or the Tatar *mirzas* in the Crimea?[4] Just the same problem arose in the state's attempt to categorize the Jews.

Economic considerations also weighed heavily upon Catherine. The expansion of the Russian state was accomplished through expensive wars which had to be paid for. The Russian treasury could anticipate greater revenues as a consequence of improved administration. The members of properly defined classes could be more effectively taxed and obligated. Under existing conditions even the Ukraine, universally admired for its fecund wealth, cost the Russian state more to administer each year than it brought in as revenue.[5] Similarly, plans for the potential reform of the Jews within the Russian Empire were never far removed from economic calculations.

The anomalies of a nonintegrated state could not but attract the attention of the reform-minded empress. In 1772 her position on the Russian throne was still insecure—her son Paul, for whom many considered her merely a regent rather than a ruler in her own right, reached his majority in that year. The experience of the famous Legislative Commission of 1767 warned against precipitate attempts at reform within Russia itself. Newly annexed territories, on the other hand, after their initial pacification, offered exceptional opportunities for experimentation. The empress need be less attentive to the opposition of special-interest groups, even nobles or quasi-nobles, on the periphery of the empire. Significantly, Catherine chose Belorussia, newly acquired from Poland, as the test area for her famous administrative reforms of 1775.[6] It was often in areas like this that the Jews were to be found, and they shared in the reformation of state and society, not as a special case, but as members of the wider community.

Catherine's reforms usually proceeded at a leisurely pace, and this was especially the case when dealing with the Jews. The Jewish population of Belorussia was small and homogeneous, and did little to call attention to itself. This important point has often been ignored by commentators who were more prone to see the inclusion of Jewish communities into the empire as a dramatic turning point. The actual size of these communities was often overlooked. To be sure, the second and third partitions of Poland brought over 400,000 Jews under Russian hegemony. The first partition, on the other hand, was of quite a different order.

Few reliable statistics exist for the population of the Russian Empire before the late nineteenth century, and statistics concerning the Jews have taken on an especially impressionistic character. S. M. Dubnow, for example, set the figure of Jews taken by Russia in the first partition at "over forty thousand families, about two hundred thousand souls," citing the anonymous "testimony of a contemporary."[7] While Dubnow's text does not make it clear whether he was referring to all of Belorussia or merely the Russian areas, other secondary sources have tended to accept his figures.[8]

The figure of 200,000 persons is much too high, especially if viewed against statistics gleaned from the official census returns which set the male population in the Russian share of Belorussia at 613,000.[9] Nearly a decade before the first partition, Polish census takers found only 21,263 Jews of over one year of age in the Polish-provinces of Witebsk, Połock, and Mścisław. Even following Raphael Mahler's reasonable argument that these figures should be increased by 20 percent, it would seem doubtful that there were more than 30,000 Jews in Russian Belorussia in 1764.[10] These figures conform to the general outlines suggested by official Russian attempts to tabulate the Jewish population. The government census, taken for tax-collecting purposes (and thus probably too low), revealed a total Jewish population, male and female, of only 14,155 in 1772 in Vitebsk (also called Polotsk) province. This represented 2.76 percent of the total population.[11] (The Polish census of 1764 showed the Jewish population in this area to be slightly more than 2 percent of the population, below the national average of 5 percent for Poland-Lithuania as a whole.) The Jews tended to predominate in only a few towns; most lived in rural areas in the villages of private landowners. Writing in 1773, the governor of Mogilev placed the Jewish population of his province at 15,935 males and 16,689 females.[12] Thus, no matter what the total number of Jews in Russian Belorussia really was, official statistics encouraged the government in the belief that its new Jewish population was not large. These results may be contrasted with the Austrian census of 1774, which enumerated 224,981 Jews in the Austrian lands of Poland,[13] or the estimates that Russia's Jewish population approached 400,000 after the third partition.

The insignificance of the Jewish population in Russian territory between 1772 and 1793 allowed the government to proceed at a leisurely pace in devising policies for the Jews. The relative indifference of policymakers was further expedited by the fact that the Jewish communities were religiously uniform, unlike the communities added after 1793 and 1795, and were spared the disturbing struggles between the Hasidim and the Mitnaggidim. The dispersion of the Jews in Belorussia was also significant. These factors tended to render the Jews invisible, to minimize the effects of occasional native hostility directed against them, and to make it easy for the government to defer to the wishes of the numerically superior Christian population in the towns on matters of economic policy. Most of all, these demographic phenomena permitted the Russian administration to utilize Belorussian Jewry as a human workshop, where it could formulate and implement a Jewish policy, free from pressure or an atmosphere of crisis.

The economic pursuits of Belorussian Jewry were varied and diverse. Jews were especially concentrated in arendator or leaseholding activities—Wischnitzer has estimated that more than one-third of Poland's Jews were engaged in such occupations—and in petty trade and crafts.[14] Jewish artisans were concentrated in tailoring and food and beverage production, but they also served as cobblers, metalworkers, woodworkers, soap and candle makers, surgeons, barbers, and brush and comb makers. It is difficult to delineate professions precisely because they frequently overlapped. Artisans might trade in goods of their own and another's making, while tradesmen did repair work, and shopkeepers performed manual labor in their off-hours. The Jewish tavernkeeper was frequently forced to seek additional employment in order to make ends meet. There was also a fairly large class of beggars and vagrants who depended on the organized charity of individual communities for support. At the other extreme of society there was an elite of well-to-do merchants and businessmen whose wealth distinguished them from the community at large. There were also members of professional groups, doctors, teachers, and religious functionaries, who enjoyed differing degrees of status within the community.[15] This diversity, although frequently noted in the reports of Gentile investigators, was largely ignored by the lawmakers of Catherinian Russia. Instead, legislation invariably focused upon the Jews in the guise of merchants (*kuptsy*) or townspeople (*meshchane*), although, as will be shown, a significant percentage of the Jews did not fit the occupational or residential criteria for these estates.

The style of life of the Jewish community was dependent upon the nature of the land and the people among whom the Jews lived. Russia's new territory amounted to about 40,000 square miles (as opposed to the 100,000 square miles gained in the second partition and 45,000 in the third). This area was particularly unproductive: the soil was poor and rye was the staple grain and the major component of the peasant diet. The area lacked good communications, so the rye was often converted into vodka rather than being sent to market. While some scholars have warned against exaggerating the poverty of the area, most contemporaries emphasized the wretched state of the peasantry, the more so since the region was the center of a series of serious crop failures and consequent famines in the period after the Russian acquisition. Aside from a few towns, such as Vitebsk and Mogilev, the territory was overwhelmingly rural.[16]

The attitudes of the local population toward the Jews were a significant factor in the development of Russian policy, and it must be stressed that these views could hardly be called "Russian." The ruling group was either Polish or Polonized Lithuanian, and usually members of the Roman Catholic Church. The peasantry, cut off from the Great Russian

"The Twelfth Cake," a contemporary print satirizing the first partition of Poland.

territories since the thirteenth century, had developed a distinct language and culture. The religious vicissitudes of the Orthodox peasantry were also unique and constituted a heritage different from that of medieval Muscovy. The Orthodox Church in Belorussia had briefly recognized the Metropolitan of Moscow after the collapse of the Church union in 1448, but by 1596 it had its own "metropolitan of Kiev and all Russia," under the control of Rome. Thus, whatever the attitudes of the Great Russians toward the Jews, it would be a fundamental mistake to impute them indiscriminately to the inhabitants of what had been the Polish-Lithuanian state. The greatest practical distinction between the two was that while Great Russian attitudes toward the Jews were of a preeminently theoretical nature developed in the absence of a Jewish population, Belorussian attitudes grew out of the Jewish-Gentile symbiosis that had existed in the area for centuries and that was based not upon abstractions but upon the actual interrelationships, cultural and economic, of the area.

The immediate concern of the Russian government in 1772 was the preservation of order in the newly annexed areas. This preoccupation pervaded the instructions given by Catherine to the new governor-general of Belorussia, Count Z. G. Chernyshev. The territory under Chernyshev's jurisdiction was divided into two provinces (*gubernii*), Mogilev and Polotsk (or sometimes Pskov, and later Vitebsk), each with its own military governor. By treaty Russian control over the region commenced on 1 September 1772, and Chernyshev was ordered to take possession of the whole area by 8 September and to "maintain order and tranquillity." The new borders were to be demarcated, local taxes directed to the appropriate Russian authorities, and control extended over all existing courts of law. The central government was clearly apprehensive about the reaction of the local populace to Russian occupation. Chernyshev was ordered to demand immediately a formal oath of allegiance to the empress, which was to be sworn by all classes of the population. Those unwilling to take such an oath were to be permitted to leave the country.

To allay the expected hostility to Russian rule, especially from the Polish nobility, the government hastened to assure all classes of society of its good intentions. Upon the commencement of the occupation, Chernyshev promulgated a proclamation (generally known as the *plakat*) addressed to the native population. It assured that all would be free to profess their religious beliefs, a promise apparently designed to quiet the fears of the Roman Catholic nobility. All citizens were also guaranteed their property rights. Not only would all classes continue to enjoy whatever special prerogatives or privileges were associated with their respective classes under Polish rule, but they would also receive all the rights which accrued to citizens of the Russian Empire. In return the new citizens were commanded to display a "true and unshakable loyalty" to their new ruler by an oath of allegiance.[17]

Besides singling out the Belorussian nobility and clergy for assurances of the government's goodwill, Chernyshev's proclamation also devoted an entire section to the Jewish population, perhaps to dispel fears of an impending expulsion, or to specify to the natives that the Jews were also to be tolerated.

> In the course of the solemn affirmation to each and all of freedom of religious practice and noninterference in property rights, it is understood that the Jewish communities [*evreiskie obshchestva*] dwelling in the towns and on the lands joined to the Russian Empire retain and preserve those freedoms which they now enjoy by law regarding the control of their property, because the humanity of Her Imperial Majesty will not permit anyone to be excluded from Her all-encompassing generosity and from the welfare to come under Her benevolent protection, as long as they, for their part, with the appropriate compliance of loyal subjects, live and pursue their present trades and business according to their callings [*po zvaniiam svoim*]. Courts and tribunals shall be continued in their existing places under the name and authority of Her Imperial Majesty, with the observation of strict justice.[18]

As the first edict establishing a legally tolerated Jewish presence in Russia, the wording and content of the proclamation have drawn appropriate attention. N. N. Golitsyn's interpretation, reflecting the Judeophobia of the 1880s, attempted to justify future Russian disabilities imposed upon the Jews. He argued that the proclamation was a form of contract between the Jews and the Russian government, and the subsequent violation by the Jews of the injunction to live as "loyal subjects" fully entitled the government to impose disabilities upon them. Golitsyn denied that the proclamation promised much beyond complete religious toleration and property rights: guided by the lesson of "Jewish insubordination and lawlessness in the past," Catherine had retained old laws restricting Jewish movement to the Russian interior and had imposed a secondary legal status upon them as indicated by the use *po zvaniiam*.[19] The term *zvanie* could be understood as referring to one's occupation or to membership in a distinct social group or estate (the Russian *soslovie*). Golitsyn assumed the latter meaning. The logical consequence of Golitsyn's argument is that from the very first, Russian Jews were saddled with legal disabilities and that the origin of the restrictive residence laws that became the Pale of Settlement are to be sought in 1772 rather than later. Gessen correctly noted, however, that this was never the interpretation placed on the proclamation by the Russian authorities in Belorussia. They clearly understood *po zvaniiam svoim* to mean "the trades in which the Jews usually engaged," rather than "in the ranks of a group of restricted citizens."[20] Nor did the government ever refer to the *plakat* or to a broken contractual agreement in the future when imposing restrictions or disabilities upon the Jewish population.

Similar ambiguity attended the use by Chernyshev of the term *obshchestva*. Was this to be understood as "society" in the sense of "population," or in the form of social institutions such as the kahal?[21] If the *plakat*'s confirmation of the Jewish court system implied the continuation of at least some of the autonomous rights exercised by the Jewish kahal under Polish rule, it is significant that the kahal itself was nowhere mentioned in the proclamation. In short, the proclamation cannot be seen as the definitive legal statement on the Jews by the Russian government. It was a temporary expedient designed to place minds at rest. Events soon showed that the Russian government would no more honor these vague promises made to the Jews than those it had made to the Poles. But in 1772 the regime could easily give an apparent promise of wide autonomy, the more so because Russian administrators had little conception of what Jewish autonomy had actually entailed under Polish rule.[22]

Interestingly, the reference to *evreiskie obshchestva* in the proclamation represented one of the first times that this term was used instead of the more common *zhidovskie*.[23] It is sometimes claimed that this distinction was made because *zhidovskie* had a pejorative connotation in Russian, although this was not the fact in 1772, or Chernyshev presumably would not have employed the term in subsequent decrees.[24] Richard Pipes conjectures that the imperial government used the term *Evrei* (derived from "Hebrew") in order to emphasize the status of the Jews as an "ordinary religious minority rather than a special nation-caste."[25] While this would have been consistent with usage in both medieval and contemporary Europe, such an assumption implies a greater precision in terminology than was displayed elsewhere in the proclamation. In any event, it was the term *Evrei* which became standardized in legal usage, while *Zhid* acquired a pejorative connotation, particularly through its use in nineteenth-century Russian literature and polemics.[26]

Finally, it is worth noting that the Jews, unlike the rest of the population, were not specifically commanded to take an oath of allegiance. This may have been a simple oversight, or it may have been more. In Western Europe little confidence was placed by the Christian community in private or civic oaths sworn by Jews, and this omission might have been a reflection of a similar Russian belief. (Subsequently, in 1808, the question of Jewish oaths became a controversial subject in the Russian Senate, as will be seen below.)

With their inclusion under the general provisions of the *plakat*, for the moment the status of the Jews was as regularized as that of any other group among the Belorussian population. The Jews were still to make the acquaintance of the Russian administrators, invariably military men; who now took up their posts. Like the good servants of enlightened absolutism which they were, Chernyshev's subordinates began to assemble information and statistics on all the Belorussian population, including the Jews.[27]

One of the first such reports dealing specifically with the Jews was written in 1773 by the governor of Mogilev province, M. V. Kakhovskii.[28] This report is significant as a depiction of the initial impression of Russian administrators confronting Jews for the first time, impressions which would not be significantly changed throughout the following century. The report further reveals that at the very moment the Russian government was apparently confirming the prerogatives of the kahal, its agents were criticizing that institution in the harshest of terms.

On one level, Kakhovskii was obviously shocked to encounter a people who seemed so culturally alien. He conceded that the Jews were a sober nation, but this was virtually their sole redeeming virtue, for they were also "lazy, deceptive, somnolent [sonlivyi], superstitious, given to uncleanliness, and unskilled in the management of their domestic affairs; they are all newcomers [prishel'tsy] who multiply where government is weak and justice is not served; by fraud they live off the labors of the peasants . . . as a lazy people who are not concerned with cleanliness; they do not keep order in either their dwellings or their persons; everything is filthy and in disrepair."[29]

Kakhovskii's revulsion at Jewish life was the familiar phenomenon of culture shock, the reaction of an individual facing the new, the strange, and the bizarre. His hostile description became a staple of Russian literature, which occasionally depicted the Jews as exotic, more often as ignorant, superstitious, and dirty.[30] The traditional dress of Orthodox Jews (which was to have such a strong negative effect on the young Adolf Hitler on the streets of Vienna over a hundred years later), the uncut beards, the earlocks, the incomprehensible "jargon" of the Jewish masses, all produced a violent reaction.

Kakhovskii was the first Russian observer to explore the nature of the kahal. He noted that wherever the Jews lived they were governed by their own elected elders. The people so elected were well-to-do (dostatochnye) "but no less skilled in the Talmud, and dexterous in everything."[31] Kakhovskii correctly noted that they were the real power in the Jewish community, exceeding even the rabbi in influence, and dominating every individual Jew. In Kakhovskii's view, the elders sought to control all litigation in the courts, either by restraining individual members of the community from litigation or by subverting justice through bribery, coercion, or perjury should a case somehow reach a Gentile court. This concern with the judicial process becomes clear when Kakhovskii's report is examined in detail. All other concerns were subordinated to an extensive indictment of Jewish malfeasance in trade and commerce. Jews were depicted as continually before the courts because of deceitful practices, violating contracts, false bankruptcy, etc. Kakhovskii presented in embryo the first Russian portrait of what was to become the overriding Jewish stereotype in Russian culture, the *torgash*, or petty tradesman.

As Kakhovskii described the Jews, they were a parody of King Midas: everything they touched turned to fraud. In an oft-quoted line he saw the Jews as "a new type of cheat, for each transaction in which they are involved provides another dishonest variant."[32] First and foremost they were guilty of trading in goods of shoddy quality which they nonetheless contrived to sell at inflated prices. Their trade was based upon credit and high volume, and often involved collaboration with Gentiles. When these overextended credit operations collapsed, as they frequently did, it was the Gentiles, not the Jews, who suffered. If the Jew was not able to avoid court, and the energies of the kahal were insufficient to subvert a just verdict, the Jewish tradesman fled or went to jail (where the kahal continually interceded for him) or, having placed his assets in another's name, he declared bankruptcy. Yet Russian merchants had no choice but to trade with Jews, because of the system of trade monopolies devised by the kahal. There were allied crimes, but counterfeiting and the smuggling of specie abroad held pride of place. Even where laws existed to prevent such trickery, the Jews managed to circumvent them. Barred from some cities by special privilege, they gained admission as the agents of the szlachta, "and complaints spring from the cities about this."[33]

Nor were Jewish activities confined to the cities. "They lead the peasants and the landowners into extreme ruin, and so it can be said that the landowners are their bailiffs, and the peasants their involuntary workers, and the Jews are their lords. . . . "[34] This ruination was achieved by the leasing of tolls and mills, the distillation and sale of spirits, the extension of easy credit at outrageous rates of interest, and general fraud and deception.

> And so, as clearly shown above, the Jews, with their big families, find sustenance in these places not through work but only through fraud; by establishing high prices for their goods, and low prices for peasant products, [they take] unusual rates of interest from the peasants, and a new rate of interest on top of that; and all necessary sustenance is given to the Jews, as well as clothing, and a princely [*znatnoe*] dowry for their daughters.[35]

Whatever might have been Kakhovskii's qualifications to be a serious student of the Jewish community, his preoccupation with the commercial villainies of the Jews strongly suggests that he relied for his information on complaints from mercantile circles in Belorussia. The precision of his charges, the extensive description of Jewish chicanery in the courts, and the use of Russified versions for specific Hebrew terms (such as *khazakh*

[Heb: *ḥazaqah*] for communal trade monopoly), as well as the shortness of time with which he could have become acquainted with the wide range of Jewish life, all reinforce this suspicion. Of the remaining groups in Belorussia, the peasants were never consulted on anything, and the clergy's complaints tended to be of a different nature. The Polish szlachta, whom the report accused of being in collusion with the Jews, could be inspired to denigrate the Jews, as will be seen, but only with good reason. In short, the government's first informants almost certainly were drawn precisely from that group which was most often in direct rivalry with the Jews and was most energetic in seeking restrictions upon their activities. Kakhovskii's official report elicited no response, but it marks the germination of enduring Russian attitudes toward and assumptions about the Jews.

Unlike subsequent commentators, Kakhovskii proposed no specific measures to remedy these problems, and it is in fact questionable whether his report ever reached the higher authorities in Petersburg. Certainly the central government continued to show itself exceedingly ill informed about the Jewish population. On 16 June 1782, for instance, ten years after the Russian annexation of Belorussia, the Senate confessed that it knew nothing of the Jewish law courts which existed—with the permission of the government—to settle disputes involving Jewish litigants alone, although this was one of the major prerogatives of Jewish autonomy. The Senate claimed not to know the principle on which these courts had been permitted to the Jews, or even how they operated.[36] To be sure, the Senate soon began to investigate the legal basis of Jewish self-government and economic activity, especially in the period from 1785 to 1786. Still, it was not until the Senate received the extensive report of I. G. Frizel, governor of Lithuania province, in 1798, followed shortly by the reform project of G. R. Derzhavin, that any significant information was available to those who were supposed to be making decisions regarding the legal rights of the Jewish community. It is not surprising, therefore, that the first years of Russian rule were marked by vagueness and inconsistency in administrative policies.

As the government first directed its attention toward the Jews, it encountered the problem of the legal status of the kahal. Although nothing at all had been said of this institution in the proclamation announcing the annexation, the government remained concerned, as always, for an orderly flow of taxes from the new population. Thus, in a decree of 13 September 1772, governor-general Chernyshev announced that all Jews were to be assessed a head tax of one ruble, and registered in kahals "which are established under the supervision of the governors."[37] The continuation of the kahal structure was born of economic necessity, but soon the authorities recognized the kahal's efficacy as an agent of social control over the Jewish masses as well. A Senate decree of 17 October 1776 confirmed Chernyshev's command that the kahals register every

Jew, serve as the agency for the payment of the head tax, and supervise Jewish movement by providing passports for all Jews who wished to travel.[38]

While it is questionable whether the Russian government initially recognized the significance of retaining the kahal, its agents in Belorussia and the Senate in St. Petersburg soon began to renege on the prerogatives thus granted, especially Jewish communal courts. Officials at many levels initiated a desultory campaign against kahal autonomy which lasted until the abolition of the kahal in 1844. This was a phenomenon quite understandable in the context of the administrative development of the time, and it had little to do with Jews as such. One of Catherine's chief concerns throughout her reign was the problem of effective government in so vast a nation as Russia, where the absolutist centralizing regime was frequently at odds with local interests and priorities. Catherine sought to achieve a kind of balance between these forces, surrendering a measure of authority in areas better served by locally elected officials, while keeping the overall system under the supervision of agents of the central government. (This was a compromise which enjoyed indifferent success.)[39] The Jews were no exception: what the government ultimately did was to deprive the Jews of one sort of unrestricted autonomy while attempting to integrate them into a second, governmentally devised one. This was a transformation that took time, and public order required the temporary continuation of the kahal with many of its powers intact. While the government subsequently restricted the kahal, this temporary reprieve for its functions had a powerful effect. By the middle of the eighteenth century the kahal structure was in crisis, undermined by social conflict between rich and poor, and religious conflict between Hasidim and Mitnaggedim.[40] Now, instead of the complete breakdown of the traditional kahal structure which these stresses portended, the kahal was given the support of the Russian government. Official sanction served to resist the impending disintegration and to restore, at least partially, the viability of the autonomous community. This was an immediate and significant legacy of Russian rule.

With the growing tendency to restrict the autonomous kahal, the decisive question in the development of Russian-Jewish relations centered on the position that the Jews were to occupy in Russia's legally stratified society. If the Jews were to be assimilated they would of necessity have to be included in an existing Russian class (the estate or *soslovie*) or have a new category created for them. The search for a suitable solution to this problem was to dominate the relationship of the government toward the Jews under Catherine and her immediate successors.

The first tendency of Russian jurisprudence was to confirm the existing Polish view of the Jews as a unified class, an entity separate and distinct from the Gentile majority. Thus, the proclamation announcing the annexation of Belorussia spoke specifically to a number of estates, including

Count Z. G. Chernyshev, first Russian governor-general of Belorussia.

the Jews. The implied existence of a separate estate composed entirely of Jews—without distinction between individuals due to occupation or wealth—was especially evident in the tax rates announced for Belorussia. Peasants were assessed seven grivna (or seventy kopecks) while merchants were to pay a tax of one ruble twenty kopeks. In effect, two major categories were thus created: rural-peasant and urban-merchant (besides the chronically ill-defined group of nobles, who paid no taxes). The Jews, as a distinct fourth group, paid a head tax of one ruble.[41] A separate rate for Jews was also included in decrees in 1776 and 1779.[42] Despite these precedents suggesting a separate category for all Jews, the government began to move in a different direction in the 1780s. More and more, Jews were viewed as belonging to one or another of the existing and fairly well-defined Russian urban estates, and they were given the right to enter the subdivision most appropriate for them. This legal evolution was not accomplished smoothly or consistently.

It is not difficult to see how the Jews came to be viewed as urban dwellers. They were very visibly involved in commerce and in crafts. The most appropriate legal categories for such people in Russian society were the *kupechestvo*, a class of merchants subdivided into "guilds" on the basis of declared capital (after 1775), and the *meshchanstvo*, or "townspeople," a catch-all class containing most other merchants, craftsmen, shopkeepers, laborers, and "others." Such people ordinarily but not necessarily lived in urban centers. In an effort to encourage town growth in Russia, Catherine's legislation, especially that of 1775, emphasized the urban nature of these classes. Members were carried on the census and registration lists of a city or town and were discouraged by law from relocation or from residence in nonurban areas or on private lands, such as noble estates. Even though the Jews were viewed as a separate and rather ill-defined group, the law treated them as an urban class. Thus, a decree of 1776 which granted privileges to Jewish converts to Christianity also ordered the Jews to register in an urban center.[43] As a result even Jews living in the countryside were registered in a nearby town. This registration in towns of people who were in reality rural inhabitants later caused severe legal difficulties.

The legal "urbanization" of the Jews took on special impetus after 1780. In that year Catherine, in response to requests which the Jews themselves transmitted through Chernyshev, permitted the enrollment of Jews in the ranks of the merchantry in Mogilev and Polotsk provinces.[44] In a decree of 10 March 1781, it was established that Jews enrolled in the merchant class (*kupechestvo*) were to pay taxes identical to those levied upon Christians of the same guild.[45] Subsequent legislation made it clear that Jews so enrolled were to enjoy the rights of Christians in their entirety. This was to extend to taxation, electoral rights, eligibility for offices elected on a guild basis, and, in the case of members of the merchantry, freedom from personal obligation for military service.

As the Jews entered these classes they attempted to participate in the appropriate electoral activity. They were supported by the government in this endeavor: in a letter in the name of the new Belorussian governor-general, P. B. Passek, the procurator-general of the Senate, A. A. Viazemskii, explained that "if Jews, enrolled in the merchantry by the free agreement of society, are elected to some post in fulfillment of the imperial instruction [the Statute on the Provinces of 1775] then they shall not be kept from the actual functions made incumbent on them by their post."[46] It soon became apparent, however, that even at the time when the central government appeared wholeheartedly in favor of Jewish participation in the activities of existing classes, irregularities were tolerated which weakened Jewish electoral power.

This initial attempt at integration was ultimately undone because it was founded upon the mistaken view that the Jews were primarily merchants and townspeople, a misconception inspired by the government's economic pipedreams. Despite Catherine's legislative policies, Russian towns and trade centers remained in need of citizens who could actually function as an urban middle class. The admission of the Jews into the Russian social structure was seen as helping to satisfy this need. As a result, Russian law tended to deal only with that minority of the Jewish population that actually engaged in pursuits associated with merchants and townspeople while ignoring the fact—already observed by Kakhovskii—that the majority of Jews simply did not fit the broadest criteria for inclusion into these groups. There were not many Jews who could meet the stiff financial requirements for the three merchant guilds, which ranged from 1,000 to 50,000 rubles. The remainder of city society, Jews included, could be classified as townspeople (*meshchane*), an extensive category including artisans, small merchants, tradesmen, and ultimately almost everybody else, excluding noblemen and peasants, who might happen to live in a town. In theory, then, all Jews were enrolled in one or another of these classes and in some town.[47]

But this was only an illusion. The bulk of the Jews did not live in or near the towns at all, but on szlachta estates, and especially in the *mestechko* or *shtetl*, the diminutive "Jewish town," often created especially for them by the landowners, and having close economic ties with the surrounding countryside; in other words, in precisely those rural areas where urban society was forbidden to dwell. Consequently there existed "townspeople" registered in towns but living in villages and engaging in activities characteristic of the arendator: keeping taverns or leasing the right to distill vodka, money changing, or serving as stewards on private estates. None of these pursuits were associated with the usual occupations of the urban classes. Had the government been content to permit the continued existence of this illusory "urban" class, the status quo, however unstable, might have been maintained. The moment the government attempted to enforce existing laws relative to them, however, the illusion dispersed. In this way the enforcement of these unworkable laws by the new governor-general of Belorussia, P. B. Passek, created a crisis.

In 1782, in compliance with Catherine's oft-stated wish that members of the urban estates actually reside in towns, resettlement of merchants and townspeople was begun in Olonets province (where there were, incidentally, no Jews).[48] The authorities of the two Belorussian provinces, under the direction of Passek, thereupon began a similar resettlement. At first the law was applied to Christian and Jew alike, but it soon turned into an attempt primarily to resettle Jews. These phantom townspeople were removed from their rural economic pursuits and relocated in centers too small to accommodate them physically or economically. At the same time the landowners lost their traditional agents and middlemen, and this threatened to have negative effects on the rural economy.

Passek also directed the enforcement of other laws concerning the Jews. On 3 May 1783, regulations on the distillation of alcohol were promulgated in Belorussia, designed to control somewhat the widespread practice of this activity by all classes, including even the clergy. The regulations gave the right of distillation in the countryside only to the landowners. In the cities and towns it was permitted to the urban estates, under the control of the municipal authorities, with the profits going for the needs of the town in general and the requirements of the magistracy in particular.[49] On the rural estates, therefore, only the landowner could control distillation, a welcome and useful financial boon in areas like Belorussia which lacked a significant market for surplus grain. The regulations said nothing about the ability of the landowners to exercise this right as they saw fit. Consequently the szlachta and the magnates continued as before to lease their rights to Jews, thereby continuing Jewish activity in distillation and the retail trade in alcohol. Passek, on the other hand, interpreted the law to mean that members of an estate not enjoying distillation rights could not exercise them even under lease, and he moved to restrict this activity of the Jews. As a result of Passek's interpretation, those Jews not actually being resettled—and such a project could not proceed at a very rapid rate—found themselves deprived of their livelihood. The Polish landowners of Belorussia had been willing to accept a confirmation of their trade monopoly which had been given them by the regulations of 3 May, but they bridled at the loss of their Jewish factotums. When the Jews complained of Passek's actions to the Senate, they presumably had at least the tacit support of the Polish gentry.

The Jews had an additional complaint against Passek: his toleration of the irregularities that had begun to appear in the exercise of Jewish political rights. In the cities of Belorussia, Christian members of the merchantry and *meshchanstvo* had reacted with displeasure and protest to the participation of Jews in class elections to urban office, to the posts of *burgomistry* (mayors), *ratmany* (members of the municipal council), and judges of the estate courts. This opposition was understandable given the long tradition of economic rivalry with the Jews, exacerbated by religious and social prejudice. The provincial authorities, seeking to keep the peace, unilaterally responded by devising a special formula for such elections: in towns where Jews were in a majority, electors were chosen to select municipal officials; in towns where the Jews did not have a majority, no electors were used. This resulted, as might be expected, in unequal Jewish representation. In cities such as Vitebsk, where Jews were in a majority, not a single Jew was elected to office.[50] In response to these irregularities the Jewish communities of Mogilev and Polotsk sent a representative to St. Petersburg to complain of these practices and to seek the intervention of the central government.

The motives of the kahal leadership in making this appeal were threefold. They desired the cessation of resettlement, which obviously ran counter to the best interests of Jews in the countryside and which threatened the security of the Jews already living in towns. Secondly, they hoped to defend the economic position of the Jews and even to strengthen it if possible. Thus Jewish representatives in St. Petersburg asked not only that Jews be permitted to lease distillation rights, but also that they might acquire them personally, a privilege for which they offered to idemnify the government. Thirdly, the kahal leadership sought to improve the position of Jews enrolled in the urban estates by gaining representation for those "not having a defender" because of the electoral system. It was recognized that only through representation in the estate courts could Jews hope to find justice in their mercantile disputes with Christians. The willingness of the Jews to participate in such affairs was wholly economic in motivation and did not reflect a desire for closer social ties with the Gentile majority. Indeed, the leadership was equally determined to preserve its traditional authority, and thus petitioned the Senate for a continuation of special Jewish courts for the settlement of civil suits between Jews. This, of course, had been a vital component of Jewish communal autonomy in Poland.

The petition of the Jewish communities against Passek provoked an extensive review of Jewish complaints. On 26 February 1785 and on 10 March 1785, Catherine brought these accumulating Jewish complaints to the attention of the Senate with the reminder that on the basis of past decrees, the Jews were also to be treated "without distinction arising from race or creed." The Senate investigated the evidence in the case, examining the petitions the Jews had addressed to the empress, Passek's own report of his actions, the opinions of the governors of Mogilev and Polotsk provinces, and information provided by a kahal representative named Tsalk Faibishovich. All parties in the dispute were thus well represented. The result was the reinterpretation of some of the principal laws dealing with the Jews, although only specific problems encountered by the Belorussian administration were addressed and not the whole corpus of Russian law dealing with the Jews. Still, the Senate's decisions did provide further regularization of the legal position of the Jews and may be viewed as integral to the developing current of legal thought which sought the creation of a Russian *Rechtsstaat*. The *Rechtsstaat* was envisioned as a political system based on a code of written law, granted to the various estates by the monarchy.[51] At the same time several of the conclusions reached by the Senate worked against the formulation of a clear and precise legal definition of the status of Russian Jewry.

Not surprisingly, the Senate began by rejecting the Jewish offer to buy the personal right of distillation. Quoting the regulations of 3 May 1783 the Senate declared that in the countryside only the landowners enjoyed distillation rights. At the same time, the Senate reminded the Jews that persons enrolled in the towns (as the Jews presumably were) shared equally with the Christian townspeople in the financial benefits which accrued to urban society from the profits of the liquor trade. But if Passek was justified in preventing independent Jewish distillation and sales, the Senate admitted, he was not justified in hindering or regulating the leasing of such rights by the landowners. Those Jews who held valid leases, even if registered townspersons, were not to be disturbed or hindered. The wording of the 3 May regulations was clear, so the Senate actually had little difficulty in arriving at such a conclusion. The decision itself was probably aimed not so much at placating the Jews as in stilling the alarm of those landowners who would have lost revenue without the aid of their energetic Jewish middlemen. While forced now and later to tolerate this situation, the Russian government nonetheless always looked with disfavor on the large number of Jews in the liquor trade. Most reform projects in the future aimed at shifting Jews from this trade to other, more "useful," pursuits.

The question of resettlement did not permit so easy an answer, because here Passek was definitely within the spirit and the letter of the law as it was being enforced in other provinces. Nevertheless the Senate recognized the necessity of some sort of compromise, especially as it was evident that in most towns there was little possibility that the Jews could find either housing or employment. The Senate therefore hit upon a novel interpretation which had never been applied to Christians facing resettlement. It was not necessary, said the Senate, for the authorities to resettle the Jews "prematurely." Instead, Jews holding valid passports from the kahal were to be allowed "temporary residence" in the countryside, provided that they continued to pay whatever taxes might be levied on them. While this interpretation provided a temporary solution, it was to prove unsatisfactory in the future. On several occasions the central government decided, often as a punitive measure, that resettlement was no longer "premature," although the conditions that impeded resettlement in 1785 continued to exist.

The resolve of the government to continue the trend of social integration can be detected in the attitude of the Senate toward the system of separate Jewish courts requested by the kahal leadership. Such courts would have provided the kahal elders with powerful means of control over the community itself and would have enhanced Jewish autonomy. The Senate refused to make such a concession, thereby repudiating the implied promises made by the decrees of 1772 and 1776. The Senate found that the Jews did not require separate courts because they fell under the provisions of the Charter to the Towns of 21 April 1785. As a result, Jews were allowed election as burgomasters and councillors of the *magistrat* (a corporate body charged with extensive police power) and the city commission, or *duma*, "in equal proportion with every other group." The decision of the Senate thus declared openly what had been merely implied in the Charter to the Towns. Although the Jews as a special group were never mentioned, the charter provided special regulations for the non-Russian Orthodox—complete religious toleration, the right to swear oaths by their own rites, etc.—and the Senate resolved any doubt that the Jews were to enjoy the appropriate rights and responsibilities. Special Jewish courts would be redundant, according to the Senate, since the Jews could appeal to the existing courts and be judged in their own language, according to article 127 of the Charter to the Towns.

This last decision raises several problems. Article 127 in full reads:

> Should there be settled in a town five hundred or more families of outsiders [*inogorodnykh*] or foreigners, then one half of the Municipal Magistracy can be made up of Russians and the other half of foreigners; that is: the number of Russian burgomasters and councillors remains as it is now, but the outsiders and foreigners are allowed to elect the same number and to join with the former and to judge any case coming before the Municipal Magistracy, Russians in Russian and foreigners in their own language (and the same thing is to be understood for the artisan guilds).[52]

In citing this article the Senate clearly had in mind the latter provision permitting the Jews to be judged in their own language. But on what basis was article 127 applicable to the Jews in the first place? Earlier, in article 124, the Charter to the Towns had promised the free exercise of religion to "the heterodox, to those from other towns and to foreigners [*dozvoliaetsia inovernym, inogorodym i inostrannym*].[53] These categories apparently meant the non-Russian Orthodox already living in a particular town (i.e., native-born non-Orthodox), native-born non-Orthodox or non-Russians who transferred their residence from one Russian city to another (although the term *inogorodnye* did not of itself carry either religious or national connotations), and foreigners, respectively. The failure of article 127 specifically to include in its provisions the term *inovernye* as did article 124 is more than a question of semantics. The exclusion suggested that the Jews were included under the provisions of article 127 because they were viewed in legal terms as foreigners and not because they were granted these rights already as non-Russian Orthodox citizens to whom article 124 applied. This point is crucial when viewed together with another decision of the Senate at this time, a refusal to allow Jews to enroll as merchants and townspeople outside of Belorussia "because a special imperial ukase does not enjoin it, without which the Senate cannot act."[54] In other words, in spite of all assurances to the contrary, the Jews could still be viewed collectively as a separate estate. If an individual had indeed been a "merchant" or a "townsman" instead of a "Jew," then such an interpretation would have been impossible: he would have possessed the legal right to enroll in *any* urban center in the empire if he could obtain the internal passport necessary for such a move.

It was exactly this ambiguity surrounding the applicability of the Charter to the Towns which permitted Russian administrators at this time and in the future to misinterpret those rights granted to the Jews.[55] A petition sent to the Senate in 1802 by the Jews of Kamenets-Podolsk, for example, noted that the former military governor of Volynia and Podolia, I. V. Gudovich, had at one time permitted local Jews to occupy half of the elective offices in the towns where they were residents on the grounds that, according to article 127 of the Charter to the Towns, such representation was permitted foreigners.[56] Thus the ambiguity of the law had given rise to a "false precedent," an apparent legal precedent which later was shown to be based on a misreading of the original intent of the law and was overturned. The Senate initiated this "false precedent" in 1786, and it was carried on by Gudovich, either imitating the Senate or misreading article 127 in his turn. After 1802 the precedent disappeared, and the Jews were definitely *not* considered foreigners during the reign of Alexander I. [57]

Although the implication that the Jews were foreigners was never fully developed, the accompanying legal precept that the Jews were a special group to whom everything was forbidden unless specifically allowed did serve as a real precedent, to be restated by Catherine herself in 1791, and to pass firmly into Russian law. Some historians have emphasized this point and have seen this declaration as the starting point for the body of discriminatory legislation heaped upon the Jews in the nineteenth century.[58]

Yet, in the context of the times, the Jews were in no way a special case. Western concepts of class privilege—to say nothing of "natural rights"— were lacking in the Russian legal tradition, where the survival of the state was tied to the meticulous exploitation of all the resources of the land and the population. Privileges and responsibilities alike were assigned by the state to individual estates, and efforts were made to discourage movement from one to another. Relocation from one place to another by individual members of a particular class was likewise frowned upon. A particular group could undertake a specific economic pursuit only if designated to do so by the state, and, conversely, whatever was not expressly permitted was understood to be forbidden.[59] The Senate's treatment of the Jews in this way served, therefore, to anchor them securely in the context of Russian jurisprudence. The negative aspect of the Senate's interpretations became apparent only with the passage of time, and the rest of the Senate's decisions may be viewed as conscious attempts to placate the demands of the Jews and to encourage their gradual integration into Russian society. While the Senate had decided that the urban estate courts superseded the secular functions of the Jewish community rabbinical court, the *bet din*, it permitted the continued operation of the *bet din* for matters involving rite and ritual. In the Jewish community, where religious considerations frequently intruded into the secular realm, this was surely half a loaf as far as the kahal leadership was concerned. In the future, in fact, hostile Russian publicists frequently complained that the *bet din* continued to exercise all its original functions unhindered. The Senate further enhanced the existing power of the kahal elders by granting their request that they be allowed to apportion all taxes—except the fixed tax of 1 percent of declared income from the merchantry—as they had done in the past. From the Senate's point of view such a concession was no more than another attempt to bring the administration of the Jews into line with that of other estates. In justifying its acquiescence to the request, the Senate observed that a similar system of apportionment was permitted to Cossacks, townspeople, and state peasants in the Ukraine. The kahal leadership, from its side, retained a valuable economic weapon to use against community malcontents.

To encourage the Jews to enter Russian life, the Senate also declared the abrogation of all existing Polish laws which made distinctions between Christians and Jews, thus in a sense violating the promises given to Polish society in 1772 that all of its privileges would be fully maintained. The Senate resolution was thus an amalgam of disparate tendencies, a premonition of the wavering attitude which the government manifested toward the Jews for the duration of Catherine's reign.

In the years following the Senate resolution, Jews continued to seek the advantages promised to them by the Charter to the Towns of 1785. The optimistic assurances of the Senate that they might participate in class activities on equal grounds with Christians began to founder on the traditional enmity of merchant Poles toward the Jews, especially since this economic competition was exacerbated by religious prejudice. This was most obvious in community elections. In 1786, for example, the office of the Belorussian governor-general intervened in order to secure the election of Jews to posts in the magistracy in the towns of Belorussia. In June of that same year, after the promulgation of the Senate resolution, kahal representatives complained that not only were Jews being denied election in Vitebsk, but Jewish electors were being forcibly driven from electoral meetings.[60] In an effort to placate the Gentile majority, the governors-general repeatedly diminished representation by Jews through administrative rulings.[61]

While such restrictions originated, it is true, not in the capital but in the provinces, they nonetheless represented a gradual change in Russian treatment of the Jews. The 1770s had been characterized by indulgent toleration as the government largely concerned itself with domestic order and financial benefit. The 1780s saw repeated attempts to meld the Jews with existing Russian estates. The 1790s, the period of the second and third partitions, witnessed the inclusion of a much larger and less homogeneous Jewish population into the empire. It was this period which gave rise to overt discrimination against the Jews for the first time.

The first such incident grew out of a trade dispute between Belorussian Jewish merchants and tradesmen in the "inner" Great Russian provinces. In 1790 the merchants of Moscow complained to the sovereign about the infiltration of Jewish merchants into the city. These Christian merchants were apparently encountering the same problem that had vexed their Polish counterparts before the partitions, competition from cheap Jewish goods. The Muscovites in their petition argued that the Jews were selling goods so cheaply that they must be contraband, although there was no evidence advanced to support this claim. Furthermore, they noted, the Jews were notorious for clipping coins and would thus debase the currency. At the same time the Moscow merchants denied that religious prejudice motivated their request. Even if this disclaimer was insincere, it is interesting that they felt compelled to make it. One of the most conservative social groups, in the very heartland of old Muscovy, was specifically eschewing religious intolerance toward the Jews. Responding to the economic charges of the Muscovites, some Belorussian Jewish merchants formally petitioned the empress that they be allowed to register in the ranks of the merchantry in Smolensk and Moscow.

Catherine's response, in a decree of 23 December 1791, was a return to the Senate precedent of 1786: "We find that the Jews do not have any right of registration in the merchantry in inner Russia's towns and ports and only by Our ukase are they permitted to exercise the rights of citizenship and [the privileges] of townspeople in Belorussia."[62] That this regulation was not intended as a punitive measure is indicated by the fact that at the same time Catherine permitted the enrollment of the Jews in the merchant classes of Ekaterinoslav and the Crimea, those areas of New Russia where Jewish settlement had been permitted in 1769.

The decree of 1791 was one of the cornerstones upon which the so-called Jewish Pale of Settlement (*cherta osedlosti*) was subsequently erected. The Pale, as it evolved in the nineteenth century, was an overtly discriminatory corpus of legislation which restricted the places of residence of Jews to the Russian provinces which had been annexed from Poland, and to New Russia. (The Kingdom of Poland, where different legislation was in effect for Jews, was never part of the Pale.) A consistent attempt was made to keep the interior of Russia free of Jewish settlement. Even within the Pale, Jews encountered further restrictions, at various times being banned from living within fifty versts of the frontier and from engaging in various professions or owning land. In the 1880s further modifications of the Pale sought to remove the Jews from the countryside. The Pale was undoubtedly the single most repressive and burdensome component of Russian anti-Jewish legislation.[63] The decree of 1791 was of great consequence and the motivation of the government in promulgating it a question of vital significance.

It must be stressed, therefore, that the intentions of Catherine and her advisers—as evidenced by discussion of this topic within the State Council—were not marked by malice toward the Jews. Catherine had energetically encouraged and promoted the rise of a native merchant class in Russia, as typified by her legislation of 1785, with its numerous privileges and prerogatives. Just such a body of merchants existed in Moscow, and it was hardly compatible with the intentions of the government to subject them to potentially destructive competition. The very existence of legislation designed to regulate Russian economic life demonstrated Catherine's belief that the domestic economy was something the state could help to direct and control. Restricting Jewish merchants from Moscow was just such a controlling act. They were banned not because they were Jews but because they were unnecessary competitors.[64] To this could be added the legal tradition of preventing the movement of members of the urban estates from one area to another, which was at least as old as the *Ulozhenie* of 1649.[65] So ingrained was this idea that in the reign of Paul I the Senate was obliged to instruct the authorities of the provinces of Mogilev and Novgorod-Seversk that merchants, regardless of nationality, were allowed to move from one province to another on the basis of the Charter to the Towns of 1785, although it was again noted that townspeople did not enjoy this right.[66] Further, settlement was occasionally permitted (as in 1794) in those hitherto exclusive provinces where it could be shown that Jews had lived in the past. The best example was the area around Kiev.[67] Only after the second and third partitions, when a rapidly expanding Jewish population was encapsulated within the Pale, did such restrictions begin to prove inconvenient to the Jews, and even then the government continued freely to grant exemptions by which merchants might travel to the interior on business. A system of formal exemptions was included in the Statute of 1804.

If restrictions on Jewish mobility did not have a discriminatory intent, the same could not be said for a new tax statute promulgated for the Jews on 23 June 1794. At the same time as it enlarged the territory where the Jews might enroll in the urban estates, it imposed a double form of taxation upon them:

> The Jews are allowed to pursue the activities of merchants and townspeople in these provinces: Minsk, Iz'iaslav, Bratslav, Polotsk, Mogilev, Kiev, Chernigov, Novgorod-Seversk, Ekaterinoslav, and the Tauride region, enrolling in towns as townspeople and merchants, and We command that from the aforementioned Jews who wish to utilize such permission there shall be collected, commencing

the first day of next July taxes [in an amount] double those levied upon townspeople and merchants of the various Christian confessions; those who do not wish to remain are given the liberty, on the basis of the Charter to the Towns, to leave Our Empire upon payment of a three-year assessment of the double tax.[68]

Unlike the decision barring Jewish merchants from Moscow, which had been aimed at the Jews in their role of economic rivals rather than as a heterodox religious community, this new decree implied punishment for religious belief. Even if the law was essentially motivated by economic considerations, as most commentators have argued, it nonetheless discriminated on religious grounds against the numerically superior Rabbinite (as the traditionalist Jews were sometimes called in Russian law) by granting special exemptions to the Karaite Jewish sect.

Previous enactments of a double tax by Russian lawgivers had combined fiscal and religious objectives. Under Peter I such a tax had been levied upon the religious dissenters known as Old Believers, as a form of harassment and, like so much else in Peter's reign, a source of revenue.[69] This duality of purpose reappeared in Catherine's enactment. If the double tax was not a punishment for religious heterodoxy it must have seemed so on 8 June 1795 when the government exempted the Karaites from the tax, with the proviso that the exemption did not apply to Rabbinical or Hasidic Jews. The Karaites, who were primarily settled in the Crimea, were frequently treated as a special case by Russian legislators, especially in the future when discriminatory legislation was often imposed upon the main body of Russian Jewry. Karaite legends traced their settlement in Russia to the pre-Christian Diaspora and enabled the Karaites to claim innocence of "Christ's murder by the Jews." Conveniently for the sect, it also rejected the Talmud, which was increasingly seen as a compendium of antisocial superstition, intolerance, and ignorance by Russian officials. Still, it should be noted that the Karaite dispensation came a year after the promulgation of the double tax and then only after a petition of the Karaites themselves was presented to the Senate through the governor-general of New Russia, Platon Zubov.[70] The exemption appears to have been an afterthought and a response to a specific set of local conditions rather than part of a larger, coordinated policy. The exemption was also an affordable luxury, given the numerical insignificance of the Karaite population, listed as under five thousand persons by the Ministry of Interior in 1790.[71]

Despite the implications of religious discrimination, economic motives were clearly tied to the legislation. A contemporary of these events, Nota Notkin, a Jewish contractor who served as an important source of information on the Jews for Russian officials and who moved easily in high bureaucratic circles, provided one such explanation. According to Notkin the government was hoping to encourage the Jews to emigrate in larger numbers to New Russia, parts of which had recently been captured from the Ottoman Empire, since the second partition of Poland had greatly increased the number of Jews in Russia's western provinces.[72] Presumably by emigrating they would have received the privileges, including tax exemptions, which the government was offering new settlers. Gessen supports Notkin's conjecture by connecting it with an order from the central government to the governor of Minsk province in 1795. It suggested that the time had come to resettle those Jews resident in the countryside who had been left *in situ* by the Senate decree of 1785. Now, however, they were to be relocated to the urban centers of the province "so that these people might not wander about to the detriment of society and so that by taking up commerce and various trades and crafts they might work for their own advantage and for the utility of society."[73] Since the towns of Minsk province were no more ready to accommodate an influx of Jews than those of Mogilev and Polotsk provinces had been ten years before, Gessen argues that this act was designed to coerce the Jews into relocating to New Russia.[74]

It is true that the government was eager to colonize the empty South, and especially the Crimea, which had been formally annexed by Russia in 1783. Yet upon closer inspection Gessen's argument is less convincing. If the government really sought to encourage resettlement, it was strangely vague on the subject. The decree establishing the double tax made no mention of exemptions or how they might be won. The resettlement instructions to the governor of Minsk came almost a full year after the promulgation of the double tax and were addressed to only one of the provinces where the Jews were permitted to live. Finally, it was noted in the exemption decree for the Karaites that the local authorities were to take special care that non-Karaites not insinuate themselves into the privileged community. This could have occurred in the Crimea only if Jews settled in the area, an action which the government was presumably encouraging. In short, under the provisions of the decree of 8 June 1795, Jews who did resettle in the South were specifically *not* released from the double tax. These facts would seem to invalidate the Notkin-Gessen resettlement thesis. But what then *was* the motive for the tax?

Matthias Rest has advanced convincing evidence of the true economic motives underlying the double tax by noting that the decree was part of a series of tax measures, all designed to restore to order the finances of the empire after years of warfare with the Ottoman Empire and the Polish insurgents.[75] The double-tax ukase was one of a series of seven consecutive decrees submitted to the Senate by Catherine on the same day. Their interconnection is obvious, since several of the decrees made specific reference to others in the series. The first decree announced a new revision of souls in order to assess tax payments more equitably and also set uniform tax rates. The subsequent laws dealt first with the peasantry, then with the merchantry, and finally with the Jews, in a way which suggests a logical progression from the general to the specific.[76] The economic motivation is clear; what is missing is some explanation as to why the Jews were singled out for the dubious honor of helping replenish the empty coffers of the state. It can only be conjectured that Catherine was perhaps unwilling to state publicly and definitively that the progressive rubric "without distinction because of race or religion" was no longer to be a feature of her legislation. The tax itself produced occasional confusion even among the financial agents of the empire. The government repeatedly promised to abolish the tax in the next decade (contingent upon the good behavior of the Jews), while never setting a specific date. Yet when the Jews petitioned the government for the abrogation of the tax in 1812, the Ministry of Finance could only explain that it was unaware that the tax was still being collected![77]

Whatever the motivation of the tax, there can be no doubt that it was a heavy liability on the Jews. It placed them at a competitive disadvantage not only vis-à-vis Christians of all denominations but other non-Christian groups as well, since the Jews were the only non-Christian minority saddled with the tax. Contemporary observers, Jew and Gentile alike, unanimously agreed that the tax was a very severe burden. Its effect was compounded by the fact that the newly annexed Jewish communities in the provinces of Vilna, Minsk, Volynia, and Podolia were all affected by it.[78]

The double tax easily lent itself to continued use as a repressive measure against Jews. The Council of Ministers, in a meeting on 15 March 1824, forbade the settlement of foreign Jews in Russia, accusing them of immigrating to Russia in order to escape military service in their home countries and to secure the privileges which the Russian government gave to settlers. Allegedly they then established themselves near the frontier for the purpose of smuggling. Those already settled were threatened with removal away from the frontier and with a double tax.[79]

There is one final problem encountered in trying to define the legal status of the Jews under Catherine. It was noted above that the dominant integrationist trend pursued by the government was in time qualified by special enactments. This was again the case with the question of military service. As far as can be determined, after 1772 the Jews were never called upon to perform military service, although there was no precise statement of this fact before 1794. This was consistent with Western European practice, which viewed the Jews as useless for military service. It was believed that the Jews were cowards by nature, that they would not fight on the Sabbath, and that their distinctive customs could not be successfully adapted to military life.[80] (The exception was the Austrian Empire under Joseph II, but even there they were not at first used as combatants.)[81] In addition, the exemption for Russian Jews could have been influenced by the fact that they were all enrolled in the urban estates.

Members of the Russian merchantry (*kuptsy*) were exempted from personal military service upon payment of a special tax of five hundred rubles for each recruit for whom the locality would have been responsible. But on the other hand, Russian townspeople (*meshchane*) were *not* exempt from military service, and most Jews were enrolled in this estate.[82]

In any event, decrees of 7 September 1794 and 21 January 1796 formally stated that Jews were to pay the five hundred rubles in lieu of service. These decrees introduced another note of ambiguity into the legal definition of the Jews. The decree of 1794 announced that Jews as well as merchants were to pay the tax, failing to clarify whether this meant only Jews enrolled in the merchantry or Jews as a general group. The decree itself stated only that the tax should be collected "from the merchantry . . . and from the Jews."[83] This decree apparently posed problems of interpretation for officials charged with administering the law, because on 21 January 1796, a new law specified that this included the Jewish burghers as well.[84] Such an exemption was a differentiation of Jewish from Gentile townspeople, since the latter did serve. Under both Paul and Alexander the government consciously refrained from attempts to make the Jews serve in the military in any way except as auxiliaries. While the exemption itself was a valued concession in the eyes of Russian Jewry, its motivation was undergirded by an unflattering view of them by Russian officialdom, and this would have negative consequences in the future. In this exemption of the Jews from military service, then, two tendencies can be seen at work: on the one hand the Jews were still viewed as a collective, a class unto themselves since they had *all* been exempted from service; on the other hand the government was still attempting to regularize their position within Russian society by precisely delineating their obligations.

There was never a completely successful attempt to define the legal status of the Jews in Russia between 1772 and 1796. Initially Russian legislation retained the Polish conception of them as a separate class, distinct from the Gentile majority, but this view hardly lasted a decade. There followed attempts to integrate the Jews into existing Russian estates (or subcategories of estates), but such efforts were hindered by a number of factors: the desire of the Jewish leadership to maintain as much as possible the past autonomy of the Jewish community (supported in this quest by the community as a whole), the hostility of the native Christians toward the participation of the Jews in the civic life of the cities, and the fact that many Jews could not satisfy the professional, financial, or residential criteria which defined Russia's two urban classes. The official attempt to "classify" the Jews therefore continued under Catherine's successors, Paul and Alexander.[85] At the same time, Russian commentators made a greater effort to examine Jewish life, and Russian attitudes toward the Jews were refined.

4

The Discovery of the Jewish Question in Russia, 1796-1801

One of Catherine's legacies to her son Paul was the need to administer the large number of Jews gathered into the Russian Empire under the final partitions of Poland. (Gessen's incomplete figures show 151,277 male Jews registered in the *kupechestvo* and *meshchanstvo* in all of Russia between 1797 and 1800.)[1] This was not an easy task. The areas of the *Rzeczpospolita*, or Polish Commonwealth, where these Jews lived had been torn apart by war and disorder for over three years. Included were regions that differed greatly from one another: parts of Belorussia, Lithuania, the Ukraine, and Kurlandia, as well as lands of ethnic Poland. Culturally variegated, much of this area had also been part of the old Grand Duchy of Lithuania. Although the residents of these new Russian territories had been guaranteed religious freedom, the Jews were not mentioned in any of the annexation decrees, as they had been in 1772. Keeping in mind the now-established principle that everything not specifically guaranteed to the Jews was denied them, this was a significant omission—all the more so because the legal system of the grand duchy, which treated the Jews as an exclusive category, was retained. Legal conflicts between Christians and Jews were not long in coming, although they did not attract the attention of the capital until early in the reign of Paul's successor, Alexander I.

The government of Catherine had pursued a confused policy toward Polish-Russian Jewry. The main intent of the government, especially when dealing with the relatively small Belorussian Jewish population, had been integrationist, aimed at incorporating the Jews into existing categories of Russian economic life while allowing them cultural and religious autonomy. Attainment of this objective was hindered by various factors: anti-Jewish feeling on the local level in Belorussia; economic rivalry between Christian and Jew; the existence of larger Jewish communities in the areas seized after 1772, to which the Russian government did not automatically extend the rights allowed to the Jews of Belorussia; and the attempts of the conservative Jewish community to resist and circumvent the diminution of its traditional political autonomy. These difficulties were compounded by the inability of the government to assign the Jews to other than preconceived categories. By the conclusion of Catherine's reign, the government, oblivious to its own inconsistencies, sponsored what were in effect two Jewish policies. The first was a continuation of the openly stated promise of equal treatment before the law. The second was a pragmatic policy of unequal treatment when the need arose, a policy marked by capitulation to the special interests of influential elements of the Christian population, be they merchants or landowners. The reign of Paul introduced two important innovations. Officialdom at last made a serious effort to gain some knowledge of Jewish life and, in partial consequence, made attempts to devise new categories into which the Jews might be fitted.

The first years of Paul's reign saw a continuation of the earlier duality, with the integrationist impulse alternating with or accompanying discriminatory restrictions. Paul continued the double tax,[2] and the government no longer intervened forcefully against the violation of Jewish electoral rights. On the other hand, Paul's administrators were generally careful to ensure that no additional liabilities were attached to the Jews. On several occasions local administrators were strictly cautioned by the central government to treat the Jews within the letter of the law. In 1796 the governors of Mogilev and Novgorod-Seversk provinces were advised to stop restricting the right of Jewish merchants to travel from one province to another. (The decree noted further that townspeople, Christian or Jewish, did not possess this right.)[3] In 1797 the governor of Podolia province was ordered not to resettle Jews enrolled as townspeople who had recently settled in the town of Kamenets-Podolsk without permission, although a strict interpretation of the law would have required this.[4] In 1800, prompted by Paul himself, the Senate held that landowners did not have the right of trial and punishment over Jews settled on their estates.[5] The pattern of these decisions revealed a desire to treat the Jews moderately and fairly.

Nonetheless, the lack of comprehensive information about Jewish life within the central bureaucracy continued to hinder effective administration. During Paul's reign, for example, the governor of Kurlandia province asked the Senate for policy guidelines with regard to the Jews of the area who were long, albeit illegally, resident and whose mobility impeded effective taxation. The Senate was forced to inquire of the Kurlandia authorities about all aspects of Jewish life, betraying a total lack of prior information or knowledge.

Emperor Paul I

The Kurlandia authorities replied to the Senate's request by submitting a report filled with negative assessments of the Jews and their activities. They argued that the Jews had no legal rights of settlement except around the town of Gazenport (Hasenpot, Aizpute), where they enjoyed special privileges. (This ignored the fact that the Jews could point to de facto residence in Kurlandia for over two hundred years!)[6] The authorities complained that the Jews could be taxed only with difficulty because of their migratory nature. They denied that the Jews were economically useful to the area: Jews were concentrated in petty trades, especially the inevitable liquor trade, as well as in the sale of used goods. Jewish participation in such pursuits, it was claimed, arose because they abhorred honest work such as manual labor or agriculture.[7]

In response to this report, a group of unidentified Jews from Kurlandia sent a petition to the Senate's Section of State Revenues. Primarily, the petition requested the creation of a kahal structure for the Jews of Kurlandia, which could then be made responsible for collecting taxes, for the settlement of minor disputes, and for the enforcement of Jewish communal law. The petition thus envisioned the establishment of kahals where none had ever existed. It is questionable whether this petition spoke for all Kurlandia Jewry, which as a group was generally too inarticulate and disorganized to have sought such overtly political goals. The petition further requested that Jewish merchants and townspeople in Kurlandia be granted the same rights as their coreligionists in Belorussia.[8] This request provides a clue that the petitioners were probably Kurlandian Jewish merchants and tradesmen who had much to gain from the creation of such a system. Certainly it was this social group that dominated the kahals when they were established in Kurlandia.

The Senate replied by permitting the creation of kahals in Kurlandia while stipulating that kahal jurisdiction extended only to religious matters. As in Belorussia the Jews were considered an urban class. They were ordered to enroll in the urban lists, whereby they were subordinated to urban judicial and administrative bodies while at the same time permitted to participate freely in class elections. As had been the case in Belorussia in 1785, the Senate halted resettlement of Jews illegally resident in the countryside, and they were allowed to receive passports for "temporary" settlement outside the urban centers. While Kurlandia's Jews thus received rights similar to those of their Belorussian brethren, they were saddled with the restrictions as well: Jews were ordered to pay the double tax, or its equivalent for three years if they wished to emigrate. One special exception was made: Jews who could prove their inability to pay this tax were allowed to leave without payment.[9] This exemption was abolished the following year as the government became more aware of the services that Jews, even poor Jews, could be made to perform for the national economy. This Kurlandian episode reveals that the government, through the Senate, was still attempting to treat all the Jews of the empire uniformly, despite or perhaps because of ignorance of regional variations in the cultural or economic life of the various Jewish communities.

The Senate's newfound interest in the Jews was not restricted to Kurlandia. Attention was also directed to the Jewish communities of Belorussia and Poland. But it should be noted that the Senate did not display excessive initiative: new considerations of the "Jewish problem" grew out of concerns directed toward a larger, more complex "peasant problem" in those areas where the Jews were permitted to reside.

The provinces of Belorussia shared in the chaotic events that marked the decline of the Polish Commonwealth. The attendant military maneuvers exacerbated the traditional maltreatment of the local peasantry by the landowning classes. These factors, coupled with the primitive agricultural techniques of peasants working on soil of marginal fertility, produced a continuous cycle of momentary prosperity alternating with widespread poverty throughout the eighteenth century. For most contemporaries it was the valleys, rather than the peaks, that predominated.[10] The last decade of the eighteenth century witnessed an agricultural depression. The countryside was burdened by military operations during the last two Polish partitions. Added to these troubles was an epizootic in 1795 which took a heavy toll of livestock and further impoverished the peasantry.[11] In 1797 there was famine in some areas, and in May of that year Paul commanded the governor of Minsk province, Zakhar Karneev, to assemble the marshals of the nobility to discover the causes of the famine and possible means of alleviating it. The first report of the marshals was forwarded to Paul by Karneev on 13 July 1797.

This report, written in Russian and Polish, analyzed a number of factors contributing to the agricultural crisis. At least part of the problem, the marshals believed, lay in the nature of the peasants themselves.

> Due to the unhappy fate of this area, the peasants, having little agricultural skill, cannot hope to attain a decent state, and their ignorance is the reason for their inability to establish sound agriculture. For all this, however, knowledge itself would prove insufficient to change them since other burdens, arising from different circumstances, interrupt their activities and make them despair of ever attaining a decent state. Changes and revolutions in this area, the billeting and movement of troops, and all those things that require various individual services prevent the peasant from caring for his home and his farm, and diminish the reserves needed for a decent situation. Crop failures often occur in many places because of sandy and low-lying land, and this is accompanied by a decline in cattle, and these things destroy in people the incentive for hard work. Trade is inadequate in many places, and in several there are difficul-

ties in supplying products by road, and this too does not help the
peasant to improve his situation.[12]

As a compilation of the woes of rural Russia, these complaints anticipated the "crisis in serfdom" which Soviet writers have discerned in the
decades preceding the peasant emancipation.[13] In order to complete the
picture, however, the marshals should have mentioned the demands
which the landowners themselves placed on their peasants. Such burdens
were quite diverse. They ranged from money payments to a variety of
labor services, such as fieldwork and the even more onerous cartage
duties. The landowners also enjoyed numerous product monopolies on
their estates. Peasants had to pay a special fee to escape the pervasive
restrictions of these monopolies. The possession of a tiny hand grind-
stone, for instance, necessitated a payment to the leaseholder of the
milling monopoly.[14] The peasants were obliged to purchase monopolized
products, such as vodka or salt, whether they wanted them or not, and at
the landowner's set price. There were variations on this technique: peasants had no choice but to sell their products to the landowner, again at his
price. The greatest demands were placed on the peasantry when the estate
was leased, a problem which even the Minsk marshals identified. Most
leases were short-term by law, and as a result leaseholders often attempted
to extract maximum profit as rapidly as possible, to the future detriment
of the entire estate. When a landowner unilaterally raised the price of the
lease—as many were wont to do—the increase was passed along to the
peasants. On a short-term basis even the ruination of the peasants worked
to the landowners' or the lessees' benefit: they could cheaply buy up grain,
cattle, and other products which the peasants had pledged for debts. On
more than one occasion, the peasants offered to pay the estate owner to
release them from the authority of his own agent, the leaseholder.[15] By no
means were all leaseholders Jews, but their concentration in petty leaseholding, especially the liquor trade, made them very visible. They could
furnish a convenient scapegoat for the very landowners whom they served
as agents.

The Minsk marshals focused on this aspect of the problem. In addition
to the poverty caused by ignorance and nature there was "the more serious
problem of the Jews, who are proprietors of taverns and inns in circum-
vention of the requirements that they live in the city, and who lead the
peasantry into debt and drunkenness, to the detriment of agriculture."[16]
The Jews were not alone in their exploitation of the peasants. The marshals also complained of an overabundance of priests, for whom the normal incidence of baptisms, weddings, and funerals did not provide a
sufficient income and who were thus forced to extort unreasonable fees for
their services. Finally, the report explained the abuses which arose from
estate leasing. Thus, initially, the role of the Jews was only one factor

among many which were held responsible for rural impoverishment. The treatment this original report received in the capital, however, soon emphasized the charge of "Jewish exploitation."[17]

Emperor Paul acted quickly upon reception of the marshals' report. On 28 July 1797, the materials from Belorussia were sent to the procurator-general of the Senate, A. B. Kurakin, for investigation by the Senate. At the same time Paul instructed Kurakin to notify Karneev that "he, through his office, should take actions similar to those measures proposed by the marshals regarding the limitation of the rights of the Jews, who ravaged the peasants, and the clergy, who oppressed them by their immoderate extortions, and regarding the terms of leases."[18] The Senate in turn, on 3 August 1797, asked for more information from the Minsk marshals regarding the problems of the peasantry. The marshals, now sensing what the central government desired, considerably revised their original description of the activities of the Jews. They reported that "the inhabitants of Minsk province are found in the greatest poverty not only from frequent crop failures, but also because the landowners keep Jews under leases in taverns in their villages, and by selling liquor to the peasants on credit for which the peasants pledge things they need, they [the Jews] lead them into squalor and make them incapable of engaging in agriculture." To remedy this situation the marshals asked for renewed enforcement of the decree of 31 March 1755, which, they argued, forbade the Jews to distill spirits.[19]

The Senate now extended its study to a wider field. In April of 1798 the governors of the other "Polish provinces" were asked to submit recommendations for the improvement of the life of the peasantry. The responses to this order reinforced the view that had begun to emerge from the Minsk report, namely that the Jews were a principal cause of rural poverty. However, while the opinions of the marshals of various provinces offered very little that was new, the accompanying reports of Russian officials analyzed the "Jewish problem" in more than cosmetic fashion.[20]

The marshals of Podolia province, for instance, echoed the charge of their Minsk counterparts that it was the Jewish hold on the liquor trade that was responsible for peasant destitution. They made no recommendations for restricting this activity, however, an omission perhaps best understood by recalling that the Jews were their employees. Instead the marshals merely thanked the government for leaving the control of distillation in the hands of the nobility. Only their own careful supervision of the trade had prevented the complete ruination of the peasantry by the Jews, they announced. The marshals did make one proposal concerning the Jews. They requested that the Jews be restricted from engaging in "uneconomical foreign trade," the sale of Russian agricultural products abroad. They suggested that the Jews instead be encouraged to take up agriculture. The landowners perhaps had in mind the formal enserfment

of the Jews on their estates, a threat which the Russian government continually recognized and opposed.

The comments of the vice-governor of the province, Aleksei Iuzefovich,
qualified the marshals' report. He suggested that instead of merely restricting Jewish foreign trade, the government should encourage the landowners to engage in it themselves. Iuzefovich recognized the repercussions of making peasants of the Jews. He noted that such a plan was in
apparent contradiction to the decree of 3 May 1975, which treated the
Jews as an urban class by providing that they be subordinated to the city
magistracy (and not the landowners) and that they be settled in the towns.
Russian officialdom had yet to go beyond the view that the Jews could be
anything else than an urban people.[21] Only with the report of the marshals
of Lithuania province did this view undergo modification.

All the governors polled had responded quickly to the Senate's command, creating the suspicion that at none of their meetings had the marshals attempted to go deeply into problems posed by Jewish economic
activity. The one notable exception was Lithuania province,[22] from whose
marshals the Senate was forced, on 23 November 1799, to demand haste.
The governor, I. G. Frizel, excused the delay by explaining that the
marshals had been slow to complete their task and that their replies had to
be translated from Polish into Russian. In retrospect, however, it appeared that Frizel was himself engaged in a comprehensive survey of
Jewish life in partitioned Poland and that he was forcing the Lithuanian
marshals to devise remedies more wide-ranging than had been produced
elsewhere. Frizel accompanied the marshals' report with a survey of his
own, the first comprehensive program advanced for the reform of Jewish
life in Russia.[23]

Fifteen Lithuanian marshals jointly responded to the Senate's request
for recommendations. Three of them believed that reform was impossible
since the Jews were too deeply involved in the rural economy. All the
marshals agreed, however, that some modification of Jewish employment
in the liquor trade was desirable, presumably by eliminating the means by
which the Jews circumvented regulations in collusion with the landowners. The marshals recommended that Jews be prohibited from distilling or tavern-keeping even in the name of the local szlachta. Should
such a rule be promulgated, the marshals acknowledged, serious problems
would arise from the necessity of transferring the Jews who would lose
their livelihood to the urban centers, which were still too small to absorb
them either physically or economically. The result would be the creation
of a permanent pauper class. Therefore the marshals suggested that Jews
who were unable to resettle in the towns be permitted residence on public
and private land, as free agricultural laborers not bound to the soil. (There
already existed in Belorussia analogous groups of rural people, found
primarily on magnate estates, engaged in agricultural labor or petty trade.

They were known variously as *pokhozhikhi*, *zakhozhikhi*, and *brodiachi*, and included runaways, immigrants, transients, and petty szlachta. After the annexation of Belorussia, all such people not recognized as serfs were placed in a special category of "free people" (*vol'nye liudi*). This was not a large group.)[24]

The marshals also attacked the cultural and political autonomy of the Jews. They recommended the compulsory abandonment of the "untidy" dress of the Jews, which further served to alienate them from the Christian peasantry. So too they advocated the abolition of the kahal, which, they argued, gave the Jews great power and allowed them to circumvent governmental restrictions. Instead, the Jews should be divided into separate and distinct legal categories.[25] The opinion of the Lithuanian marshals surpassed, in its depth of criticism and espousal of innovative reforms, the remedies previously submitted to the central government. The report of Governor Frizel, which accompanied that of the marshals, went further still.

Frizel never explained in his report why he took so unusual an interest in the position of the Jews in Russia, although his recommendations show some acquaintance with both historical and contemporary responses to the "Jewish Question." The suspicion, suggested by his Germanic name, that Frizel was a bureaucratic "Stolz" in the midst of the Russian "Oblomovs" is belied by his typically Russian service career. Frizel was born into a noble family in Estland in 1740. At the age of fifteen he was already a sergeant in the army, where he served in the infantry, the musketeers, and the hussars, often holding administrative posts. At the age of twenty-four he was made an adjutant on the staff of Major-General Peutling. In 1790 he served on the commission that oversaw peace negotiations with Sweden. He entered the civil service in 1794, and it was in his civil posts that he had the most opportunity to observe Jewish life in partitioned Poland. In 1796 he served as vice-governor of Vilna province, and in 1798 he was appointed civil governor of Lithuania province. His advancement under Paul was evidently not continued under Alexander, since the last reference to him is encountered in 1802, when he was mentioned as the former governor of Lithuania province.[26]

Frizel began his report with a sweeping demographic and historical examination of the Jews. He observed that the Jews had apparently dwelt in Poland for over five hundred years but still remained "Asiatic" in appearance, and maintained a "typically Asian laziness and slovenliness." These traits led them to engage in exploitation or activities which either necessitated fraud or required little physical labor. The Jews had been treated with indifference by past Polish governments, and they had taken full advantage of this latitude. In Poland the Jews had been free men, unrestricted by law and free to enter any occupation they desired. They thus gained control of the provisioning trade and of virtually all activities involving the handling of money. Under these conditions, more and more Jews were attracted to Poland, where they found "a veritable earthly paradise." The government of the Jews had fallen into the hands of religious leaders, patriarchs, and rabbis who dominated education and morality by their "absurd teachings." Frizel lamented the control such charlatans had over the simple creed of the average Jew, which they turned to their own base advantage. Yet so great was the fear of their curses that no one protested their impositions and excesses. The exploitive activities of the religious leadership were aided, abetted, and surpassed, moreover, by the secular leadership of the kahal elders. In Frizel's view the kahal had originated solely as a device for protecting the affluent in the community, especially in the apportionment of taxes. Accordingly, a general reform was necessary, to halt the thievery of the elders, to protect the average Jew from their oppressions, and to ensure the usefulness of Jews to the state. Frizel offered such a reform. It took shape as a critique of the religious-secular life of Russian Jewry, an analysis of their economic role in society, and a set of concrete reform proposals.

Frizel presented a harsh picture of Jewish religious life. He was a witness to the disintegration of Jewish religious unity resulting from the rise of Hasidism, and his outlook was clearly influenced by this religious civil war. According to Frizel, scriptural interpretations which varied from teacher to teacher provided the basis for Jewish religious law. Since the kahal was an autonomous institution, and since the Jewish clergy was nonhierarchical, conflicting interpretations were held by different communities. This situation encouraged the rise of charlatans and false prophets who traded on the credulity of the simple people, usually for their own economic benefit. Frizel did not specify any particular sect or religious leader, but he was apparently referring to the Hasidic movement and its individual leaders, the *tzaddikim*, some of whom did indeed prosper on the gifts and offerings of their devoted circle of followers. The result of this, said Frizel, was doctrinal chaos, intrigue, and confusion. "Looking at this aspect of the Jews it cannot be said that anyone, merely by dressing like a Jew and not believing in Christianity, is a member of the same faith."[27]

Despite the high incidence of theological bickering, each area of Jewish settlement had at least one rabbi who could command respect and who collaborated with kahal officialdom. Just as the rabbi was the chief spiritual authority, so secular concerns were in the hands of the elected kahal elders. Frizel was most taken by the negative side of kahal activity, and he displayed special concern for the average Jew, whom he depicted as completely in thrall, spiritually and physically, to the kahal leadership, "prisoners of fear and ignorance, without any morality, without any dignity or self-respect, without education."[28] All areas of public life fell within the purview of the kahal, ranging from criminal law and litigation to economic concerns such as control and oversight of contracts between its members and outsiders. The Jews were kept separated from surrounding Christian society, not only by the strictures of custom and religion, but by the impenetrable Jewish language. Jewish society took care that every young Jew was kept within this charmed circle through a process of early indoctrination and education. Frizel, like future Russian commentators, scorned the education which Jews received within the community. Ignoring the fact that most adult Jews could at least read and write after their education in the Jewish primary school, or *heder*, he complained of the emphasis on study of the Talmud and careful textual analysis of the Bible. In Frizel's opinion this training was not socially useful, since it did not inculcate virtues or morality and, most especially, "love of order." Frizel was a typical representative of the cultural-integrationist stand which dominated Russian views toward the Jews until the second half of the nineteenth century. Jewish education was valueless, Jewish speech was jargon or, worse, a protective and isolating cultural wall, and Jewish dress was unhygienic and alienated Jew from Gentile. The Jewish problem would be solved only when the Jews became culturally identical to Great Russians.

The role played by the Jews in the Russian economy was, of course, the motive force for a reform project in the first place, and Frizel explored the economic role of each group within the Jewish community. Frizel divided all Jews into one of four occupational categories: merchants, craftsmen, tavern-keepers, and "others."

In Frizel's judgment only the merchants were unquestionably useful to the Russian state. He recognized that such Jews were the most important agents of the import-export trade in the region, and he saw nothing wrong with leaving this activity in their hands, unlike the Podolian marshals who had desired that such trade become the prerogative of the landowners. Yet Frizel included one proviso: given the tradition of dishonesty and chicanery in Jewish commerce, special caution must be taken against deceptive practices. Frizel was especially concerned by the frequent bankruptcies which afflicted Jewish trading houses engaged in the speculative import trade.

Frizel was more ambivalent about Jewish artisans. It has already been noted that the artisan trades attracted many Jews even though such employment frequently failed to provide adequate income and created unnatural competition in areas of concentrated Jewish habitation. Frizel advanced several explanations for this. First of all, he reported, the Jews were overrepresented in crafts which required minimal work and strength—he commented elsewhere on the "innate laziness" of the Jews—such as tailoring, cobbling, goldsmithing, stone carving, and jewelry work, as opposed to blacksmithing, carpentry, joining, and masonry. An additional part of the problem was the inadequate training of most Jewish artisans. Instead of the training that Christian guildsmen theoretically received, the Jew usually began his career with only minimal experience. This problem arose from a social peculiarity, the habit of early marriage, which necessitated support of a family very early in life. Frizel did not condemn the artisan class so much for sharp practices and unfair business techniques as for shoddy, substandard work. He respected these Jews for at least attempting honest work, however poor the result.

Such could not be said for the third and largest class, that of the Jewish tavern-keepers. Frizel repeated the charges of the Minsk marshals: the Jews dominated the liquor trade; they ruined the peasantry by offering liquor on credit; no one who went into debt to the Jews could ever escape their power. At the same time Frizel made the important observation that for all their bad influence on the peasantry the Jews themselves were not visibly better off. The Jewish public house and the squalid Jewish village were slovenly and filthy; the Jews themselves lived close to destitution. He noted that the income they drew from their tavern-keeping was seldom enough to support a family and that many taverns were run by women, while their husbands found work elsewhere in order to supplement the family income. Although Frizel did not specifically say so, the implication was that the fault lay in the system of which the Jews were a part, rather than in some peculiarity of the Jews themselves.

Frizel had no use at all for the final "class," a motley of idlers, recipients of public charity, money-changers, and "factors," a term which in Polish means men for hire for any activity, including those which were disreputable and illegal. He claimed that it was impossible to find one Jew deceiving, robbing, or murdering another Jew without the aid of a factor. Though it hardly excused their activity, Frizel pointed out that such men were forced to perform this work as the only hope of earning money to pay their taxes, especially the double tax. He believed that the eradication of this "class," as well as the entry of all Jews into activities which would be of utility to the state, could come about only through a general raising of their moral and economic position. Frizel then suggested how such an improvement might be achieved.[29]

Reflecting the Mendelssohnian approach, Frizel argued that the enlightenment of the Jews must begin with their religion. The government should continue to display tolerance in a general way, and should permit the Jews to retain any legitimate religious liberties. At the same time, the government would have to be more alert for any religious activities that ran counter to its best interests. A halt had to be made in the religious civil war. In some unexplained fashion the government was to oversee and guarantee the existing beliefs of the Jews, and then strictly forbid any innovations that might lead to unrest, ignorance, or fraud. With this in mind, the government was to abolish the language barrier behind which the Jewish authorities conducted their business. Henceforth, all activities of internal administration in the Jewish community were to be conducted in Polish (a reminder that Belorussia and the Ukraine were still far from Russified).

Frizel recognized that these measures alone would be insufficient to raise the moral status of the Jews. Like many reformers, he pinned his hopes on the next generation, suitably educated for its role. The government should require the education of Jewish youth in public schools with curricula encompassing more than religion. "When they receive enlightenment and morality here they will shun those features of their life which were formerly so characteristic among them."[30]

Another problem of a religious nature was the early marriage of Jewish youth, sometimes at age seven or even younger. This custom produced a number of complications. Young men, marrying early, had no time to master a skill before they had to support a family. While early marriages were good for increasing the population—although Frizel, like his contemporaries, decried the rapid growth of the Jewish population—the strain of early and frequent childbearing had an adverse effect on women who were often "old at thirty." The rapidly expanding family was very difficult to support. Frizel, imitating Austrian authorities, argued in favor of age requirements for marriage, preferably twenty years of age, accompanied by a demonstrated ability to support a family. Unlike the Austrian legislation, however, this recommendation did not have as its aim the limitation of the Jewish population.[31]

Frizel recognized that an improvement in the socioeconomic status of the Jews would have to accompany these cultural reforms. He envisioned an expansion of the economic pursuits of the Jews. As a result, Frizel's report is of added significance for understanding the development of Russian attitudes toward the Jews. On the one hand, Frizel's work helped to enlighten the central government concerning the conditions of Jewish life in Russia, since it was studied by the reform committee of 1802. On the other, it advanced the government's growing awareness that the existing classification of the Jews as "urban-mercantile" was insufficient. It further suggested the format a reclassification might take.

Frizel's plan called for the division of the Jews into three classes: merchants, artisans, and agriculturists. The Jewish merchant, in this schema, was to possess complete equality with Christians of the mercantile estate. This meant the removal of any distinctions that might have survived in the face of the theoretical equality that Catherine had long since guaranteed. Frizel did not elaborate, so one is left to wonder how he would have dealt with the restrictions on Jewish participation in elections and officeholding which had become a commonly accepted tactic used by local government to ensure domestic peace. Likewise, Frizel wished to extend equality to Jews enrolled as townspeople along with the right to register in the Christian artisan guilds. In all, there was little that was new in Frizel's treatment of merchant and artisan Jews, save an apparent call for a more just application of general laws governing all members of these estates.[32]

The suggestion that some Jews might be made into peasants was new, if already prefigured in the requests of some of the marshals of the nobility in their reports to the government. The Jews of Poland had traditionally been barred from buying or owning land, and since they remained at the same time a free people, they had never been enserfed. The conditioning of centuries was difficult to overcome, and even when the Jews of Poland were allowed in the last years of the independent commonwealth to acquire land for their own use there was little response. Nor did it ever occur to the first Russian administrators that any Jew was other than a member of the urban classes. As such, they were forbidden to buy or own land in the Russian village or, more correctly, to own serfs. For Frizel, however, all Jews who were not members of the first two classes in reality as well as in name were to become members of this new, specially created "class" of free Jewish peasants. Frizel pointed out that there was no shortage of arable land in the empire where the Jews could escape both overcrowding and their traditional fiscal alliance with the Polish landowner. Frizel was careful to specify that those Jews who did settle as agricultural laborers on private estates would retain the right to move to another area after the census and after a settling of accounts. Finally, to encourage the new agriculturists and to help them financially Frizel suggested a ten-year exemption from state taxes.[33] Frizel's plans for the creation of this new class of Jews left much unsaid. He seemed to have forgotten or ignored the already existing invitation of the government to the Jews in 1795 to settle in New Russia. He neglected to mention where he thought resettlement might take place and made no recommendations as to the training or supervision of the Jewish peasant.

Frizel was more specific in his treatment of the kahal. Since he recommended the complete civic and fiscal equality of Christians and Jews, the kahal as a tax-gathering agency was no longer needed. Similarly, all civil litigation and all criminal trials were to take place in the appropriate estate court. Its functions displaced, the kahal was to be abolished, and with it "a thousand abuses." Frizel specified that the debts the kahals had acquired would of necessity have to be paid. For this, he suggested the retention of the existing kahal "basket tax" (korobochnyi sbor), an excise tax on kosher meat and other necessities. In this way, over a period of years, fiscal obligations would be satisfied.

For all the confidence Frizel placed in his plan, he recognized the difficulties involved in carrying it out. For instance, he asked for a two-year period of grace during which the Jews in the liquor trade might settle their accounts with the szlachta and sell off their distillation apparatus, thereby avoiding the consequences of precipitate action. Frizel also proposed some cosmetic reforms such as the prohibition of the characteristic dress of

Russian-Polish Jews which so offended the sensibilities of sophisticated Russians. Despite the trauma certain to accompany such radical changes, Frizel had few doubts that his plan could be successfully carried out under the supervision of a few experienced persons, especially if they in their turn were assisted by "learned and enlightened" Jews within the community itself.[34] With this hope, Frizel consigned his proposal to the consideration of the government. It was soon joined by another, authored by Gavriil Romanovich Derzhavin.

In contrast to the "Teutonic" Frizel, Derzhavin was born in Kazan in 1743 of parents who had some Tatar blood in their background. More is known of Derzhavin's life and career than of Frizel's, because of his subsequent distinction as a man of letters and from his own evidence, the *Memoirs* (*Zapiski*), a tendentious but fascinating account of his life as an administrator and favorite under Catherine, Paul, and Alexander. Like Frizel, Derzhavin had administrative experience, serving as governor of Olonets (1784) and Tambov (1786) provinces, neither of which, incidentally, had a Jewish population. As an examination of his *Opinion* ("*Mnenie*") reveals, Derzhavin harbored some religious prejudices against the Jews, and his *Memoirs* recounted incidents which apparently reinforced such prejudices while at the same time transferring them to a more secular plane. On those few occasions in his *Memoirs* when Derzhavin did speak of Jews—and his firsthand dealings with them seem to have begun only in 1799—he depicted them individually in a very unfavorable light, almost always engaged in shady or criminal dealings. For example, the first reference to Jews in the *Memoirs* was an indictment of Prince Potemkin for conniving at the sale of two thousand souls on Zaporozhian land by Prince Viazemskii to one "Stiglitz, a Jew," a transaction of dubious legality.[35]

In 1799 Derzhavin was sent by the Senate to investigate complaints made against Simon Zorich, a Shklov landowner and a former favorite of Catherine, by the Jews who lived on his estate. Derzhavin asserted that this was a plot both to remove him temporarily from the capital and to enable another royal favorite to pick up the estate of Zorich on the cheap after its confiscation. Derzhavin acquitted Zorich with the justification that the Jews had wronged him as much as he had wronged them. Indeed, Derzhavin at first attempted to avoid passing judgment on Zorich at all. In 1799 several Jews in the Belorussian district of Sennensk were arrested on a charge of ritual murder. Derzhavin wrote to the tsar questioning whether he should proceed with the Zorich case, since it depended upon the testimony of Jews at a time when all Jews were being held in disrepute because of the charge against them. If the claim was true, contended Derzhavin, the Jews were beyond the pale of civilized life and could not be trusted as witnesses.[36] After his second trip to Belorussia, Derzhavin claimed that an attempt was made to discredit him and his proposals for Jewish reform when they were under consideration by the Senate, by the

G. R. Derzhavin, poet, senator, and would-be reformer of Russian Jewry.

circulation of a tale that he had beaten a pregnant Jewess at a distillery and caused her to lose her child.[37] Finally, during the meetings of the reform committee, Derzhavin asserted that he had been offered a bribe by the Jews and argued that other members of the committee, especially Speranskii, had accepted one.[38] Derzhavin disliked and distrusted Jews individually and collectively.

Derzhavin's first experience with the organized Jewish community occurred in 1799, during his trip to Belorussia. From this journey dates his

enthusiastic search for a solution to the "Jewish Question," which Derzhavin understood as the protection of the Christian population from the
exploitive devices of the Jews, accompanied by the task of making the
Jews useful to the state. The impetus for the composition of his reform
project was yet another famine in Belorussia, this time in 1800. On 16
June 1800, Derzhavin received a letter from the emperor, informing him
in part:

> It has come to our attention that in the Belorussian provinces there is a
> grain shortage, and that some landowners, out of boundless avarice,
> leave their peasants without assistance with their food supply; [and]
> we send you to investigate such landowners, and where there are
> peasants requiring aid from them for foodstuffs [who] are unaided, to
> place the estate under trusteeship and to supply the peasants with
> their master's grain, and should this prove insufficient to supply them
> from the village magazines at the landowner's expense.[39]

There was no reference to the Jews; rather, the government originally
held the landowners responsible for the unhappy condition of the peasants. Paul's command was communicated to Derzhavin by the procurator-
general of the Senate, P. I. Obol"ianinov, who enumerated the steps
Derzhavin was to take in carrying out the emperor's order. Obol"ianinov
added a curious postscript to these intructions:

> Since according to our information a major cause of the exhaustion
> of the Belorussian peasantry is the Jews, who extract their profits
> from them, the Most High will is that you deliver a personal opinion
> and report on their pursuits, in order to prevent this general harm
> and that you give your opinion on the general conditions there.[40]

The source and motivation of this postscript are unknown, although
some historians have suggested that it was included by way of collusion
between Obol"ianinov and Derzhavin, in order to give the latter a mandate to examine the Jewish question. In any event it served to divert
attention from the landowners to the Jews. Although Derzhavin did take
vigorous measures against the landowners on several occasions, his chief
preoccupation was with the role of the Jews and the composition of his
Opinion.[41]

Since Derzhavin had little precise knowledge of the Jews, he had to
acquire a rapid orientation about Jewish life, based on interviews, historical documents, and personal observation. As Derzhavin described it in his
third-person narrative:

> Likewise, at the time of his travels, he collected information from
> judicious citizens, from the Jesuit Academy, from every office, from

nobles and merchants and the Cossacks themselves, regarding the
manner of life of the Jews, their trades, deceits, and every contri-
vance and trick whereby they deceived and stripped the ignorant
and poor inhabitants, and by what measures it was possible to defend the ignorant rabble from them, and to direct them to an honorable and blameless way of life, settling them in their own towns and
villages, in order to make them useful citizens. . . .[42]

Derzhavin was remarkably unselective in the material upon which he
based his historical view of the Jews in Poland; he examined a random
sample of Polish laws regarding the Jews and took note of Governor M. A.
Kakhovskii's report of 1773, as well as some decrees of Count Chernyshev. Derzhavin also included in an appendix a series of fanciful items
about Jewish rites and beliefs, including some which purported to show
Jewish guilt in several recent cases of ritual murder, together with a
translation of a Jewish book, *Shevet Eguda*, supposedly glorifying the
clever escapes of guilty Jews from ritual murder accusations. (All of this
was material which Derzhavin had procured during his visit of 1799, in
the midst of the Sennensk ritual murder trial.)

Derzhavin's *Opinion* at times took on the aspect of a lurid exposé, the
author adopting an air of righteous indignation as he "discovered" one
perfidy after another in Jewish life. In one other aspect the *Opinion* differed from Frizel's report: Derzhavin relied heavily on suggestions and
recommendations of Jews themselves. He even asked the kahal leaders for
recommendations for the modification of Jewish life and received, in so
many words, a polite invitation to mind his own business. Much of Derzhavin's suggested reform was based on the advice of two rather untypical
Polish Jews. The first was Nota Khaimovich Notkin (sometimes known as
Nata Notkin, or Nathan Shklover), a businessman known in governmental circles and an indefatigable partisan of Jewish reform. His proposal
that Jews might form a useful factory-worker class was incorporated into
Derzhavin's *Opinion* and thence into the Statute of 1804.[43]

The second adviser was more exotic for the time and place: Dr. I. Frank,
a Polish Mendelssohnian from Kreslovka. Learning, as did Notkin, of Derzhavin's work on a reform project, Frank sent a Mendelssohnian program to
the senator in September of 1800. The spirit of the Enlightenment via the
Jewish "Berliners" is evident in his analysis of the Jewish community:

All agree that only a good man can be a good subject, that only good
moral beliefs create civic virtue. And since the general opinion holds
that the moral character of the Jews has been changed for the worse
and that because of this they appear as bad and harmful subjects,
there thus springs up the question: can they be corrected morally
and thence politically?[44]

Through a survey of Jewish history, Frank explained how the Jews had come to be regarded as poor citizens in the modern period. Following Mendelssohn, he argued that the "primeval purity [of the Jewish religion] rested on a simple deism," but that it had been corrupted by the earliest Jewish teachers, who were simply charlatans working for their own advantage. They distorted the true spirit of Jewish dogma by "mystical-Talmudic" misinterpretation of the Holy Scriptures and

> instead of a practical and social virtue, they retained absurd, meaningless formulae for prayer and empty rituals for devotion and, led on by personal advantage, directed the blinded nation toward whatever they wished, through the sacred murk of superstition. In order to protect the nation from enlightened aspirations they introduced rigorous laws which isolated the Jews from all other nations, inspired in Jews a deep hatred toward any other religion, and by superstitious notions erected a high wall, separating Jews from other people.[45]

The Jews suffered for their exclusiveness by serving as targets of the hatred of Christians. Christians forced Jews to pay dearly for any toleration which they extended, and as a consequence, contemporary relations between Christian and Jew rested only on considerations of fiscal advantage. The resultant need for money complicated the problem, forcing the Jews into constant money-grubbing and toward the pursuit of any profitable activity, no matter how socially degraded. "Trade and usury feed petty egotistic passions, baseness, and ignoble motives and kill any impulse toward great deeds and moral improvement," argued Frank.

The key to moral redemption lay in a return to the original purity of the Jewish religion, a return expedited by the adoption of the ancient Jewish tongue—"scales fall from his eyes and he clearly sees then the stupidity of the Talmud, and he hurries irresistibly toward moral revivification." Frank had in mind biblical Hebrew which he hoped would displace the Yiddish "jargon" spoken by Polish Jewry. Hebrew study alone was not enough, however, and Frank invoked the example of his idol, Moses Mendelssohn:

> By just such means did Mendelssohn enlighten himself, and afterward he had recourse to such means in order to enlighten his German fellow believers, and the most fortunate success crowned his endeavors. He called for the study of the Jewish and German languages, published a highly exact translation of the Old Testament, and the more this translation was read, the more highly rose German Jews in their moral development.[46]

The solution for Frank lay in opening public schools which would teach in the Russian, German, and Hebrew languages, with access to state service for especially talented Jewish students.

Derzhavin's sources for his *Opinion* were very eclectic, for he drew on the experience and legislation of the Roman and Byzantine empires, as well as contemporary Prussia, Austria, and even revolutionary France. Yet Derzhavin's basic premises always rested on the Mendelssohnian precepts of Dr. Frank. He especially took to heart the latter's warning that improvement would come only far in the future.[47]

Derzhavin had originally received his commission to investigate the famine in Belorussia, and by July he was actively taking measures on the spot. He also began to collect the reports and evidence that were to provide the sources of his *Opinion* and assembled all of his information in Vitebsk by September 1. Since Derzhavin returned to the capital in October with his *Opinion* already complete (although it may have been subsequently revised), the task, even for so prolific a writer, was a hurried one.[48] The *Opinion* examined the conditions of Belorussia, the reasons for the famine, and the history of the Jews in Poland, and it proposed a reform filled with minutiae. In his collected works the *Opinion*, with appendices, runs to just over a hundred folio pages. The full title of the work is revealing: "The Opinion of Senator Derzhavin regarding the avoidance of the grain shortage in Belorussia by curbing the mercenary trades of the Jews, and regarding their reform, and other things."

Although Derzhavin blamed many of the problems of the Belorussian peasants and of Belorussian agriculture on the Jews, he was dissatisfied with all classes of society. He stood as a Great Russian nobleman judging the Belorussian peasant and the Polish magnate. The conditions that he found violated Derzhavin's own conception of the proper economic role to be played by both groups as well as the relationships that should exist between them. He was disgusted by the "laziness" that he believed characterized the peasants, while he was also distressed at the apparent irresponsibility of the magnates, as evidenced by their disregard for the welfare of the peasants. Derzhavin was a strong partisan of the Russian pattern of noble serf-holding, and Belorussia failed to conform to the idyllic Russian model he created in his own mind. Derzhavin, in addition, always remained a foe of the Russian court nobility, whom he accused of manipulating the government for their selfish aims and, incidentally, of blocking his own career. The Polish nobility presented an archetypical picture of such an irresponsible aristocracy.[49]

Derzhavin contrasted the Belorussian peasant sharply with his own image of the Russian serf. The latter he saw as industrious, with a genuine aptitude for agriculture. The Russian never surrendered to the vicissitudes of fate: in times of want he turned to handicrafts for support, and seldom failed to fulfill his obligations. The Belorussian peasant, on the other hand, was lazy, an inept agriculturalist incapable of surviving by handicrafts. He was forced to beg the landowners for grain, not for seeding, but for food. Derzhavin was also repelled by the low standards of conduct that were manifest in peasant life. Not even Derzhavin was prepared to eulogize the Russian serf as a model of sobriety, but he indicted the Belorussians for the "disorderliness" of their lives, and especially for drunkenness. At harvest time, for example, they spent their time in revelry and drinking, buying liquor from the Jews and getting into debt to them. Holidays also provided a similar excuse, so that the peasant was not only in debt, but often too ill to work. (At times the *Opinion* anticipated a nineteenth-century temperance lecture.) Why were the Belorussian peasants so different from their Great Russian counterparts? For Derzhavin the answer was simple: too much freedom. Derzhavin both exaggerated the number of "free people" (those with the right to change residence) in Belorussia and condemned any deviation from his ideal of a rigidly enserfed peasant population. According to Derzhavin the peasants could move from one magnate's estate to another and would attach themselves to one leaseholder after another in order to get money to pay their taxes. Nearly transients, they displayed no pride in nor desire for a settled life and lived aimlessly, "from day to day."[50]

If the Belorussian peasant was thus undirected and shiftless, the source of the problem, for Derzhavin, was to be found in the magnate class. Derzhavin differentiated between the petty Polish szlachta, the landowners of only limited means, and the magnates, aristocrats with large landholdings. The latter had been the dominant social and economic group before the partitions, and they remained a major force in the Belorussian countryside afterward. The szlachta were also guilty of improper treatment of the peasantry, but Derzhavin thought they were only following the lead of the magnates, who, for their part, had a special obligation to set a proper example. Unlike Russian landowners, however, they showed no concern for the well-being of their estates or their peasants. Derzhavin considered them guilty of neglecting the essential duties and responsibilities that should maintain proper order and balance in the countryside. Instead of personally settling on their estates and administering them, or at least delegating control to a member of their family, the magnates leased out their estates on a short-term basis, an abuse lamented in the reports of other investigators. By leaving their peasants at the tender mercies of the lease agent, the landowners failed to assume their proper obligations. They were ever ready to sacrifice peasant well-being for financial gain, a typical example being their willingness to tolerate the activities of the Jews as distillers and tavern-keepers, although the latter ruined the peasantry by encouraging drunkenness. The magnates found still other means of exploitation, such as the trade monopolies they often imposed on their estates, discussed above.

Derzhavin quickly identified in his own mind the principal sources of travail in the countryside, especially since they emanated from a foreign class of Polish aristocrats whom he personally disliked. His intended reform never rose above his bias in favor of the serf-holding system. If the cause of agricultural ruin was the indifference or lack of responsibility of the landholding class, Derzhavin's response was to give this class even more power, and in effect to force it to face its duties.

> The improvement of the character and situation of the peasant ought likewise to be entrusted to the landowner. They know the population's qualities, propensities, behavior, economic practices, belongings, shortcomings, and requirements. They can rectify the bad in them and affirm the good by prudent admonition, diligent supervision, active assistance with their needs, and appropriate punishments. . . .[51]

Derzhavin was enough of a realist to understand that moral persuasion alone would not suffice to work the desired transformation. He relied instead upon restrictions and regulations that he himself might have found intolerable if applied to the Russian noble landowner. (This propensity to discriminate against the Polish landowner continued into the next century, apparent in the Statute of 1804.) Derzhavin recommended control of the liquor trade, arguing that the government should demand that distillation be strictly confined to the magnates and not leased out to anyone else, especially Jews. Violators were to lose the right of distillation forever. It is interesting that Derzhavin should consider the liquor trade, which he associated with the Jews, before more tangible problems such as leaseholding; this was a preoccupation which was shared by the framers of the Statute of 1804. In the case of leaseholding, Derzhavin was determined to end the extensive exploitation and subsequent ruination of estates by effectively abolishing the leaseholding class. He did this by requiring that property be leased only to another magnate and for periods of not less than nine years. Even then an agreement would have to be signed pledging the renter to protect the well-being of the estate, and Derzhavin even envisioned inventories that would be taken before and after the lease period. Other types of magnate exploitation were also banned: Derzhavin threatened a three-year confiscation of any estate where the landowner forcibly controlled the sale of peasant products, to be accompanied by permission to the peasants to settle elsewhere.[52]

Only tangentially was the *Opinion* concerned with the well-being of the Belorussian countryside, or even with the establishment of a proper socioeconomic relationship between peasant and landowner. Derzhavin's chief preoccupation remained the Jews, and he had in mind for them a thoroughgoing social, economic, and cultural transformation. As a preliminary he delivered an extensive critique of Jewish life, as viewed from three perspectives: religious, civil, and economic.

There has been a tendency in the historical literature, exemplified by Orshanskii and Dubnow, to dismiss Derzhavin simply as a religious Judeophobe. The nature of Derzhavin's antipathy toward the Jews is more complex than such a characterization implies. Derzhavin's thought represented a transition from the older, essentially religious anti-Jewish tradition of the past to a culturally oriented variant which developed in Russia (and elsewhere) in the nineteenth century. Derzhavin's religious prejudices often underlay or reinforced his condemnations of secular shortcomings which could, at the same time, be regarded independently of religious considerations. The Talmud, for example, was treated as both a religious and a secular document. Biblical exegesis became muddled up with the economic antipathy of the Polish mercantile classes and the Mendelssohnianism of Dr. Frank. Russian Judeophobes of the next century, with a more homogeneous ideology, characteristically cited Derzhavin's attacks on Jewish economic and cultural life while excising his religious pronouncements.

Derzhavin began the reform section of his *Opinion* by defining the character of the Jewish people. He saw them as a people of contradictions: predestined by God to rule, they had been scattered and humiliated under foreign domination yet still ruled over the people among whom they lived. They had always displayed a dichotomy in their nature: "on the one hand they are called a nation chosen by God, and on the other ungrateful, obstinate, cunning, faltering and debauched." They were motivated at times only by enmity toward other human beings, a hatred fueled by the Talmudic interpretations of their rabbis, who were able to hide these ideas from Gentiles behind a wall of incomprehensible Hebrew.[53] How could it be otherwise, asked Derzhavin, when the Talmud promised them dominion over all other nations? Consequently, the Jews lived day to day on the basis of their exploitation of the surrounding Christian community, while they waited for their Messiah. Unlike the God of the Christians, "who is a spirit of truth and virtue, who will unite heaven and earth, the Jewish Messiah is a worldly leader who will bring them temporal rule and glory, and who will rebuild the temple of Solomon."[54] While throughout the *Opinion* Derzhavin stressed the exclusivity of the Jews, manifested in their hatred of Gentiles, he never completely escaped the fear that the Jews also represented a corrupting religious influence on Christians, a charge firmly rooted in the Russian religious tradition. Derzhavin, citing similar decrees from the Byzantine Empire, would have forbidden any Jew to keep Christian servants, and he demanded that Jewish criminals who were exiled to Siberia not be allowed to take their wives, lest they multiply and "corrupt the Northern Empire." In support of this Draconian measure Derzhavin recalled the heretical Strigolniki and the Moscow-Novgorod "Judaizers" as evidence of the threat posed to Orthodoxy by Jewish proselytizing. He took care, too, to cite the fiercely anti-Jewish *Enlightener (Prosvetitel')* of the abbot Iosif of Volokolamsk.[55]

Derzhavin's attitude toward the religious training and education of Judaism was a curious blend of Christian religious prejudice and the enlightened Mendelssohnianism of Dr. Frank. Virtually paraphrasing Frank, Derzhavin complained that in Jewish schools, through a system of Talmudic interpretation and the imposition of sterile laws and customs, the common people were induced to follow "hollow rites and hatred of other peoples," while their children were reared in "naive restrictions," not guided by rules of good conduct or personal honor. Derzhavin, like virtually all other Russian observers, decried the Jewish educational system, especially the intense specialization on Talmudic exegesis. "For their Talmudic studies they pay dearly, but nobody regrets it. I saw from dawn to dusk old men and youths putting on airs and trembling with wails before their books." Other forms of learning fared no better under Derzhavin's analysis. He dismissed the activities of the Kabbalists, for instance, as "hocus-pocus and black magic."[56]

Derzhavin especially faulted the Jews' respect for Judaic Law and its traditions. He saw the result of strict and literal adherence to its tenets in such abuses as frequent, unhealthy fasts and the system of early marriage. Judaic Law was capable of giving rise to even more pernicious practices. While Derzhavin never went so far as to accuse the entire Jewish community of supporting ritual murder, he did believe that individual fanatics were the perpetrators, and that they in turn were protected by the community. Whatever distinctions between individuals and the community he made in the body of his text were more than balanced by the blood-curdling revelations of the appendices. Derzhavin claimed that these accounts were gleaned from Jewish lore and the experience of recent history, and that they proved the continual practice of human sacrifice by some Jews.[57] (They were, in fact, typical examples of Polish-Western religious Judeophobia.)

Derzhavin spoke only briefly and superficially about the Hasidim, whom he characterized as *Raskol'niki*, using the Russian term for Russian Orthodox schismatics. He believed that they differed from Orthodox Jews chiefly on matters of ritual. For all his condemnations of the role played in Mitnaggedim society by the rabbi, Derzhavin was oblivious to the fact that this role was one of the chief points of contention between the two groups of loyalists. Instead he mistakenly equated the rabbi and the Hasidic *tzaddik*—Derzhavin used the term "patriarch"—who was the spiritual adviser of the Hasidic faithful. Derzhavin misread the struggle between the two camps in other ways as well. Neglecting the important elements of social strife that marked the conflict, Derzhavin attributed the bitterness between the two sides to the success the Hasidim had in enticing the children of Orthodox Jews, especially the rich, to join the sect, so that the money thus brought in could be used for "secret schemes" in Palestine.[58]

In the course of his critique of the cultural life of the Jews, Derzhavin also detailed those political and economic features which he thought worked against the general good, both of the Jews themselves and of the wider Gentile community. These criticisms are already familiar from the works of Kakhovskii and Frizel. Derzhavin believed that the Jewish masses were dominated by the kahal leadership, armed with intimidating weapons like the power of excommunication. The kahal elders kept the community in superstitious terror, while simultaneously exploiting it by means of numerous taxes, unfairly levied. The kahal also oversaw the economic relations of Jews and Gentiles, chiefly by means of a system of communal price fixing. It was thus necessary, in Derzhavin's view, to break the power of the kahal, in order for the Jews to aid the economic development of society and rise above their depraved cultural level. To do these things he envisioned a sweeping reform which would alter the political, socioeconomic, and cultural state of Russian Jewry. The principal focus of this transformation was to be an elaborate bureaucracy headed by a special Gentile official, the Jewish "protector," who was apparently to have been directly subordinate only to the tsar himself.

Besides describing in detail the bureaucracy which would have to be created, Derzhavin advanced an elaborate justification for the destruction of the old system. This portion of the *Opinion* is particularly interesting because of its formulation in embryo of concepts that became mainstays of Russian Judeophobia in the nineteenth century: the idea of the closed Jewish community, a state within the state which was international in its connections and communications, and a hindrance to any attempt by the state to make the Jews good citizens. It was this belief that formed the basis of a celebrated Russian book on the Jewish international conspiracy, Iakov Brafman's *Book of the Kahal* (*Kniga kagala*) of 1869.[59]

Derzhavin asserted that the kahal had been left intact by the annexation manifesto of 1772 primarily to serve as a tax-collecting body, a function it still performed. He described the kahal's power over spiritual and civil matters: oversight of cemeteries, education, marriage and divorce, ritual slaughter, and religious rites on the one hand, and litigation, wills, the police, and communal and state tax gathering on the other. From Derzhavin's point of view the aggregate power exercised by the kahal elders was doubly dangerous. The kahal was a "state within a state" and served as an agency for exclusivity, within which the religious leadership could foment hatred and suspicion of other peoples. The kahal also served as a vehicle for the repression and exploitation of the poor by the rich. Through taxation and community pressure, people were kept in their place, and the occasional dissident was easily controlled by excommunication. Derzhavin was much impressed by the efficiency of the kahal in pursuit of its activities, and contributed his mite to the development of the myth surrounding the allegedly universal power of this Jewish institution: "Any command, order, request, etc. of the kahal is carried out with such speed and exactness so as to evoke amazement. They are all in communication with each other."[60] Consequently, if religious considerations had been insufficient to convince Derzhavin of the need to abolish the kahal, secular ones would have sufficed. A fundamental aspect of the projected reform of the Jews was to be its abolition. In so doing, Derzhavin sought to dismantle the whole structure of Russian legislation concerning the Jews inherited from Catherine's reign.

Together with abolition of the kahal, Derzhavin advocated the abrogation of the prerogatives possessed by the autonomous community, including all internal taxes, fines, and levies. Taxation in the future would be regulated through the particular estate to which an individual Jew belonged. This was not another attempt at integration, because at the same time that Derzhavin demanded that all litigation and criminal justice take place in the estate courts, he called for the cessation of the election of Jews to estate offices or to the magistracy. All legal matters were to be settled in courts in which the Jews had no representation. Derzhavin aimed at the physical separation of Christians and Jews as well. He invoked the expulsion order of 1727 and its successors in forbidding, with few exceptions, any entry by Jews into the Great Russian provinces. Wherever they might be allowed settlement, the Jews were to be carefully supervised in order to prevent improper conduct. Thus, the gendarmarie, rural police, and landowners were charged with supervising the religious beliefs of the Jews in order to prevent the introduction or cultivation of pernicious beliefs. Likewise they were to demand a higher standard of sanitation from the Jews, whose way of life and habits were known for "slovenliness and filth." Derzhavin also required the abandonment of the distinctive dress of the Jews, which he saw as a badge of exclusiveness, and which had always been indicted by Russians as unhygienic. Derzhavin thus hedged all aspects of Jewish civil life with restrictions and policed them with outside supervision. Recognizing the duality of functions, religious and civil, that the kahal performed, he extended government control to religion as well, utilizing a variety of agents from within and without the community.[61]

Derzhavin's religious reform would have created a rigidly hierarchical structure for Jewish religious life, with a strict chain of command, and with ample means to ensure continual supervision by civil representatives of the Russian state. The bottom of the pyramid was occupied by "schools" which in fact resembled the old local communities, established whenever the next-highest agency, the "provincial synagogue," saw the need. All the schools in a particular province would be subordinated to that province's synagogue. The schools were to be staffed by rabbis and their assistants, elected by the vote of the "Jewish community," the election then being confirmed by the governor or the land captains (for town or estate respectively). The schools were to be responsible for overseeing ritual, worship, and education, as well as registers of births, deaths, and weddings. Religious disputes were to be brought to the schools first, but appealed to the provincial synagogue. The school was conceived as a kahal-style organization shorn of all civic autonomy, but still overseeing certain civil functions for the government, as well as fulfilling the functions of a religious community.[62]

The provincial synagogue not only was to serve as an appeals court, but was charged with extensive supervisory functions as well. Staffed by five judges, elected by the schools and confirmed by the Jewish protector, it was also responsible for overseeing the individual schools. It would function as a supervisory institution under provincial officialdom.

As the head of this highly centralized system, Derzhavin created a body he called the Sendarin. It was evidently supposed to be a modernized version of the Great Sanhedrin of Jerusalem, which Derzhavin had encountered in the Scriptures. While this institution might have provided a nice historical touch, its proposed functions had little in common with any contemporary institution among Russian Jews. The Sendarin was to be composed of five "scribes," who would be chosen by the protector. A chief rabbi was to be elected from this group by the schools and synagogues, their choice being confirmed by the tsar. The justification that Derzhavin provided for the creation of a supreme spiritual head—an office foreign to the traditions of Polish Jewry—provides a key to his inspiration for this system: "We permit a *mufti* for the Islamic peoples, and so why not a leader for the Jews?" Specifically Derzhavin was imitating, at least in part, the creation of a similar "Spiritual Muslim Assembly" by Catherine in 1788–1789.[63] The Sendarin was to be a religious court of last appeal, and the final supervisory institution staffed by Jews. It was to meet under the watchful eye of the government.[64]

It has already been noted that Derzhavin envisioned the creation of a protector who was to preside over all aspects of Jewish life. Derzhavin's inspiration may have come from the recent creation, in 1795, of an analogous post, that of "guardian for new settlers," charged with the oversight of foreign colonists in New Russia.[65] New Russia was also the area where Derzhavin proposed to resettle many of Russia's Jews. While the duties he envisioned for the protector were substantial, Derzhavin did not indicate on what level of the bureaucracy he was to operate. There was no suggestion, for instance, as to what collegium or to what branch of the Senate such an official might be subordinated. In some respects the protector would have been a "procurator of the Holy Synod"[66] for the Jewish religion, while in others a governor-general whose powers, applicable to Jews wherever they might be settled, would have transcended provincial boundaries. It has been suggested by some historians that Derzhavin designed the post of protector for himself,[67] and certainly the concentration of enormous power in the hands of one man suggests that Derzhavin hoped that the protector might avoid the numerous jurisdictional disputes that had so often marred his own bureaucratic career.[68]

Having mapped out the process by which the Jews were to be administered, Derzhavin went on to explore the changes that would be necessary in their social and economic organization. Like Frizel, he attempted a more precise definition of the Jews than had been achieved during Catherine's reign. He confirmed Frizel's discovery that the Jews were something other than merely a component of the stereotypical urban estates. Derzhavin went far beyond Frizel, however, in devising radical reform of Russian Jewry incorporating a much broader reclassification of the Jews, and envisioning the wholesale resettlement of most of Belorussia's Jewish communities.

Derzhavin undertook a close examination of the occupations dominated by Jews. It goes without saying that Derzhavin offered negative assessments of most of these enterprises. His condemnation of the Jewish liquor trade was hardly unusual, but he also faulted all other Jewish pursuits. He claimed, as had Frizel, that the Jews dominated the easiest handicrafts, but he also dismissed the utility of those Jewish trading and commercial ventures which were usually conceded even by hostile commentators to be needed services. For Derzhavin, their utility was more than balanced by the Jews' propensity for price fixing, cornering the market, and driving up prices. Derzhavin decided that the Jews should find other occupations. While in Belorussia he interrogated the kahals on the provincial and district level, tendentiously questioning them as to whether the Jews could support themselves better by agriculture, animal husbandry, or handicrafts, rather than by extortion of the peasantry. Not surprisingly, Derzhavin received answers that were, to him, unsatisfactory. The kahals without exception denied the charge of preying on the peasantry and reminded Derzhavin that their way of life was permitted by law. In short, they preferred their economic position just the way it was. They further pointed out that Derzhavin might better look for peasant exploitation in the irresponsibility of the landowners.[69]

There was one exception. Nota Khaimovich Notkin, mentioned earlier, dispatched to Derzhavin a copy of his own reform proposal, which he had already sent to the tsar in 1797 and which, with commendable tenacity, he would subsequently send to Victor Kochubei for consideration by the Jewish Committee of 1802. If Derzhavin's Mendelssohnian ideas come from Frank, there is no question that Nota Notkin's project confirmed, if it did not inspire, his resettlement project and his attempt to reclassify the Jews. Simply summarized, Notkin called for the resettlement of the Jews in colonies around the Black Sea, where fertile soil and proximate harbors

held out great economic promise. He urged the creation of textile, spinning, and rope mills and sail-making factories, where the Jews were to
work. This is apparently the first suggestion that Jews be employed as
factory hands (although at this time "manufactory" still implied a large
workshop and not a mechanized mill). It was an idea whose time had
come: the insistent needs of factory owners for workmen, coinciding with
a period when the government would only with reluctance permit non-
gentry to buy factory serfs, suggested to the government a possible remedy. The decision to make factory workers out of the Jews, an integral
part of the Statute of 1804, was to initiate a new trend in the heretofore
static Russian Jewish policy.[70] Derzhavin utilized Notkin's idea in ways
that betrayed the spirit of the latter's intentions, for his proposals anticipated the use of constraint and massive, forced resettlement.

Under the supervision of the Jewish protector, Derzhavin envisioned
the creation of a special commission in Belorussia for the settlement of all
debts owed by Jews to Christians, in a fashion somewhat similar to the
system employed in the wake of Jewish emancipation in Revolutionary
France.[71] This commission was also to decide which Jews, by virtue of
being engaged in profitable and useful occupations, could be allowed
continued residence in Belorussia and which Jews should be resettled
elsewhere, preferably in the Black Sea region which the government was
attempting to populate. Derzhavin's comments and examples were all
drawn from his knowledge of the Jews of Belorussia, and it was never
quite clear whether he intended it to apply to the remaining Jewish communities of partitioned Poland, although logic would suggest that this was
indeed the case. Derzhavin had no use for temporizing while the settlement of financial claims was taking place: if Christians owed more to Jews
than Jews owed to Christians, resettlement was to begin; if the reverse was
the case, Christian claims were to be paid from the traditional levies and
exactions formerly collected by the kahal leadership.

Derzhavin's plan would have abolished at a stroke the right of the Jews to
engage in the liquor trade and to serve as leaseholders. While the resettlement was being planned these newly unemployed people were to become
one vast labor gang, which could be "put to work by the government, in the
winter scutching flax and hemp, in the spring opening navigable water-
ways, in the summer dredging the canals. In advance of these labors a
contract should be drawn up, so that while on the one hand these people do
not starve to death, on the other hand they do not turn to robbery and
activities as bad as they were in before."[72] While temporarily employing the
Jewish masses in this way, Derzhavin would have required a new, accurate
census of the Jewish population. Derzhavin was hardly the first observer to
note that the official figures then extant were an underestimation, since the
community concealed indigents and newcomers in order to lessen the general tax burden. Derzhavin sought to guarantee a more accurate enumera-

tion by rigorously punishing any kahal elder found guilty of falsifying figures, and by promising to remit the double tax forever when it was complete, and to grant dispensation from all taxes after resettlement, for three or six years. In the course of the census every Jew was to receive a Russian family name or sobriquet. This was an obvious imitation of Joseph II's activities in Austria, as Derzhavin himself admitted.[73]

Of great consequence for the future fate of Russian Jewry was the creation by Derzhavin of new classes for the Jews, along with the retention of the older merchant and burgher classifications. All Jews were to select one of four classes (with further subdivisions), each of which had financial as well as professional criteria. The classes were "merchants," "townspeople," "villagers," and "settlers and their workers."

The Jewish merchant class that Derzhavin described was identical to the corresponding Russian class, complete with three "guilds" or subclasses defined by declared income. This was not a simple restatement of the status quo because, it will be remembered, Derzhavin advocated the abolition of the existing rights of Jews to stand for election to civil or judicial estate offices, or even to participate in the elections. The Jewish merchant, experience indicated, would have been left to the mercies of unsympathetic Gentile competitors.[74]

The Jewish townspeople (*gorodovye meshchane*) would have corresponded roughly to the traditional Russian *meshchanstvo* estate in which most Jews were already technically registered. This estate was to be strictly regulated in every town, however, with half of those enrolled to be engaged in crafts or trades, the other half in limited local trade at fairs and in other cities. Although formally registered in the artisan guilds (*tsekhi*), they were also restricted from any participation in judicial or civic activities.

Legitimization of a specific class of Jewish villagers (*sel'skie meshchane*) was a departure from the existing norms of Russian law. Although Derzhavin argued that in the past the Jews had been in the countryside illegally (despite the resolutions of the Senate), he apparently recognized the services that the Jews performed there and resolved to regularize their status. While Derzhavin still viewed the Jews as a trade-artisan class, he introduced an important innovation by suggesting that they might be divided into two distinct groups, one rural and one urban. These village Jews were not to engage in the traditional exploitive occupations which Derzhavin so despised. Instead he expected them to build workshops and manufactories and engage in linen-making or sail-making, weaving, tanning, ropemaking, and other similar occupations. The village Jews would be allowed to construct their workshops on state land or, if they so desired, by contract on the estates of landowners. Derzhavin's recommendation was clearly inspired by Nota Notkin. What is important, however, was the appearance of this concept in the recommendations of a respected government official.[75]

The same could be said for Derzhavin's fourth class, the "settler-propri-
etor" (*poselianin-khoziain*). The conception of this estate was a reflection of
the century-old current of Enlightenment thought that urged the return of
the Jews to their biblical pastoral occupations. Still unwilling to permit the
Jews to acquire land, Derzhavin wished to create a class of well-to-do
renters, the class prerequisites being an income of at least fifty rubles for the
purchase of farm implements, and the acquisition of four laborers, either
drawn from family members or on hire. Their land was to be procured on
contract from landowners, who were charged with overseeing and supervising these Jewish tenants, evidently with an eye to encouraging diligence
and preventing their retreat into shady economic activities. Some commentators have suggested that the implications of Derzhavin's scheme would
have resulted in the enserfment of the Jews.[76] This tendency can be seen, for
instance, in the requirement that the landowner pay the state taxes for the
Jews. Whatever might have developed from such arrangements, Derzhavin
himself had no such intent. Contracts were to specify the mutual responsibility of Jew or landowner for a stipulated length of time (although not less
than ten years). The Jews were to be considered free men, *not* serfs, and
were to retain the right to transfer their settlement after the expiration of the
contract. There was nonetheless some ambiguity in the application of these
rules to the Jews on the southern frontier, since many of the requirements
for this estate obviously referred to Belorussian conditions. For instance,
there were probably insufficient Christian estate holders in New Russia to
furnish large amounts of rentable land to the Jews, and there were even
fewer cities which could be expected to absorb an influx of burghers. The
details suggest that the emigrating Jews would have been able to acquire
their own land, but Derzhavin was never clear as to their precise status or
class.[77]

It is questionable whether Derzhavin's resettlement scheme, which
would have deposited thousands of Jews on the shores of the Black Sea
and would have commanded them to metamorphose into farmers or factory workers, could ever have succeeded. The unfortunate results of later
resettlement experiments support this assessment, especially since the
government was always reluctant or unable to deliver on promised financial support. Nonetheless, the grandiose *Opinion* did serve an important
role as a source of information, however inaccurate, for later regimes.
Derzhavin had crystallized the twin ideas that the Jews might be made
over into farmers or factory workers. In this way, the *Opinion* served as a
catalyst for an important attempt at reform under Alexander I.

Derzhavin's reform proposal covered most facets of Jewish political,
social, and economic life, but, mirroring the advice of Frank, he held to
the principle that no fundamental reform was possible until the Jews were
"morally reeducated." Without this transformation all the complex civil
and economic reforms would be useless. Rhetorically, at least, the most

important part of the *Opinion* was article X, "On the Moral Education of the Jews and Their Enlightenment." As noted, it was simply an unsophisticated rehash of Mendelssohnian principles, as purveyed by Dr. Frank. An examination of this article is nonetheless warranted because the rhetoric, and many of the proposals, were to pass directly from the *Opinion* to the Statute of 1804.

Paraphrasing Frank's letter, Derzhavin invoked the example of Mendelssohn and attempted to explore the significance of his work for Russia, using Prussia as an example of a nation where "moral reform" had already succeeded. Derzhavin would have permitted the continuation of education of Jewish youth, upon whom the ultimate hopes of reform were to be fixed, in the *heder* schools, until the age of twelve. Instruction here was to be given in the "uncorrupted Jewish language" (Hebrew) over the tenets of religious belief, "avoiding harmful discussions." The Jews would then pass on to public schools where they would be trained in Russian, German, and Polish, reading and writing, arithmetic, "and other skills required by their station." This was vital for their future economic progress, since Derzhavin also required that all transactions between Christians and Jews be carried out in one of these three languages. For those who had tangible evidence of their moral enlightenment, various rewards were offered, such as exemption from the wedding tax or monetary grants. After ten years of demonstratively upright conduct, they would be permitted to engage in trade or commerce outside the area of restricted residence which Derzhavin would have informally maintained, and even to occupy low-level positions in state and local government (e.g., post carriers, medics, customs-house guards, etc.). Although Derzhavin usually followed the lead of Prussia or Austria, he was reluctant to consider the Jews for military service, since he believed that, with few exceptions, their history indicated that they were disposed to be cowardly, and unwilling to fight on Saturday even if it meant their conquest. Instead, Derzhavin envisioned their use as noncombatants, such as medics or musicians. Finally, to those isolated few of exceptional achievement, Derzhavin would have made available—but only by a specific imperial decree—university education.

Inasmuch as Derzhavin barely trusted the enlightened new generation, it is not surprising that he was doubly wary about the old, whose moral redemption might not be so easily obtained. He therefore envisioned a Jewish press, carefully supervised and censored, to print books of uplifting moral and religious content. All the spiritual and intellectual activities of this group were to be overseen and regulated by teams of enlightened Jews and knowledgeable Christians. Nor, for all his reforming zeal, did Derzhavin ever suggest or foresee a time when such strictures might be lifted or modified. Unlike Frizel or the Mendelssohnians, Derzhavin aimed at segregation, not integration. This was to be achieved not only by religious separation but by physical segregation on a massive scale symbolized by resettlement. Reform would never really be complete: if the Mendelssohnians argued that the innate potential of the Jew, like that of all men, is perfection, Derzhavin retained sufficient religious pessimism to hold the opposite view. At best the Jew, purged of fanaticism and hatred of Christians, could become "useful" to the state. "And Paul the First will receive eternal praise as the first Russian monarch to fulfill the command 'Love your enemies; do good to those who hate you.'"[78]

Consensus exists among the historians of Russian Jewry that the reports of Frizel and Derzhavin were of great significance for the subsequent fate of the Jews in the empire. Less accord accompanies judgments as to the precise nature of this significance.[79] Scholarly disagreement is not to be wondered at: it is surprisingly difficult to fix a precise point for the ideas of Frizel or Derzhavin on a continuum stretching from "friendly to the Jews" to "hostile to the Jews." Those who have attempted to do so have invariably been forced to oversimplify in order to characterize. It is more accurate to say that the two reformers served up an ideological goulash, featuring ingredients from the diverse traditions discussed in Chapter 2. Their work is a clear reflection of the innate contradictions in Russian policy toward the Jews.[80]

While the intent and motivation of Frizel and Derzhavin can be debated, on one point there is no doubt—together they defined the "Jewish Question" in Russia. Heretofore the state approached the Jews with the intention of identifying the social estate into which they could most conveniently be fitted, and of achieving the maximum of their economic potential. This was neither more nor less than the attitude underlying the treatment of other groups in Russian society. The work of Frizel and Derzhavin, on the contrary, demonstrated to the governing elite that the Jews were a special case, that Jewish life in Russia was anomalous, and that unique policies were required to govern them. Jews did not fit into a well-governed state because, in their present condition, their life was incompatible with either good government or the public weal.

This was the view of the Jews that came to dominate official attitudes and public opinion throughout the nineteenth century. First and foremost, the Jews were seen as parasites and exploiters, from whose activities the population—and especially the rural population—had to be protected.[81] Two examples at the beginning of the century illustrate the phenomenon of the Jews becoming the scapegoat for rural and urban distress. In March of 1800 the Senate was again concerned with economic problems in Belorussia, on this occasion a shortage of salt. Senator Il'inskii was commissioned to write a report. In his discussion of the problems of the local population, Il'inskii suddenly veered from the topic at hand to offer gratuitous criticism of the Jews of Belorussia. Echoing Derzhavin, Il'inskii complained that the Jews were improperly engaged in the liquor trade, that they were living illegally in the countryside, and that they lived through exploitation of the peas-

Metropolitan Platon of Moscow

antry. He urged that Jews be banned from the liquor trade and forced to resettle in urban areas.[82] In 1804 the Russian Orthodox Metropolitan of Moscow, Platon, visited the shrines of Little Russia and wrote an account of his travels. He was particularly struck by the activities of the Jews of the western provinces, and he offered a scathing portrait of them. Platon ignored religious considerations and instead condemned the Jews for all the economic shortcomings of the Ukrainian peasantry.[83] As these episodes attest, whether discussed by statesmen or clerics, the Jewish Question in Russia was perceived as a secular, socioeconomic problem.

While identifying and decrying the stereotypical Jewish exploiter and his abnormal role in the national economy, Frizel and Derzhavin also served as conduits for a broad spectrum of reformist ideas, including those of the French Enlightenment and the Jewish Haskalah. Their central model and inspiration, however, was the enlightened absolutism of Austria and Prussia, the well-ordered police state at its zenith. Both Frizel and Derzhavin have been criticized for their propensity for "government by *règlement*." It would be more appropriate to remember that this approach represented the most up-to-date form of contemporary political theory and was in striking contrast to the theologically motivated policies toward the Jews which had dominated the previous century. The irony was that, as we shall see, the Frizel-Derzhavin proposals—classic statements of the German Aufklärung tradition—were destined to be reworked by individuals more responsive, rhetorically at least, to the traditions of the French Lumière.

There was a darker side to these proposals, especially in the case of Derzhavin. The abstract, biblical, "Russian" religious prejudices which Derzhavin brought to his work were quickly deleted when those of a more secular cast of mind set to work on his ideas. In just the same fashion, when future generations of Judeophobes rediscovered Derzhavin, it was as the prophetic critic of the secular power of the kahal, not as the religious bigot. Yet Derzhavin disseminated religious ideas of a different sort: the most sophisticated Judeophobia of Poland, with its stories of ritual murder and Talmudic hatred of Gentiles. These ideas were dismissed by the Enlightened, but they acquired an underground life of their own, just by being restated by an authoritative figure like Derzhavin. In the future, when the moment was right, they reappeared and flowered. As Paul's reign approached its violent end, the task fell to his successors to distill what they could from the legacy of Frizel and Derzhavin.[84]

5

A Phantom in the Air: The Statute of 1804

T sar Alexander I, who came to the throne upon the assassination of his father Paul in March 1801, was filled with reforming zeal. The early years of his reign, before the distracting intervention of foreign events, were marked by the enthusiastic pursuit of internal reform, including the creation of a Russian constitution and the emancipation of the serfs. Most of Alexander's grander proposals for social and political change stumbled over the realities of Russian life, but an attempt to reform Jewish society was implemented in 1804. The Statute of 1804 is significant not only for the history of Russian Jewry, but also as a means for examining the methods of Alexandrine reform.

By 1801 it was difficult for Alexander's administrators to ignore the Jewish Question even if they had wished to do so. The extension of electoral rights to Jews in urban centers gained during the second and third partitions of Poland provoked incidents which required the arbitration of the Russian government. Elections, held under the rubric of the Charter to the Towns, were often marked by irregularities and even violence as Christian townsmen resisted the participation of Jews. Faced with outraged Christian sensibilities, Russian governors attempted to preserve the peace by administrative rulings governing electoral procedures. Such actions required the confirmation of the Third Department of the Senate, which also received protests from Jews who had been denied their promised rights.

On 20 August 1802, for example, the Senate heard a report from the governor-general of Volynia and Podolia provinces, A. G. Rozenberg, on municipal elections. Rozenberg noted that his predecessor, I. V. Gudovich, had intervened in elections in response to complaints from Jews that they were being denied electoral participation. Gudovich had cited article

Emperor Alexander I

127 of the Charter to the Towns, which permitted foreigners to occupy half of the elected class offices, in permitting equal representation to the Jews, with the proviso that the head of these institutions (e.g., courts, city councils) had to be a Christian.[1] (This was the "false precedent" discussed in Chapter 3.) Rozenberg found flaws in the Gudovich system. He claimed the Jews were using their organized electoral power to elect Christians who were ignorant of the law, or even illiterate, so that municipal government was run, de facto, by Jews. In reponse to such abuses the governors of Podolia and Volynia had instituted new rules whereby no more than one-third of the offices in a municipality might be filled by Jews. Rozenberg refined this system further by stipulating that Christians and Jews were to elect their candidates in separate curiae, thus depriving the Jews of the opportunity to influence the election of Christians.[2] On 7 October 1802, the Senate confirmed this ruling of Rozenberg and sent a decree implementing an identical electoral order to the provinces of Mogilev, Vitebsk, Kiev, Minsk, Grodno, and Vilna.[3] (This action soon elicited complaints, in November of 1802, from the Jews of Kamenets-Podolsk. The new system was being abused by the Christians, they claimed, who even elected nonmerchants to office and who used their domination of office ruthlessly to collect tax arrears from Jews while ignoring those of Christians. They asked the Senate to explain to them why this discriminatory system was being permitted, since even criminals at least had the charges revealed to them.)[4] Finally, on 9 December 1802, the Senate specified that these regulations applied to urban centers in Grodno and Vilna provinces, which together composed the governor-generalship of Lithuania.[5]

These pronouncements by the Senate precipitated another crisis. The military governor of Lithuania, Baron L. L. Bennigsen, replied to the Senate decree of December 9 with a request for clarification. The Charter to the Towns had not been automatically extended to all the lands taken in the later partitions, and Bennigsen pointed out that a dual court system continued to exist in the towns of Lithuania, based on the ancient prerogatives of Magdeburg Law. A magistracy existed for the adjudication of civil suits, while a *voitovsko-lavnichii* court served for criminal cases. Since the Senate did not mention these courts in its decree, did it mean to abolish the *voitovsko-lavnichii* courts, and if not, did this mean that Jews were to be admitted to them?[6] This query was accompanied by anguished protests from the cities of Vilna and Grodno that the Senate was violating the traditional prerogatives of Lithuanian cities, which had been confirmed by the Russian crown. The petition of the Vilna *meshchanstvo* emphasized the fact that the Jews had never possessed electoral rights in that city and warned that Jews would exercise a deleterious influence, since they "lacked a conception of morality." Public confidence in the institutions of self-government would be destroyed once they passed into the hands of persons unequal to Christians in faith or social standing. Foreigners would lose any desire to settle in a city governed by Jews, and Vilna would eventually become a town inhabited only by Jews.[7]

It was not this grim vision of Vilna's demise which moved the Senate so much as the legal argument that Jews had never enjoyed the right to participate in municipal government in Lithuania. When Bennigsen confirmed that Magdeburg Law had been in force well before the Russian annexation, and that Jews in the past had no electoral rights in municipalities under its jurisdiction, the Senate decided that it had no option but to stipulate, in a decree of 25 August 1803, that the one-third rule for the election of Jews was in force only where the Jews had possessed electoral rights in the past, and was not to be construed as granting electoral rights to the Jews of Lithuania. This interpretation elicited a counterappeal from the Jewish communities of the Vilna and Grodno provinces on 31 August 1803. Citing Catherine's decrees of 1794 and 1795, which permitted the election of Jews to civic office under the Charter to the Towns, the petition requested that such rights be standardized for all Jews in the Russian empire.[8]

New complaints about the situation of the Jews also emanated from the Ukraine. In a report to the central government in 1802, the civil governor of Kiev province, P. Pankrat'ev, noted the unsatisfactory consequences of past efforts to expel the Jews from the countryside. He detected an accelerating impoverishment of the Jews as a consequence of the double tax and—a newly discovered factor—the need for Jews to rent land and housing from the Polish landowners.[9]

This confusing exchange of decisions and appeals led the minister of internal affairs, Viktor Kochubei, to suggest to Tsar Alexander that the Senate clarify the entire issue of Jewish electoral rights. In response to an imperial command of 15 December 1803, the Senate attempted to comply. It carefully retraced the courses of events, explaining the mistaken assumptions underlying the decree of 9 December 1802 which required its repeal. The Senate report accepted the legal principle that the Jews were to be denied any rights or privileges which were not specifically granted to them in a particular area. The Senate conceded that on the basis of the laws of 8 December 1792 and 3 May 1795, the Jews possessed the prerogatives of all other townspeople in Belorussia (or more specifically, in the territory of the second partition). This did not extend to Lithuania, where the indigenous legal system, which denied representation to Jews, was still in force.[10]

While perhaps the correct decision on the basis of legal precedent, the Senate findings created a multitude of additional problems. The Jews of Lithuania were left to the mercies of their Christian competition: although legally defined as merchants and townspeople, "bearing equally all state and civil obligations with their confreres living in other provinces," they were excluded from participation in judicial and administrative bodies to which they were subject. In old Poland this unequal legal status had been compensated for by the governmentally approved activities of the autonomous kahal, but in Russia the edict of Catherine of 3 May 1795 had specified that thereafter the activities of the kahal were to be confined to those of a religious nature. There was no indication that this limitation of kahal power did not apply to the otherwise disenfranchised Jews of Lithuania. A fuller interpretation was clearly needed.

The vehicle for Jewish reform was a special committee created by Alexander on 9 November 1802, the "Committee for the Organization of Jewish Life," or Jewish Committee. The origin and specific mandate of the committee remains somewhat obscure. According to the introduction to the Jewish Statute of 1804:

> Because of complaints repeatedly reaching us and the Governing Senate concerning the various injustices and disorders detrimental to agriculture and to the commerce of [Our] subjects in those provinces where the Jews dwell, We recognized the need, by a ukase of 9 November 1802, given the Governing Senate, to create a special committee to examine the relevant matters and to recommend measures to correct the existing state of the Jews.[11]

The complaints mentioned might have been the earlier reports of the marshals of the nobility, or perhaps the appeals to the Senate regarding Jewish electoral rights, or merely the accumulated sentiment that reform of the Jews was necessary. The motivation might well have come from Derzhavin himself, who had been appointed Alexander's first minister of justice in 1802 when the system of ministries was introduced. According to Derzhavin's own account, the committee was formed specifically to implement his reform project and was supposed to work through his ministry.[12] Such testimony must be viewed cautiously, however, since Derzhavin wrote after the fact, in an attempt to show how the committee had betrayed what he believed to be its duty to bring the Jews under proper control.

In contrast to Derzhavin's claim, it is apparent that from the first the committee considered a number of rival plans and had no compunction about revising or ignoring major elements of Derzhavin's proposal. The committee even dealt with features of the Belorussian economy which had no relation to Derzhavin's *Opinion*. This was the problem of the *chinshevye* nobles, a group of impoverished nobility with no resources except their pedigree, whom the Russian government sought to transform into peasants.[13] This would suggest that the task of the committee was a good deal more ambiguous and less definite than Derzhavin imagined.

Had the committee's chief objective indeed been the implementation of the *Opinion* it would have been difficult for the tsar to have appointed a membership less calculated to cooperate with Derzhavin. With one exception they were men whom Derzhavin grew to hate, men who represented to him all the negative aspects of the central administration surrounding the tsar. The lone exception was Count V. A. Zubov, the brother of Catherine's last lover. He died on 21 June 1804, before the final report of the committee was submitted, and played only a minimal role in the deliberations. A direct rival was on the committee in the person of the minister of internal affairs, V. P. Kochubei. Derzhavin's relations with Kochubei and his ministry were clouded by a series of jurisdictional disputes.[14] If Derzhavin merely disliked Kochubei, he reserved a special hatred for the minister's close collaborator and assistant M. M. Speranskii, whose brilliant career in the Russian administration was already well under way. According to Derzhavin, Speranskii "led him [Kochubei] around by the nose." What was worse, Speranskii was allegedly a mercenary Judeophile. In his memoirs Derzhavin accused Speranskii of accepting an enormous bribe from the Jewish communities to sabotage the reforming efforts of the Committee.[15] Derzhavin's anguish was increased by the fact that in the work of the committee, as in many other matters, Kochubei relied heavily on Speranskii.

The remaining members of the committee were Prince A. A. Czartoryski and Count S. O. Potocki. Both were Poles and as such were particularly detested by Derzhavin. The former provincial had an obsessive hatred for "wily Poles," whom he usually viewed as traitors, intent on preserving the well-being of their dismembered country at the expense of Russian interests. The participation of these two men was the basis for Derzhavin's charge that his *Opinion* had been robbed of all its efficacy by a "Polish plot." The "plot," aided by the culpability of the Russians on the committee, was supposedly aimed at preserving the economic status quo in the Russian-Polish borderlands, a status quo based on the financial exploitation of the peasants through the Jewish agents of the magnate landowners. Both Czartoryski and Potocki, because of their large holdings in partitioned Poland, and their family connections, were members of this exclusive class. Whether they were committed to any particular retention of the existing status of the Jews is questionable. To exacerbate matters further, Derzhavin and Potocki were involved in a celebrated quarrel over the prerogatives of the Senate in 1803. The dispute was both bitter and public, and it led Derzhavin publicly to question the patriotism of Potocki on several occasions.[16] Marred by such obvious incompatibility, the sessions of the committee were at times stormy and the remaining membership could not have been saddened to see Derzhavin leave state service and his position on the committee on 8 October 1803, for reasons having no relation to the Jewish Committee.[17] He was replaced on the committee by the new minister of justice, P. V. Lopukhin, who played a minimal role.

M. N. Speranskii, shortly after his service on the first Jewish committee.

Contrary to Derzhavin's negative evaluations, his opponents on the committee were men of impressive experience and ability, highly placed in the confidence of the tsar. In contrast to Derzhavin they possessed cosmopolitan perspectives, broadened by education and travel. Viktor Kochubei (1768–1834) studied in Sweden, France, and Switzerland and journeyed throughout the continent. Until Paul's death he served in the sensitive post of minister to Constantinople, and on 8 September 1802, he was appointed minister of internal affairs. More important, he was a member of the "Secret Committee" of Alexander's closest confidants

(N. N. Novosil'tsev, Count P. A. Stroganov, and his fellow member on the Jewish Committee, A. A. Czartoryski). This group worked extensively on the secret reforms of the young emperor.[18]

Prince Adam Czartoryski (1770–1861) was the descendant of an ancient Lithuanian family and one of Alexander's closest early collaborators, especially in the field of Russian foreign policy. Well educated and urbane, he had first come to Russia during the partitions as a hostage and later chose to make his career there, consciously working for the restoration of a Kingdom of Poland under Russian protection. Far from engaging in a plot to circumvent the emperor's wishes, he had been included on the committee because of his knowledge of Polish conditions.[19] Alexander expected reform to take place with the cooperation and support of the Poles and was intellectually far removed from Derzhavin's paranoid views of them. Whatever their bias might have been, Czartoryski and Potocki were still better equipped to speak on problems in partitioned Poland than was the parochial Derzhavin.[20]

Count Severyn Potocki (1762–1829) had studied abroad in Lucerne and Geneva. In his youth he had been an ardent Polish patriot and had played an active role in the reformist Quadrennial Diet. He became acquainted with Tadeusz Czacki, who had been the vigorous champion of Jewish reform in the Diet. Potocki allied himself with those Poles who placed their hopes for national restoration on the Russian throne, and he began a career in Russia in 1793. His friendship with Tsarevich Alexander later led him to high office. Among his other duties, he was an active member of the Russian Senate.

Kochubei, Czartoryski, and Potocki all had much in common. Each was a committed liberal of the type that abounded in the early years of Alexander's reign. Their common outlook included a commitment to the traditions of French rationalism, with its emphasis on education and "enlightenment" as prime movers in the betterment of society. Potocki's place in Russian history stems primarily from his educational efforts. In 1802, he was appointed to a special Commission on Schools within the Ministry of Public Education. He later served as head of the Khar'kov Educational District, from 1803 to 1817, where he was chiefly occupied with raising the quality of Khar'kov University to Western European standards. In the Senate he worked in the Third Department, which was responsible for science, education, and the arts, as well as questions concerning the status of the Jews.[21]

Czartoryski too was deeply involved in educational activity, having been appointed in 1803 to direct schools in the Polish provinces. He very consciously used these schools for the advancement of Polish nationalism, especially at the University of Vilna. According to Czartoryski:

> The University of Wilno was exclusively Polish and during the next four years the whole of Russian Poland was covered with schools in

which Polish feeling freely developed itself. This University, to which I appointed the most distinguished literary and scientific men of the country, and some eminent professors from abroad, directed the movement with admirable zeal and intelligence, and its consequences, which the Russians afterwards deeply regretted, seemed at that time to flow naturally from the Emperor's generous intentions with regard to the Poles.[22]

There is much that one can infer from Czartoryski's statement: if schools could be used to make Poles good citizens of Poland, could they not as well be used to transform Jews into good citizens of Russia? This was clearly the intent of the educational provisions of the Statute of 1804, especially their insistence on the teaching of European languages.

Kochubei too dealt with questions of public education, and in 1801 he was appointed a member of the Committee of Education in the regions of New Russia and Astrakhan. Derzhavin likewise recognized the efficacy of education, so on this question at least there was unity of mind. In the same year that the Statute for the Jews appeared, Alexander sponsored a massive university reform which shared many affinities with the goals of Jewish reform. It is not surprising that the first ten articles of the Statute dealt with various aspects of Jewish education and enlightenment.

Other individuals also played an important role in the workings of the committee, but their activities are less well documented. They were representatives of the kahals of the Polish provinces who were sent to St. Petersburg. There were precedents for such activity on behalf of the Jews, the bearers of petitions against the administrative acts of Passek in 1785 being a good example. In the future, the government continued this means of consultation.[23] At first Derzhavin himself approved of the convocation of representatives of the kahals. Initially under the impression that the function of the committee would be to implement his own plan, he had proposed to call together "several elders and illustrious rabbis" and communicate to them the details of the *Opinion* in the hope of enlisting their cooperation in its implementation.[24] The actual circumstances surrounding the advent of Jewish representation were somewhat different.

In the final report of the Jewish Committee to the tsar it is noted only that the committee invited representatives of the kahals for consultations. Actually, the establishment of the committee had created widespread restiveness among the Jewish communities of the western provinces, and the committee sought to prevent panic by adopting this measure. The committee was established in November 1802 and already by December of that year the Minute Book (the community record book) of the Minsk kahal recorded:

> Due to unfavorable rumors which have spread from the capital, Petersburg, that matters, concerning all Jews collectively, have now

passed into the hands of five high officials so that they can deal with them at their discretion, it is necessary to go to the capital, St. Petersburg, and beseech our Sovereign (may his glory increase) that they not impose any innovations on us.[25]

So alarmed did the various communities become that Kochubei, as minister of internal affairs, sent a circular to the governors of the appropriate provinces on 21 January 1803. He advised them that they

> should declare and explain to the kahals and to other Jewish communities that by the establishment of a committee to oversee their affairs it was not intended to hinder their position or diminish their essential privileges; but on the contrary, through the examination of all circumstances better organization and tranquillity are sought, and because of this they should not be distracted by false rumors coming to them but should continue to attend for the present to the trades and crafts permitted to them, with firm confidence in the government. . . .[26]

At the same time the participation of deputies was given official sanction, and elections were held by each kahal. The deputies began to arrive in the capital in the summer of 1803.

There were Jews already in the capital ready to assist the new deputies. They were men acquainted with the workings of the Russian bureaucracy and possessed of influential connections. The most prominent was a naval contractor and financier named Abram Peretts. Peretts had first acquired connections with Russian high society through his family's acquaintance with Prince Potemkin. He could also boast of an acquaintance with Derzhavin and a very close friendship with Speranskii. His son was the future Decembrist Grigorii Peretts.[27]

Living in the Peretts household and serving the government as a translator was an aspiring author, Ieguda Leib-ben Noakh (Nevakhovich). Nevakhovich is considered one of the first Russian Maskilim, a claim justified by the work he wrote at this time for the committee (and dedicated to Kochubei). Entitled *The Lament of the Daughter of Judea* (*Vopl' dshcheri Iudeiskoi*) and published in Russian and in Hebrew with a slightly different text, it was the first public endeavor by a Jew to influence Russian opinion. Nevakhovich did not ask for specific legal rights for Jews but rather, appealing to general humanistic ideals, called for a fundamental change in the attitudes of Russian Christians. Written in the sentimental style of the age, the work represents a compendium of the various strands of French Enlightenment thought. Nevakhovich personified the suffering Jewish people as the "daughter of Jacob," persecuted and driven across the face of the earth until offered the tolerant refuge of Alexander's Russia. He appealed to the Russian people to confirm the confident hopes which the Jewish people placed in them. There was no longer any basis for Russian hatred of Jews, Nevakhovich argued, when Nature itself cried out against intolerance based upon religious differences. "Little innocent children, however much their parents might differ in faith, play with each other without antipathy, loving one another without the slightest hatred; but, O horrors!—they begin to speak and parents separate them, separate them forever."[28] With John Locke's epistemology firmly in hand, Nevakhovich emphasized that it was improper upbringing and prejudice that converted childhood playmates into mortal enemies. He opposed the irrationality of hatred born of religious enthusiasm by an appeal to the staples of Enlightenment Judeophilia, Mendelssohn's *Jerusalem* and Lessing's *Nathan the Wise*, and by recalling that the old prejudices had produced only unwarranted human suffering.[29]

Christians were urged to recognize the inherent potential in the Jews: "You search for the Jew in the man—no, search for the man in the Jew and without doubt you will find him." Many Christians could already testify to amicable relations with Jews, and if there were occasional misdeeds connected with individual Jews, this was the influence of past religious persecution. Jews who preserved their religion in its pure form could not be other than good persons and good citizens, for as Mendelssohn had demonstrated, Judaism contained within itself everything appropriate to a humane and humanistic code.[30]

With the deliberations of the Jewish Committee in mind, Nevakhovich appealed to the principles of Catherine's celebrated *Instruction* to her Legislative Commission of 1767. That document had demonstrated the futility of attempting to correct the faults of an entire people through intimidation and punishment. In nations such as England, Holland, and Denmark, on the other hand, civil rights had made the Jews a useful component part of the population.[31] Nevakhovich closed his appeal with an invocation of the Russian people:

Honorable Russians! Your actions are extraordinary and the greatness of your achievements diminishes or destroys the unhappiness of the peoples you have conquered. Who would be ashamed to be subject to you, when Fate herself is under your command? At your order Fate puts down her grave and terrible scepter: order her to cease the persecution of the Jewish people! I see that it is the most difficult task in the world—requiring a century at least—to change hearts and minds, but I also see that the undertakings of the Russians always achieve a swift and all but unbelievable success. The spirit of the North demands great deeds, and as a consequence it ushers in a new and brilliant epoch, which will witness a change in the way the Jews are viewed.[32]

The final member of this informal triumvirate was Nota Notkin, the indefatigable partisan of Jewish economic reform. He was invited to join the deliberations of the committee at the instigation of Derzhavin himself, and the influence of his project for the resettlement of the Jews as factory workers in the South is quite evident in the final draft of the statute.[33]

Despite the help and assistance given the kahal deputies by the "Petersburgers," there were fundamental differences separating the two groups. Peretts, Nevakhovich, and Notkin were partisans of reform and enlightenment. Their careers had taken them far from the conservative Jewish community. The Belorussian home of Peretts served as a center for Enlighteners of the Berlin school, and Nevakhovich was obviously a sympathizer. (It should also be noted that while all three men were practicing Jews at this time, Peretts and Nevakhovich later converted to Christianity.) Yet the views of Mendelssohn had not as yet penetrated very deeply into Russian-Jewish society at large. Consequently, while the "Petersburgers" stood for reform and showed a willingness to cooperate with the Russian government, the deputies acted as procrastinators and obstructionists. They relied on the traditional weapons of weak Jewish communities when faced with unappealing choices offered by an unfriendly majority. Their delaying tactics only frustrated the committee. After a first draft of the proposed statute was completed, it was submitted to the deputies for suggestions and criticism. After postponing a decision for as long as possible, the deputies finally explained to the committee that they themselves had no authority to decide such matters, and requested a six-month delay in the proceedings to consult with their respective kahals. The committee refused this request, arguing that it would lead to rumor-mongering and that, more important, it was necessary for the reform to begin as soon as possible. Instead, the kahals were invited to present their opinions on the draft to the provincial authorities. The response was a unanimous plea that the proposed reforms be postponed for a period of fifteen or twenty years. Wearied by such recalcitrance, the committee instead presented the draft of the statute to the tsar.[34]

In addition, the committee was inundated by a flood of unsolicited proposals volunteered by Russian society, a circumstance from which no reform committee ever seemed able to escape. As noted earlier, the apparent loss of these materials in the archival fire of 1862 or 1863 created a serious lacuna: their survival would have provided invaluable evidence of the attitudes toward the Jews of a wider segment of educated Russian society and shown more specifically which ideas were in the air. Instead, it is not known to what degree they influenced the decisions of the committee. A special role was also played by the proposals for reform which Tadeusz Czacki had submitted to the Polish Quadrennial Diet. Sections of the Statute of 1804 display a strong affinity with Czacki's project.[35]

Derzhavin's *Opinion* and the findings of Frizel, Czacki, and Nota Notkin were apparently the principal sources for the ensuing legislation.

It is also important to assess the orientation and outlook of the committee members as they began to formulate the statute. The committee produced several documents of great interest. They confirm the extent to which some members of the committee were reformers in the Enlightenment tradition. They sought to base the reform on the principle of "personal advantage," inducing the Jews to accept a temporary modification of their mores by the promise of a better life thereafter. Implicit in this view was the characteristic assumption that men could be improved by enlightenment and education.

The first of these documents was an anonymous memorial, entitled "Vues préliminaires sur les Juifs," which has been attributed by Gessen to Count Potocki.[36] Its author noted the awesome responsibility borne by the committee before God and society to deal with the lives of seven or eight hundred thousand people. The Jews had been harassed for more than eighteen hundred years, driven from all respectable trades, burdened by taxation, and exposed to hatred. This inevitably corrupted them, instilling vices in them which many commentators deemed to be innate. It was the task of the committee to differentiate between those vices which were developed in the Jews through persecution, and those faults which they shared with all other peoples. For example, the Jews were usually accused of being sly and dishonest, but this very slyness helped preserve them from persecution. The Jews were traditionally moneylenders because normal, honorable pursuits were closed to them, and they could not possess land. While the Jews undeniably did cheat at trade, it had to be recognized that the double tax placed an intolerable burden upon them and weakened any scruples as to how they acquired money. It was necessary to redirect the Jews away from harmful trades, such as tavern-keeping, into useful economic pursuits, especially agriculture. The author conceded that Jews hated Christians, but saw this as the natural response of a people who had been handed over to slavery and tyranny. If at times the birthrate of these troublesome Jews might seem too high, how could Russia, with its boundless spaces, complain?

In short, the Jews could be made into useful citizens by restricting their harmful activities and encouraging their useful ones. It would be necessary to permit the cautious and gradual resettlement of the Jews, as well as to give their merchants and craftsmen greater mobility, although this should be coupled with continued respect for existing municipal and regional privileges. (This was an important proviso, given the current deliberations in the Senate concerning the Lithuanian provinces.) Jews and Gentiles would have to be brought closer together. This was to be accomplished through the traditional Enlightenment panacea, education. A great awareness of superior Gentile culture would presumably encourage Jews to abandon their own cultural distinctiveness.[37]

It was a common Enlightenment theme that climate and environmental factors (which would include the relationships between Christians and Jews) ultimately determined the character of a people. Some Philosophes, such as Paul Thiry d'Holbach, argued from this that the Jews were a people hopelessly and irremediably foreign to Europe. The anonymous commentator, however, followed the tradition of Montesquieu in holding out the promise of reform not by coercion but by gradual change.[38] This attitude was quite influential in the deliberations of the committee.

The second document was the entry in the journal of the committee for 20 September 1803. It drew various Enlightenment formulae together, and its constant emphasis on moderation was a recurrent theme in all the surviving materials of the committee.

Transformations brought about by governmental force will generally not be stable and will be especially unreliable in those cases where this force struggles against centuries-old habits, with ingrained errors, and with unyielding superstition; it would be better and more opportune to direct the Jews toward improvement, to open the path to their own benefit, overseeing their progress from afar and removing anything that might lead them astray, not employing any force, not setting up any particular institution, not acting in their place, but enabling their own activity. As few restrictions as possible, as much freedom as possible. This is a simple formula for any organization of society!

In the calculation of the variables determining human action, the basic foundation ought always to rest on private gain, the internal principle which never stops anywhere, and which evades all laws that are inconvenient. Governments that have forgotten this in political institutions, or that have disregarded this truth, often have found it necessary, after great expense, to abandon their enterprise. . . . Everywhere that governments thought merely to command, there appeared only the phantom of success, which was maintained for a while in the air, and then disappeared together with the principles that gave birth to it. In contrast to every undertaking carried out insensitively are those generated by private gain, freely maintained, and only patronized by the government, which were shown to be maintained by an internal force, a firm basis established by time and by personal benefit.

In every respect the Jews should be encouraged toward education, preferably by means of quiet encouragement, organized by their own activity, and only those things should be suppressed which

depend directly on the government and which they themselves are
unable to suppress.[39]

At their labors' end the members of the committee were satisfied that
they had faithfully followed these guidelines. In the report accompanying
their draft law to the tsar, the committee proudly noted that "for all these
reasons, and from comparison of the present Statute for the Jews with all
those which in *other states* are made for them, the committee still believes
that, taking local circumstances under consideration, nowhere are there
designed for them measures *more moderate* or *more* indulgent. . . ."[40]

The extent to which such sentiments ruled the day may also be noted in
the commentary of the journal *Vestnik Evropy* upon the work of the committee. The journal examined the charges and popular superstitions directed at the Jews and ascribed them to "deeply rooted oppression, undergone by them in the course of centuries." The committee had found the
correct remedy in its emphasis on education which would make good
citizens of the Jews, just as Peter had used it to make good citizens of the
Russians.

> Can it be doubted that we in time will have our Mendelssohns?
> Alexander has ordered the opening of the doors of the universities
> and the *gimnazii* to young Jews, and has permitted them, without
> any difference, to be reared and educated equally with the native
> population, permitting the refinement of their natural proclivities
> for the fine arts in the Imperial Academy; he has given them the
> right to obtain the highest educational degree. The statute for the
> Jews approved by the emperor begins with such provisions [on edu-
> cation]; it is necessary for the state to create useful citizens, and
> moral upbringing is the only way.[41]

In return the Jews were to accept the provisions of the new law and find
a useful place in society. It was time for the Jews to forget the authors of
their unhappiness, the Roman emperor-generals Titus and Hadrian (as
well, presumably, as the Jews' supposed loyalty to Palestine), and seek
shelter under the wings of the Northern Eagle. The Jews could truly say,
"I am a son of the fatherland."[42]

While both the Jewish Committee and its critics took pride in the liber-
ality of the new code, equally significant were the committee's preconcep-
tions regarding the economic role played by the Jews in society. They
were the combined legacy of Kakhovskii, Frizel, and especially Derzhavin: the belief that the Jews were a threat to the well-being of the western
provinces. This threat could be parried only by "rendering the Jews harmless." The first priority of the government was the protection of the
peasantry; the well-being of the Jews themselves was secondary. When-

ever the committee deviated from its moderate guidelines, it was in response to this concern.[43] For all its good intentions, the resulting Statute of 1804 was a document of both privileges and disabilities, complicated by the inconsistencies and ambiguities so characteristic of Russian legislation concerning the Jews throughout the period since 1772. This is apparent from a close analysis of the new code.

The Statute of 1804 was as significant for what it *failed* to stipulate as for what it did. The entire conception of the reform was shaped by an important omission: failure to abolish the kahal structure. To be sure, the retention of the kahal pleased those most directly concerned—the Jews themselves—but its confirmation reveals much about the ultimate intentions and orientation of the committee itself.

Even in a state such as Russia where forms of autonomy and special privilege were not uncommon, the existing attitudes toward the kahal suggested that the government would seriously consider abolishing it. The whole body of evidence collected by the Russian government on the status of the kahal since 1772 seemed to point to the abrogation of the kahal. There was the example of foreign states: Derzhavin himself noted in his *Opinion* that the kahal structure had already been abolished in the Austrian Empire and Prussia. There remained as a key exhibit the most famous case of all, the emancipation of the Jews in France in 1792. This political act ostentatiously abolished the communal structure even in the face of significant opposition by the Jewish communities. The French expedient of abolishing the community while retaining the Jewish responsibility for communal debts showed further that abolition need not cause great financial dislocation if the government was willing to ignore legal niceties.

From the beginning of Russian rule the reports of officials suggested the necessity of abolition. It was certainly implied in Kakhovskii's 1773 report, while Frizel, Derzhavin, and Frank had all based the success of their respective projects on the need to replace the kahal by other political and social forms. Nor was the committee in any way unacquainted or unsympathetic with such views; they figure prominently in the committee report which accompanied the statute to the tsar. In the four different parts of this report the pernicious effects of the kahal were discussed. The first section, entitled "Principal Information Regarding the Condition of the Jews," presented a stinging critique of the kahal and the allied rabbinical power:

Ignoring obligations imposed by law, they always keep up their special administration. Secluding themselves, so to speak, from all common institutions, they always seek to keep everything secular within their kahals and everything spiritual in the synagogues. . . .

Everything that concerns their internal policing, from the collection of taxes to assessments on property, the holding of leases, and every economic matter, is always overseen and administered in the kahal. The influence of the rabbis in spiritual affairs is almost unlimited. Lacking any legal power for their decisions, they compensate, often to excess, through the forces of prejudice, superstition, routine, and oath-taking. They order collections, levied for the sick and under other pretexts, which constitute a considerable sum and also give them an additional weapon for coercion.[44]

The report not only made no attempt to mitigate these accusations but further on, in "The Procedural Order of the Committee," presented a case history of such exclusivity: the obstructionist activity of the Jewish deputies and the kahals themselves in the face of the committee's efforts. The third section isolated those chief characteristics that separated Jews from Christians and that the committee considered must be rectified before reform was possible. The first of these characteristics was the separation of the Jews from a common administration. It was noted that the Jews had always managed to maintain their separate communal life and to preserve their own rites and customs. The areas where reform was *most needed*, according to the committee, included the abolition of this Jewish independent government and the unification of the Jews with other inhabitants in a common administration.[45]

Yet after this lengthy indictment the committee still retained the functions of those same officials who constituted Jewish autonomous government. Article 50 of the statute gave to each Jewish community the right to elect one rabbi and several kahal elders every three years. While some restrictions were imposed upon the rabbinate, rabbis still possessed sufficient power and authority to aid and abet the control of the kahal over the community as a whole, especially if they were willing to resort to illegal actions, such as the imposition of the ban or communal excommunication. They had certainly proved willing to do so in the past.

The statute was largely silent on what the kahal itself could or could not do, but retention implied that it kept most of its prerogatives. In fact, while the decree of 3 May 1795 had specified that the power of the kahal was to extend only to religious matters, the responsibilities which the statute specifically assigned to the kahal restored the one function which served as the basis of the kahal's coercive power, the apportionment of taxation. Article 54 stated:

The kahals should ensure that state taxes, for as long as they remain in their present state, are properly and fully collected; they should take charge of the sums entrusted to them by the community, giving an account to the community for their use, and presenting it in

Russian or Polish to the *Gorodnichii* in the towns, to the *Ispravnik* on state properties, and to the landowners on private estates, and in every case they are subject to trial and punishment with all the severity of the law if the accounts given by them to the authorities are found not to correspond to the original given to the community. However, under no pretext should they levy new taxes unbeknownst to the authorities, under penalty not only of confiscation from them personally of everything that they have newly established, but also of trial and punishment.[46]

This general surrender of authority by the Russian government to the kahal had an additional significance. The Senate, as has been noted, was in the midst of denying the Jews equal or equitable participation in municipal self-government, in opposition to the trend in Catherinian Russia. The Senate was well aware of the committee's deliberations, and the committee was equally well informed of the latest restrictions on Lithuanian Jewry. (In sending a copy of its final report on the Lithuanian imbroglio to Kochubei, the Senate specified that this resolution was not to be confused with any ongoing deliberations in the committee, thus tacitly inviting the committee to rectify the situation if it chose.)[47] By failing to respond to this invitation with a set of uniform political rights for Jewish townspeople and merchants, while at the same time confirming and even strengthening important prerogatives of the kahal, the work of the committee displayed an exceedingly lukewarm commitment to the integration of the Jews into Russian society.

What further motives underlay the decision to retain the kahal? Is it possible, for instance, that the committee took seriously its oft-stated formulae of moderation, gradualness, and indulgence and permitted these vague principles to obstruct its better judgment? On the contrary, moderation proved dispensable when it appeared inconvenient in other contexts. In the case of the educational reforms of the statute, the liberal provisions were so hedged with qualifications and optional provisions as to lose most of their force. When dealing with the liquor trade, where immediate, uncompromising measures threatened to produce economic dislocation and social chaos, the committee refused to modify or ameliorate any of its precipitate decisions. Yet the continued existence of the obstructionist force of the kahal was at least as serious a problem facing the reformers as the continuation of the liquor trade, judging only by the rhetoric of the committee.

Could the committee have been deterred by its inexperience in matters involving the Jewish community, and thereby have been forced to retain the kahal as an advisory institution?[48] This reticence could have been further increased by the difficulties posed by the abolition of the kahals, the only communal framework for Jewish society. These arguments would be more plausible but for the attitudes of the committee as reflected in the documentation. The whole point of the statute was that the principles of self-interest, enlightenment, and education could, without fail, produce a superior type of Jew, worthy (and trustworthy) to take his place in Russian society. Frizel, Derzhavin, Frank, and even Notkin had all argued for fundamental reform. Thus, why would the Jews need the kahal if their economic interests were served and effected outside of it, in the magistracy or in the guilds? Why should they require the school system of the kahal if they were to gain enlightenment outside, in the larger Gentile community? A central premise of the reform was that the Jews, by gaining enlightenment, would reject with disgust the old manner of life, thus obviating any need for the kahal. Or perhaps that was the plan: to permit the kahal to exist as a "living fossil" until the Jews themselves rejected it, pulling themselves up by their own enlightenment bootstraps.

These paradoxes can best be resolved if it is remembered that there were *two* distinct motives that impelled the government to reorganize Jewish society. The first was to improve the lot of the Jews by making them enlightened, useful citizens, fully sharing in the life of Russian society. The second was to protect the Christian peasantry from the depredations which were associated with, and blamed on, the Jews. The former principle, examination reveals, was invariably subordinated to the latter, whether consciously or unconsciously. It was assumed that the Jews exploited the peasantry. Therefore it was necessary for immediate unwavering steps to be taken: resettlement, restrictions, strict supervision. The inconvenience to the Jewish community was outweighed by the advantages supposed to accrue to Christian society as a whole. It was also understood that the "enlightenment" of the Jews, together with their inclusion into new professions, could be accomplished only in the face of sustained opposition by the Jewish community and only at considerable expense to the central government. Here then, the principles of moderation and indulgence could and would be applied.

The question of abolition has been examined in detail because of its ultimate repercussions on the Jewish community in Russia. Abolition was ultimately to come about after a delay of forty years, in 1844. It would be carried out by the government of Nicholas I, a tsar far less sympathetic to the Jews than had been Alexander or any of his advisers. Tsar Nicholas I's policies were closer to forced assimilation than to integration. The process of integration in 1804 would have been well served by abolition. Indeed, if at any point in Russian history prior to 1917 the Jews could have begun the difficult process of meaningful integration into Russian society, free from disabilities and a special status (a debatable proposition in its own right), this moment was among the most expeditious. There was a better chance of forcing—and enforcing—such reforms in Belorussia or Lithuania in 1804, given political realities, than in the Great Russian provinces.

(It could be argued that the decision of the government to placate the Poles of Lithuania by retaining their pre-partition political privileges would ultimately have obviated such a program. Still, the government was willing to clash with the powerful landowning class over the question of tavern-keeping by Jews.) The example of the prosperous Tatar merchants in southern Russia under Catherine indicated the willingness of the regime to tolerate and integrate persons of foreign culture and religion, if they were economically beneficial.[49] It is possible that Jews, forced toward legal integration into Russian society, could have fared as well. As it was, the kahal was maintained as a powerful vested interest, an obstacle to any governmental reform good or bad, and a mark of the separate status of the Jews, until its ultimate degeneration under Nicholas I.[50] Given this state of affairs, there never existed much promise for the cultural reforms, much less integration, even if the government had been willing to advance them more aggressively.

It remains to consider the reforms which the statute did implement. Since the committee professed itself committed to the efficacy of education and enlightenment as agents of social transformation, it was appropriate, as *Vestnik Evropy* had observed, that the first section of the statute, comprising ten articles, was devoted to "enlightenment." They provide a litmus test for the confluence of rhetoric and reality which characterized the working of the committee. The first five statutes represented the integrationist trend: Jews were permitted admission and instruction, without discrimination, in every Russian primary, secondary, and advanced educational institution, and at no time in this training were they to be disturbed in their religious beliefs. These measures could be viewed as the creation of an accepted vehicle for Jewish integration or even assimilation, but a closer examination reveals the overly idealistic spirit which dominated them. To begin with, the state of public instruction being what it was in Russia in 1804, it was impossible to expect the existing institutions to deal with more than minuscule numbers, even if the Jews were willing to attend such schools. While the regime was promulgating an elaborate educational reform, it pertained primarily to advanced university education, rather than to the primary schools which would have been necessary to initiate Jewish integration.[51] It is noteworthy that the government was never to discuss this provision again in the following years of debate, much less offer to provide funds. The key to this was article 6.

If, ignoring all these inducements, the Jews do not wish to send their children to the common public schools, they may be permitted to institute their own schools at their own expense where they may be taught, and they may set the requisite taxes under the supervision of the government. Among the subjects taught must be one of these languages: Russian, Polish, or German.

The committee members should have realized that the Jews would never enter Gentile schools if they had a choice. The fear of proselytism would not be stilled by government assurances that Jewish youth would not be disturbed in their faith. Within the Jewish community there was no motive for seeking an outside secular education: what could be learned that would do anybody any good? This then was a meeting of minds, the Jewish community not wanting schools and the Russian government not wanting to pay for them. What the government really desired was one specific thing, the ability of the Jews to use a language other than their "jargon." By requiring that Jewish schools offer instruction in one or another second language, the committee was in effect grafting a syllabus of language instruction onto the already existing, and flourishing, Jewish communal school system, the *heder*. It would, however, be unfair to accuse the government of mere hypocrisy, of trying to get a revised school curriculum on the cheap. It must be remembered that a basic principle of the Mendelssohnian school was that the adoption of modern languages would free the Jewish masses from the religious obscurantism imposed by their rabbis and would provide an entree into Christian society. Following such beliefs, the Russian reformers might expect these provisions to initiate change within the context of the promised "moderation and gradualness."

There were other aspects of the enlightenment articles less optimistic in tone. Articles 7 and 8 demanded that after a six-year period, all bookkeeping, property, and commercial records were to be kept in one of the three languages. Further, article 10 demanded that after 1812 no person could be chosen as a kahal elder or rabbi if he could not read and write one of the three languages. These measures were designed to expedite the adoption of a new language by Jews, but one also detects the desire to bring suspicious Jewish business practices out in the open. It also aimed at depriving the elders and rabbis of the protective cover of Hebrew, behind which they allegedly hid their malefactions from the masses. There was one further requirement that can be viewed as mildly discriminatory: Jews who were elected to the magistracy were required to read and write either Russian, German, or Polish. This was in contrast to their Christian counterparts, who were permitted to be, and often were, illiterate. Indeed, in Lithuania the Jews had been accused of helping to elect illiterate Christians to the magistracy, the better to manipulate them. Aside from a few minor restrictions on Jewish dress—it could not be worn outside the western provinces or in meetings of the magistracy—this was the extent of Russian attempts at enlightenment.

More substantial were the efforts of the committee in the areas of economic reform and social engineering. Armed with the advice of reformers and the experience of thirty-two years, the committee set out to provide a definitive classification for the Jews. All Jews were to be included in one of four classes: farmers, manufacturers and artisans, merchants, and townspeople (*meshchanstvo*). In the very act of clarifying the status of the Jews, however, the committee was guilty of imprecision and irresolution which did not bode well for the practical application of its theoretical schemes. For example, the description of the functions and prerogatives of the classes of merchants and townspeople was nothing more than a restatement of the economic role characteristically played by these two groups. There was no effort made to clarify the ambiguities that had appeared in Catherine's reign such as the status of "townspeople" who were registered in urban centers but resident in the countryside. The new law merely stated that merchants could engage in "any sort of internal or external trade," while petty trade was approved for townspeople. The functions of the "manufacturers" were indeed new, but those of the "artisans" were handicrafts, which had always been associated with members of the *meshchanstvo* estate. A valid reason for differentiating artisans from the rest of the *meshchanstvo* would have been to grant them a distinct set of prerogatives. In one sense this was done. Regulations for travel to the interior of Russia and even to the capital were established for "manufacturers, artisans, artists, and merchants," the implication being that farmers and townspeople, who were not mentioned, did not have this right. But the issue was clouded by the inclusion of "artists" on this list; they were not a separate class, and were nowhere else mentioned or defined in the statute.

Of more importance was a disability specified for artisans. Article 23 noted that artisans could pursue any craft permitted by law and also were allowed to join the craft guilds "if this is not counter to the privileges specially given to several cities." This was clearly a reference to the Lithuanian cities and their pre-partition right to exclude Jews from municipal government, which had recently been explored by the Senate. In the course of issuing a new law code the government could have superseded these ancient prerogatives. Its failure to do so left an important group of Jews in an anomalous position, neither fully under nor fully removed from the authority of the Charter to the Towns. This decision hardly clarified the status of the Jews once and for all.

The committee's brevity and imprecision when dealing with the Jews as a trade-handicraft group can perhaps be explained by its fascination with two new groupings. They were of great significance not only because they were to provide tangible economic benefit for the state, but also because they would be needed to absorb the large number of Jews about to be displaced from their habitual niche in the liquor trade by other parts of the statute.

The idea of turning the mercentile Jews into farmers, first popularized by French Enlightenment thinkers, came to the committee via the proposals of Frizel and Derzhavin. The concept was now to receive legal approbation, initiating a century-long quest by the Russian government to turn

Jews into peasants. The statute stressed in article 12 that "Jewish farmers are all free, and are not allowed to be enserfed or possessed." The government did not wish to create another class of serfs in any part of Russia. The landowners may have hoped for this, as the historian I. G. Orshanskii contends, but the committee took specific steps to forestall it.[52] (It will be remembered that even the conservative Derzhavin was unwilling to restrict the Jews' status as a free people.) The language of article 12 was clear enough, but the committee took additional steps to prevent enserfment from happening *sub rosa*. Article 47 specified that the Jews were not under the authority of the landowner in matters of criminal justice. Article 46, which required that Jews who desired to move from one place to another present evidence from the landowner that they had fulfilled all their responsibilities to him, may be viewed as counter to this tendency. But the fact remains that the statute stated and reiterated that the Jews were free to change their place of residence. This was hardly the time or the place for the creation of a new group of enserfed peasants. The government had already proclaimed the "Decree on Free Agriculturists" on 20 February 1803, designed to set in motion the emancipation of some Russian serfs. It is also noteworthy that it was in the borderlands of the empire where serfdom was most expediently attacked. It was always easier for the government to place restrictions on Baltic or Polish landowners, as opposed to native Russians. For these reasons, the statute can be taken at its word when it envisioned a class of free Jewish farmers.

The Jewish farmer was permitted to buy land, and was placed under the provision of the Decree of 12 December 1801, which gave city classes and state peasants the right to purchase uninhabited agricultural land. The Jews were to have full rights of ownership and could even till such land with hired labor. Jews could also lease land from landowners for temporary use. In addition they were granted a rebate of taxes for five years, an added inducement to encourage agricultural settlement. Obviously, many Jews would not be able to afford land purchases, or procure a lease, and so the statute offered other options in which may be discerned the residue of Derzhavin's forced resettlement project. Jews who wished to become farmers but who were unable to secure land elsewhere were invited to move to public lands in Lithuania, Minsk, Volynia, Podolia, Astrakhan, the Caucasus, Ekaterinoslav, Kherson, and the Tauride, that is, in those areas of the empire where Jews were already permitted to live. In some areas, it was stated, almost thirty thousand desiatins (about eleven thousand acres) of land had been set aside by the government for such settlement. Although the committee did not state it, presumably the bulk of this land lay in the southern reaches of the empire, where the government was still diligently attempting to encourage settlement. The privileges offered for such resettlement—which the statute noted was to be strictly voluntary—were by and large those given to foreign settlers: free land, a ten-year period of tax rebates, and loans. These settlers were also promised freedom from the double tax. These measures are worthy of note; they permitted Jews to own land and to become peasants if they so desired, thereby reversing the tradition of Jewish landlessness which had generally held true for Central and Eastern Europe.

The government clearly hoped to derive significant benefit from the creation of the second "new" class, that of "manufacturers and craftsmen." Among the active measures of the statute, this was promoted most assiduously by the government, although rhetorical enthusiasm was seldom matched by promised financial support. The new class was largely based on the ideas sponsored by Nota Notkin. Derzhavin had included elements of Notkin's program proposing manufacturing colonies on the Black Sea in his *Opinion*, but Notkin apparently resubmitted another draft of his project to the committee. At this particular time the Ministry of Internal Affairs was especially concerned with the problem of securing a sufficient amount of woolen cloth for military uniforms. The vision of a host of Jewish factories suddenly arising through economic spontaneous generation was too appealing to ignore. The statute therefore granted the Jews the right to build "every sort of manufactory in the provinces where they are allowed to live." The government promised a loan fund of twenty thousand rubles for every province of partitioned Poland for those Jews who would undertake such projects, with clothmaking, linen-making, and tanning specifically mentioned. This was buttressed by the promise of tax advantages to Jews who engaged in factory work and of loans to land-owners who permitted the establishment of such factories on their estates. Apparently the statute assumed that Jewish workers would labor only in Jewish factories, although Russian manufacturers would have been eager to gain access to such a pool of mobile labor.

All Jews were ordered to enroll in one of these four categories, with the right to change class as circumstances necessitated. Exactly how enrollment was to take place was not explained, although the statute spoke vaguely of a census over the next two years, in the course of which every Jew was to adopt a hereditary name or sobriquet, which the statute noted would be useful "for the best implementation of civil categories, for the easiest protection of property, and for the trial of lawsuits." It was not necessary to add that such a census would also aid taxation.

A good deal of ambiguity surrounds the question of taxation as it was treated by the statute. The most pressing concern for the Jews themselves was the double tax, the ill effects of which had been discerned even by Gentile commentators. The committee evidently intended to abolish the double tax, but left much unsaid. Article 29 stated that "when, in general, every Jew manifests permanent order and diligence in agriculture, manufacturing, and trade, the government will then take measures to equalize their taxation with all other inhabitants." From this it would appear that at

some specific time, when the Jews had indicated their willingness to cooperate with the government's efforts at reform, the government planned to
abolish the double tax for all Jews. Yet in promising advantages to the Jews
for resettlement or for the adoption of a new profession, the abolition of the
double tax was held out as an immediate privilege, as in article 19 that
referred to farmers. Article 21 offered similar dispensation to Jews who
engaged in factory work, while article 24 included the artisans within its
provisions, though somewhat obscurely. In practice the double tax was
abolished sporadically. No specific date can be given after which it was no
longer collected, but by 1807 it seems to have expired de facto.[53]

No such lack of precision surrounded another feature of the statute—
the confirmation of the Pale of Settlement. The Pale had always had a
rather informal quality, arising from trial and error and administrative
decision, and not from any specific plan or policy. Heretofore there had
existed a provisional character to the Pale, and the committee might easily
have abolished it altogether and encouraged settlement in Great Russian
areas. Instead, the committee took the opposite approach and confirmed
the policy of exclusion. By enumerating those provinces and territories
where the Jews *could* trade and settle, and placing restrictions on habitation in the interior, the statute gave the Pale the legal basis it would retain
until the demise of the empire in 1917. There were exceptions allowing
merchants, artisans, and manufacturers to travel in the interior on business, but the principle remained. Even enlightened Jews were to be kept
from excessive contact with the Great Russian populace. The Pale was not
at first a serious burden, but as it was gradually reinforced by additional
discriminatory provisions, it became the single most important cause of
Jewish poverty and destitution and a spawning ground of both misery and
dreams.

It has been noted that there were two themes of reform: one designed to
improve the material prosperity of the Jews and the other, more dominant,
to protect Christians from "Jewish exploitation." This latter theme is best
illustrated by the attitude of the committee toward the Jews and the liquor
trade. In a sense the articles devoted to this trade are the key to the whole
statute. They indicate that where matters were not clear-cut, the concern of
the committee was the Christian population first, the Jews second. Allowing for the seriousness of peasant drunkenness and drinking debts, the
committee took an inordinate amount of time trying to solve a problem
which was insoluble within its context: the landowners would not stop the
production and sale of spirits, no matter whom they used as middlemen,
Gentiles or Jews. The government was unwilling to restrict this right, save
to disturb the Jews involved in the trade. It was a valueless remedy, but it
produced in the minds of the committee members the illusion of substantive
action.

Governmental concern with the liquor trade is evident from the inordinately large number of articles devoted to its various aspects. Whereas one article was devoted to the kahal and four to the joint class of merchants and townspeople, ten articles, or almost a fifth of the total, dealt with the liquor trade in some way.[54] Even while emphasizing the problem the statute was vague regarding important specifics. Article 37 provided that all contracts held by Jews in rural areas in some aspect of the liquor trade were void "after the expiration date" (i.e., they were not renewable). Article 38 stated that "all debts of inhabitants and other classes of people to taverns run by Jews are, on this basis, worthless and nonrecoverable." Did this cancellation of debts refer to the promulgation of the statute or did it refer back to article 37 and the expiration date of contracts? In the absence of a precise administrative decision, it must be assumed that at times individual Jews were forced to rely on the good graces of their debtors for the recovery of loans. There were other problems which were encountered later by officials engaged in implementing the statute, such as the correct definition of the term "lease" (*arenda*).

The most important article as regards the liquor trade was article 34. It stated:

No Jew, beginning on the 1st of January 1807, in the provinces of Astrakhan and the Caucasus, and in those of Little Russia and New Russia, and from the 1st of January 1808, elsewhere, in any village or in the countryside, is allowed to hold a lease on a tavern, drinking house, or inn, either in his own name or in another's, nor to sell liquor, nor even to live where this is done, except when passing through. This prohibition applies to all taverns, inns, and other establishments located on major roads which may not be run by the community or private individuals.

This meant that Jewish families which depended on some aspect of the trade for a portion of their livelihood would be expropriated. The government soon realized the number of Jewish families involved was considerable. In theory, of course, these were the Jews who were to compose the new class of farmers and to provide the work force for the new Jewish factories. What appeared attractive when confined to the realm of theoretical social engineering proved disastrous when put into effect with minimal preparation and funding. The net result of this reform was widespread chaos and economic dislocation.

The Jews were the chief target as far as reform of the trade was concerned, but the committee indicated, somewhat obliquely, that the problems it raised were more than a little the responsibility of the landowners. (This understanding was facilitated by the fact that the landowners in question were Poles.) Article 35 provided monetary fines, and even confiscation, on landowners who attempted to circumvent the law against leasing liquor rights to Jews. It is doubtful, however, that such punishments were often, if ever, imposed.[55]

In summary, it was the abolition of the liquor trade which was to set many of the other reforms in motion. It displaced large numbers of rural Jews who of necessity entered other more economically productive classes. Originally it was assumed that this transformation could be wrought in two or three years, by 1807 or 1808. The committee gave no hint of the difficulties which might be expected to arise.

With the economic position of the Jews in theory stabilized, the statute concluded with various societal reforms. They were designed to regulate the admission of the Jews into Russian society and to define the remaining limits of their own self-government. As Russian citizens, the Jews were promised complete protection under the law as enjoyed by other subjects of the crown. They were promised inviolability of property, freedom from discrimination and harassment, the right of movement, and rights of legal redress if they lived on private estates.[56]

As noted above, the government retained the kahal as well as many of the prerogatives of the rabbinate. Channels of governmental supervision and control were also decreed. The kahal elders and rabbis were to be elected by the community and to serve three-year terms with the opportunity for reelection. The Russian provincial authorities were given a veto, since their assent was necessary before the post could be occupied (article 50). A common warning sounded by reformers had been the power of the rabbinate, and thus a special section of the statute delineated and controlled its activities. Rabbis were strictly enjoined to judge only arguments arising from religion. They were forbidden to employ the characteristic weapons used in the past to ensure the subjugation of dissidents: excommunications, fines, curses, or denunciations. Violations were to be punished by large fines (article 51).

The committee also attempted to solve the tumultuous sectarian warfare that pitted Hasidim against Mitnaggedim. Article 53 permitted a dissident sect to establish its own synagogue and elect its own rabbi in any community. The statute specified that there be only one kahal, however. This illustrates another point regarding the deliberations of the committee. It never seemed to possess a fundamental understanding of the blend of the religious and the secular in Jewish life. By attempting to make an artificial division, the committee was confronting centuries of tradition and belief. Thus it continued the religious court, the *bet din*, oblivious to the fact that quite frequently matters which the government would consider secular were being brought before it. Likewise, the warring Jewish sects could hardly be expected to collaborate successfully in the secular operations of the kahal plagued as they were by religious hatreds. Such duties as tax assessments virtually guaranteed further contention.

The inconsistencies that marked the statute as well as its misplaced hopes were to become more readily apparent as the government attempted to implement its provisions. Although weaknesses quickly became apparent, the stress of war as well as the emperor's turn toward political conservatism and religious obscurantism by and large distracted the government from further attempts at wide-scale reform. Instead the statute endured, to be qualified by administrative decisions or ignored altogether. While the positive reforms of the statute were frequently neglected, its disabilities, such as the Pale of Settlement, were to be increasingly welded onto the framework of the law of the empire.

6

Che Vicissitudes of
Reform, 1804-1825

"Man proposes but God disposes": it is one thing to draft reforms and quite another to implement them. The outcome of the Statute of 1804 would be of interest if only as a classic example of the difficulties of reconciling the world as it is and as it should be. Yet it has an added significance because the statute was one of the few reform projects of Alexander's early reign that was actually put into force. The statute's implementation demonstrates how outside forces and internal exegencies helped to shape the ultimate form of the statute almost as much as its original designers. Most of all, the fate of the Statute of 1804 indicates what a Sisyphean task it was to provide a definitive resolution of the Jewish Question, especially when reformers mixed together the theoretical and the practical. This situation was not unique to the Jewish Question, however. Like the Statute of 1804, many of the comprehensive laws deriving from enlightened absolutism in Russia were in need of continual reinterpretation and explication once loosed upon the real world.

The reform itself, as noted in Chapter 5, was driven by two distinct impulses: "the true good of the Jews," and the "welfare of the native population." These were not antithetical propositions, but neither did they mesh together smoothly in the completed code. As a result, administrators were continually forced to choose priorities within the two categories, as well as to emphasize one theme or the other.

"The true good of the Jews" was construed as turning them into good citizens in the political sense, and was to be achieved by drawing the Jews more securely into an idealized model of the Russian social system. This objective, in turn, necessitated the societal reforms of the statute. These reforms were offered in a generous spirit, emphasizing "quiet encouragement" by the government, and the activity of the Jews themselves.[1] Such reforms had the advantage of costing the government nothing, beyond the energy required to encourage and exhort, but in retrospect they had the disadvantage of achieving nothing substantive.

The "enlightenment" provisions of the statute were stillborn, and could hardly have been otherwise. To be sure, the statute promised Jewish children open admission to all primary schools as well as full security for their religious beliefs. In the areas taken from Poland, schooling was almost entirely in the hands of the Roman Catholic clergy, which was hardly calculated to put the minds of religiously devout Jewish parents to rest. Statistics speak eloquently of the total failure of the opening of "secular," primary schooling to the Jews. In 1808 there was only one Jew in Vitebsk province attending a public school, and in Mogilev province, nine.[2] In Russia, Alexander's important university reform, which sought to create public primary schools, was only just under way. There could be no question of this system accepting any significant number of Jews, when it hardly educated any Christians. (When, in the 1870s, a Jewish influx occurred into the much better prepared Russian schools of the Pale of Settlement, it produced only alarm and exclusionary proposals from the school administrators.)[3] As a consequence of article 6 of the statute, in theory all existing Jewish primary schools added language courses in Russian, German, or Polish. No system of inspection or control was added, however, with predictable results. Even fifty years later, the Russian state was still promulgating legislation designed to force language instruction in Jewish primary schools.[4]

No young Jew, emerging from the traditional Jewish school system, with its emphasis upon the study of the Talmud, would have been qualified to seek admission to a Russian institution of higher learning, nor, ordinarily, would he have wanted to. On the other hand, the Russian state showed itself completely mystified when confronted with the anomaly of a Russian Jew with a university degree. After a Jewish native of Kurlandia province, Simon Wolf (Vul'f), completed the requirements for the advanced degree of Candidate in Law at Derpt University in 1816, the Faculty Council refused his request to pursue the doctoral degree in law, and this decision was upheld by the Russian Council of Ministers, in clear violation of article 5 of the statute. (The justification for these decisions was that the requirements for a doctorate included the study of Canon Law, which would have been contrary to the Jewish religion.) Wolf was briefly permitted state service— the only employment available for a university graduate—in the Justice College for Lifland and Kurland Affairs but was soon dismissed on the pretext that he could not be asked to work on cases involving Church law.[5] Not surprisingly, Wolf had few emulators.

Equally unsuccessful were the statute's attempts to legislate language proficiency among rabbis by threatening them with removal from office. (It was never clear how the Russian government could hope to remove officials whom it did not appoint and over whom it had no direct supervision or control.) Similarly unenforceable were demands that Jewish merchants keep their books in a language other than Yiddish. Even the practical demand that Jewish members of municipal magistracies know German, Polish, or Russian accomplished little, to judge from the continual petitions against it by representatives of Jewish communities at the Russian court. The statute had also sought to remove the most public badge of the Jews' alienation from their Christian neighbors: caftans, skullcaps, and earlocks. Yet there was seldom an imperial tour made to the western provinces by Alexander or his two successors which was not followed by an indignant query from the tsar as to why he had seen, in virtually every marketplace along the route, crowds of Jews wearing their traditional, and supposedly illegal, garb.[6]

By retaining the kahal as the semiautonomous agency for the regulation of the Jewish community, the framers of the Statute of 1804 effectively emasculated their proposed restriction of the power of the rabbinate. In theory, judicial decisions of rabbis were confined to matters of ritual and religion, as though the religious element could easily be differentiated in Jewish culture. Add to this the absence of any oversight, and it is doubtful indeed that the *bet din*, the rabbinic court, ceased to exercise its traditional jurisdiction. It may be doubted as well whether the prohibition on the power of rabbis to ban or excommunicate community members had much effect, a state of affairs recognized by the Russian government itself when, in 1817, it authorized rabbis to use the ban against Jewish smugglers.[7] Nor did rabbis in any number learn Polish, German, or Russian, since the government was still pursuing this chimerical objective as late as mid-century.[8] In the cultural realm, in short, the drafters of the Statute of 1804 permitted the Jews to move at their own pace. The Jewish community, in turn, chose not to move at all to the drumbeats of the reform.

Of the twin impulses of reform, the government was consistently more attentive to the "welfare of the native population" (as officials persisted in calling the non-Jewish population), with its reverse side of making the Jews into good citizens in an economic sense. These objectives were to be attained by the restriction of harmful economic pursuits by Jews and the encouragement of new, useful ones such as agriculture and manufacturing. In contrast to its sponsorship of the statute's educational program, in economic matters the government was willing to go far beyond "quiet encouragement" and embark upon an ambitious program of social engineering.

Before this could be done, however, the state administration was required to explain what it had wrought. This was an urgent requirement in the case of article 34 of the statute. This article forbade Jews to "hold a lease [*arenda*] on a tavern, drinking house, or inn, either in their own name or another's, or to sell alcohol, or even to live where this is done, except when passing through." The ambiguity arose from the use of the Russian term for "lease," *arenda*. In Polish this same term was used specifically and exclusively to refer to leases in the liquor trade, while the term in Russian did not make any distinction among the various forms of leaseholding. The question of what the government meant to restrict by this article is important, since the Jews also leased mills, fisheries, and product monopolies, which could conceivably come under the prohibition.

The contextual use of the term *arenda* in article 34 suggested that it was directed against the liquor trade alone. On 21 December 1805, however, the central government made clear that article 34 was to be understood in a wider sense. A decree specifically forbade Jews to purchase leases on fisheries and mills, although they were described as "honorable."[9] Nowhere in the deliberations of the First Jewish Committee is there to be found any suggestion that it was desirable to restrict the Jews from all leaseholding. Consequently, the expansion of the jurisdiction of article 34 by administrative decision was as important as the original article itself. What motivated this extension of the law?

It is conceivable that the central government was determined to sweep the Jews from the countryside once and for all, by denying them any means of support, although such a surmise lacks any documentation. Resettlement would expedite the formation of the agricultural and factory-worker classes that the government still hoped to create with the Jews, although neither the central government nor local officials made any immediate effort to do so. There is also the possibility that the restrictions were directed against the native Polish landowners.[10] Article 35 of the statute prescribed a hierarchy of punishments, culminating in the confiscation of the estate, against those landowners who permitted Jews to engage in the liquor trade on their estates. These punishments were specified even ahead of those to be assessed on guilty Jews. The First Jewish Committee had recognized the role which the Polish landowner played in the exploitation of the peasantry, and this no doubt was exacerbated by the government's distrust of the loyalty of the Polish nobility. The expanded interpretation of the article could be viewed as a subtle thrust at the Poles through their Jewish stewards. This interpretation is not strengthened, however, by the failure of local officialdom to apply the stringent measures toward wayward magnates or szlachta. There is no evidence that any Polish landowner was ever prosecuted under the force of article 35. For their part, the landowners *did* fight to retain the Jews on their estates, by contesting resettlement projects and by resisting Jewish mobility.[11] However handy the Jews might be as scapegoats for the maladministration of estates, they were themselves an indispensable component of the rural Polish economy. Whatever the motivation might have been, the welfare of large numbers of rural Jews was immediately placed at risk.

If large numbers of Jews were to lose their livelihood in the rural economy, what was to be done with them? In the long term, presumably, they would enter the newly minted classes of farmers and manufacturers. In the short term, the government decided to relocate them to urban centers where all members of the urban estates, whatever their actual residence, were legally registered. Similar resettlements had been attempted in the past, for both Jews and non-Jews, the best examples being the resettlement of non-Jewish townspeople in Olonets province in 1782 and Passek's attempt to resettle the Jews of Mogilev and Polotsk provinces prior to 1785. Never before, however, had resettlement involved such a large group of people as the Jews in all the western provinces. (The Second Jewish Committee, to be discussed below, estimated the total number of Jewish families resettled to be sixty thousand.) The small urban centers characteristic of the western provinces—themselves largely Jewish in population—could not hope to provide employment or even adequate shelter for such an influx of indigent refugees. Subsequent investigations by the government itself revealed that the ill-conceived and badly executed resettlement scheme launched by the Statute of 1804 produced a human disaster of considerable dimensions. Within two years of its inception, resettlement was in fact temporarily halted, although this was a result of political and military, not human, considerations.

Russian arms had been actively involved in the Wars of the French Revolution and the Napoleonic Wars which followed them. The Russian army had been badly bloodied in the Battle of Austerlitz (2 December 1805 N.S.), which saw the breakup of the anti-French Third Coalition. Tsar Alexander refused to come to terms with Napoleon, however, as had his coalition partner Austria, and was involved in the diplomatic maneuvers which culminated in the War of the Fourth Coalition from 1806 to 1807. It was against this background of diplomatic and military preparations that resettlement took place. Napoleon suddenly complicated matters by issuing a call for an "Assembly of Jewish Notables," drawn from the lands of the French Empire and the Kingdom of Italy, on 30 May 1806 N.S. The assembly, which met in Paris, was a device which Napoleon hoped to use to clarify the position of Jewry within those states under French control. Still, the convocation itself, and the rhetoric surrounding the meetings, could only disquiet Napoleon's enemies, each of which had a significant Jewish population of untested political loyalty. These fears grew when Napoleon announced the reconstitution of the original assembly into a "Great Sanhedrin," a term which conjured up visions of the ancient Jewish Sanhedrin of Jerusalem. Further, on 6 October 1806 N.S., the assembly invited representatives of all the Jewish communities of Europe to send representatives to the Sanhedrin, which ultimately met from February to March 1807. Napoleon used the Sanhedrin as a testing ground for the loyalty of the Jews within his own empire, but the dramatic quality of its convocation filled Russian and Austrian officialdom with alarm. On 20 February 1807, for instance, the minister of internal affairs advised the governors of the western provinces to guard against any communication between local Jews and the Paris meeting. They were advised to spread rumors that the Sanhedrin aimed at changing the Jewish religion, and at giving the French government control of those lands where the Jews lived.[12] The Russian government in this way waged a countercampaign against the sympathy which it believed Napoleon enjoyed among European Jews, beginning with a fictitious promise, supposedly made during his Egyptian campaign, that he would restore the Jewish kingdom in Palestine. Actually, East European Jewry looked with suspicion at Napoleon and displayed little interest in the Paris meeting. In 1812 the Jews of Russia usually supported the government against the French.[13]

But to Alexander in 1806, the French threat to the Jews seemed real enough. On 24 August 1806, he created another Jewish Committee, consisting of the foreign minister, A. Ia. Budberg, Czartoryski, Czacki, Kochubei, Potocki, Lopukhin, and N. N. Novosil'tsev, the former minister of justice and future tsarist representative in Poland. This new committee was ordered to investigate how the Jews might be protected from French influence and to decide whether resettlement should be delayed.[14] Unfortunately, little is known of the deliberations of this committee beyond the fact that it explored the question of resettlement "in great detail." The few excerpts that are extant from the work of the committee survive only in the report of the Third Jewish Committee. These extracts reveal that on 10 February 1807, Kochubei advised the tsar of the necessity of "delaying the resettlement of the Jews from the country into the cities and towns and of treating this nation carefully in opposition to the schemes of the French government."[15] Either impressed by the French threat or bowing to economic necessity, Alexander agreed to halt the resettlement.[16] This decision was relayed to the Senate by Senator Ivan Alekseev on 15 February 1807. Alekseev was told by the tsar that "one must take into consideration the shortness of the remaining period for Jewish resettlement, military circumstances, the existing position of the bordering provinces, and the destruction which would result should the Jews require us to use force in resettlement."[17]

Shortly after the cessation of resettlement, the Battle of Friedland, on 14 June 1807 N.S., destroyed the hopes of the Fourth Coalition and forced Alexander to seek rapprochement with Napoleon. This decision culminated in the Treaty of Tilsit, concluded on 9 July 1807 N.S. The Great Sanhedrin had been dissolved almost a year previously, and the French no longer seemed to present a threat to Russian Jews. Thus the government again returned to its *idée fixe*, promulgating new resettlement plans on 19 October 1807. On this occasion the central government was determined to act more methodically than in the past, and it called for the election of Jewish deputies from the kahals "to inform the government how best the provisions of the statute might be fulfilled." These deputies pointed out the financial difficulties posed by resettlement and asked for a postponement of several years. The government in return conceded that difficulties had arisen in the past, which it blamed on the war, and implemented a revised resettlement plan which divided all Jews residing in the countryside into three groups, each of which was to be resettled in the three following years, 1808, 1809, and 1810. The provincial governors, together with the marshals of the nobility, were designated to draw up lists making this division, beginning with a census of the Jews under their authority. These resettlement committees were ordered to take several factors into consideration in the assignment of the Jews to the various categories, in contrast to past resettlement plans, which were directed indiscriminately at all Jews in the countryside. The committees were supposed to take cognizance of the density of settlement in each locality, the number and location of taverns run by Jews, and whether or not there were Jewish leaseholders on bordering estates. In this latter case they were all to be resettled simultaneously, so that no landowner could enjoy an economic advantage over his neighbors.

The government by now recognized that resettlement could not succeed without economic dislocation, if it merely moved large groups of Jews from one place to another. The central paradox of resettlement was now made manifest: how could the Jews be resettled before they entered into the new classes that the statute had opened for them, especially when the activation of such classes was making only desultory progress? The government's new resettlement decree grappled with this problem, but with the same spirit of economy that marked so many of its efforts. The Jews who proved to be too poor to finance their own resettlement were to procure funds from the kahal, if possible. If not, they were to be settled on landed estates, where the owners were to build factories for them, or to be employed in factories created with the capital of rich Jews. Perhaps unconsciously recognizing that neither option was a viable alternative given the numbers involved, the government offered a third choice: resettlement in New Russia, Astrakhan, and the Caucasus, a movement to be financed by loans from the local resettlement committees, composed largely of the wealthier landowners.[18] Unfortunately, these landowners were no more willing to commit funds for the resettlement of their useful Jewish employees than the government itself had been. Small wonder that this more structured resettlement was as unsuccessful as those that had been attempted in the past. Barely a year later, in response to complaints from provincial governors, the resettlement was again halted.[19] A new committee, the Third Jewish Committee, was appointed to make plans for yet another attempt, but resettlement as envisioned by the statute was postponed for a decade. Nevertheless, the panacea of ridding the countryside of the presence of Jews was now firmly entrenched in the Russian bureaucratic mind, to be advanced again and again throughout the 19th century as a ready solution for the Jewish Question.[20]

Resettlement, even if improperly carried out, threatened to increase the urban Jewish population, and this fact focused attention once again on the problem of Jews' participation in municipal self-government. The conflicting administrative rulings and counterrulings of the past served to complicate rather than resolve the problem. This was explicitly recognized by the Senate when, having subordinated Jewish electoral rights to the discriminatory precepts of the Lithuanian Statute in 1803, it appealed to the drafting committee of the Statute of 1804 to make appropriate changes in order to enfranchise the Jews. Instead, the committee chose to ignore the question, and the Statute of 1804 failed to deal with it in any way. Christian rivals of Jewish tradesmen did not miss this cue. Invoking the established dictum that everything not specifically permitted to the Jews was denied them, the municipal authorities in the city of Kiev and in Taurida province attempted to disenfranchise Jewish merchants and townspeople. Their justification was that since the Statute of 1804 had remained silent on the issue of electoral rights, Jews were denied them.[21]

This left the question of Jewish participation largely in the hands of the higher provincial administration, to which appeals arising from these conflicts made their way. Thus, despite the Senate confirmation of the discriminatory Lithuanian Statute, Jews continued to serve in municipal government in Lithuania itself until 1808. In that year the Ministry of Internal Affairs forbade Jewish participation until the full implementation of the Statute of 1804 (i.e., until the final removal of Jews from the countryside). In 1816, however, the governor of Vilna province, on his own authority, permitted Jews to participate in the Vilna town council, and several served from 1817 to 1820, to the intense displeasure of their Christian counterparts, seven of whom were prosecuted in court for refusing to serve with Jews.[22]

Similar problems attended the question of the admissibility of the testimony of Jews in civil court cases, which was forbidden by the Lithuanian Statute. In 1806 two litigants in a court case in Kiev both attempted to call a Jewish witness. The Main Kiev Court and the civil governor, P. Pankrat'ev, were inclined to permit the testimony but refrained from doing so because a specific imperial decree did not permit it. Thus, once again, the precedent was set that anything not specifically permitted to the Jews was denied them. In order to secure such permission, the case was appealed to St. Petersburg. The case dragged through the Russian bureaucracy for almost a decade, provoking a vigorous debate in the Senate.[23]

The Jews were defended in the Senate by Count Severyn Potocki, a veteran of the First Jewish Committee, who proposed that Jews be permitted to testify in all situations. He was opposed by Count Vortsel'—himself of Jewish ancestry, according to Gessen—who proposed that Jews be permitted to testify only in cases in which their own interests were involved, and then only with imperial approval. One of his principal arguments was that the reliability of Jewish court oaths could not be guaranteed. According to Vortsel', the prayer "Kol Nidre," said on the Jewish Day of Atonement, released Jews from the sin of perjury committed against Gentiles. These claims were vigorously rebutted by another member of the Senate, Karl-Heinrich Geiking, a Baltic nobleman. Geiking was already acquainted with the problem because he had investigated it for Tsar Paul I in 1796. The debate between Vortsel' and Geiking is a reminder that Poland was not the only conduit for attitudes hostile to Jews into the Russian Empire. Vortsel' and Geiking were acquainted with German Judeophobia, as represented by the claim against the prayer "Kol Nidre," which went back to the German anti-Jewish classic *Entdecktes Judenthum* (*Judaism Unmasked*) by Johann Eisenmenger. Indeed, Geiking identified Eisenmenger as a source of the charge in the course of debate.[24]

In a meeting of the full Senate the arguments of Geiking won the day. A majority of senators, as well as the minister of justice, advocated the admission of Jewish testimony in all court cases. Alexander refused to confirm this decision, however, and the matter was sent to the State Council for final resolution. Once again a majority found in favor of the Jews, and the admissibility of evidence given by Jews was confirmed by an imperial decree in 1814. This was a partial, although not insignificant, victory for the Jews, but it still left much unresolved.[25] The ruling of the State Council in favor of the Jews was based on two precedents. The first was an imperial decree of Catherine II in 1795 organizing the recently acquired province of Minsk. The decree stipulated that Jews were to have equal treatment before the law, a principle already violated by the Senate decision of 1803 which gave precedence to the discriminatory Lithuanian Statute. The second precedent was the Statute of 1804 itself, which had also declared that the Jews were to be considered equal to all other Russian subjects.[26] Clearly, however, this decision was not understood in a wider sense, because neither the Senate nor the State Council addressed the ongoing problem of Jewish electoral rights. They were again left to the caprices of the local administration.

One additional ambiguity remained concerning the legal status of the Jews, the fate of the double tax imposed by Catherine in 1794. The reform committee of 1802 had promised to end this burdensome tax when the Jews had successfully made the transition to their new classes of activity, but neither date nor emancipating mechanism were included in the statute. As late as 1812, representatives of Jewish communities were still petitioning the Third Jewish Committee for the abolition of all inequalities in taxation, including the double tax. The committee replied that, based upon a query to the Ministry of Finance, the double tax was supposedly no longer being collected.[27] No specific decree ever abolished the double tax, however, so it must be assumed that abolition took place on an ad hoc basis. It is known that discrimination against the Jews in matters of taxation continued, especially in those provinces which composed pre-partition Lithuania, and where the locals continued to evoke ancient legal codes. In 1811 in these areas, both Jewish men and women were taxed according to the Polish Constitution of 1775, but against Russian practice. In 1816 Jews were threatened with a double tax on those who evaded taxes.[28]

The unwillingness of the reformers of 1804 to confront these problems—the effects of resettlement, electoral rights, taxation—is perhaps best explained by their lack of interest in the Jewish members of the urban estates. Just as the government of Catherine had been concerned with using the Jews to swell the urban centers, so the reformers of a different age wanted to use them for their own special concerns. The urban Jews would survive much as they had always done. In the meantime the Jews driven out of the countryside could enlarge the two new estates of free farmers and manufacturers, especially created for them. Unfortunately, the disastrous outcome of resettlement each time it was attempted throughout Alexander's reign demonstrated the folly of attempting to metamorphize Jewish tavern-keepers, leaseholders, and distillers into more desirable types. The statute's bright promise of economic reform came to nothing because of monetary shortages, bureaucratic apathy, and local conditions.

The most spectacular short-term failure was the attempt to create a class of Jewish yeoman farmers. Despite the enthusiasm of the "back to the soil" school of Gentile reformers, Polish Jewry was singularly ill suited for a rapid transformation into farmers. Cut off more effectively than any other group from agriculture, the traditions and experiences of the newly unemployed Jews were almost entirely mercantile. To expect them to excel at agriculture—for this was what was required in order to colonize the virgin soil of the New Russian steppes—was unrealistic. The initial fraudulent premise was reinforced by the government's willingness to offer only minimal aid. The statute offered free land for those who needed it, but it was almost without exception situated in the south. The task of relocation, the creation of farms, the supply of equipment and seed, all threatened to place financial demands on the government in the midst of wartime. The government was thus unable to supply the basic material needs of the would-be agriculturalists, much less to provide the training they required and the reform proposals assumed they would receive.

All these features were part of the melancholy story of the first Jewish agricultural settlements. Before 1806 the Jews had shown little desire to move to New Russia, but when their expulsion from the countryside began in earnest, individuals from various communities began to request agricultural resettlement. One of the first such requests was made to the governor of Mogilev, M. M. Bakunin. The manner in which it was handled is indicative of the government's failure to do anything substantial for the creation of the Jewish agricultural class beyond making the land available in the newly colonized areas of the south. Jews had already been permitted to settle in these areas for decades. Bakunin asked the minister of internal affairs, Kochubei, what to do about the request that he had received from the representatives of 36 Jewish families, who particularly asked to resettle in the south. He noted that they were destitute and would require a loan. (Article 18 of the statute had promised Jewish agricultural settlers not only free land, but the same type of loan as was given to foreign settlers, such as the German colonists along the Volga.) Instead of answering Bakunin's questions, Kochubei asked the governor to ascertain the previous occupation of these Jews, whether or not they had reliably paid their taxes, how they had come to be indigent, what they knew about agriculture, whether or not they were resourceful, whether or not they might be expected to repay the loan, and where they wished to settle. This attitude is noteworthy. Kochubei's queries were reasonable enough when dealing with foreign nationals, but as a member of the First and Second Jewish Committees, he must have been aware of the peculiar problems which would arise in relocating a nonagricultural people on the soil. Instead, he was more concerned about the possibility of the misuse of government funds than moved by the potential for Jewish agriculture. This particular group of settlers did ultimately receive funds, but only after one of its leaders, Nokhim Finkenstein, came to the capital to meet personally with Kochubei. The success of the group in gaining official help triggered requests from other would-be settlers for aid. These requests were ordinarily declined by Kochubei, who argued that adequate housing could not be built in time, but who was more concerned about a widespread effort of Jewish communities to receive aid from the state. Kochubei was not alone in his opposition. Agricultural resettlement was also opposed by the governors of Vilna and Minsk provinces.[29] The Polish landowners, for their part, were not disappointed to see such projects fail. On the whole, then, the Russian government could hardly be said to have been true to the optimistic guarantees made by the statute.

There was some actual resettlement, nonetheless, and increased pressure on the government from other groups who also wished to migrate. The experiences of the original settlers were a disappointment. Their lack of agricultural experience was complicated by insufficient assistance from the government. The harried New Russian authorities opposed the resettlement, since it complicated their own duties and offered diminishing returns at best. In a decree of 6 April 1810, the Council of Ministers acceded to their requests. It announced that the financial burden involved in the resettlement of the Jews was simply too great. Six hundred families with 3,640 members had already been resettled, while 300 additional families had made requests for aid. The project was suspended, it was claimed, because of the poor results arising from a lack of agricultural skill and Jewish "uncleanliness," which resulted in a high mortality rate among the colonists.[30] With this decree, the last energies of the Russian attempt to create an agricultural class on the basis of the statute sputtered to a halt. The idea died hard, however. Of all the proposals advanced for the economic resolution of the Jewish Question in nineteenth-century Russia, the hope of settling Jews on the land was the most recurrent, to be advanced by both Jewish and Gentile reformers.[31]

The attempts of the Russian government to encourage the second new class, that of "manufacturers and artisans," must be viewed against the background of the slow emergence of industrial enterprise in Russia. Since the reign of Peter the Great the Russian government had attempted to create or encourage the establishment of factories and workshops, with varying degrees of success. This initial industrialization was hindered by the social structure of feudal, agrarian Russia. There were four different types of manufacturing enterprises. The first were the state factories, owned and operated by the government. They were staffed with state peasants or the flotsam and jetsam of society: soldiers, vagrants, criminals, or other vulnerable types whom the government could press into service.[32] (It will be remembered that the government had ordered that Jews of Kurlandia province who were unable to pay their taxes were to be attached to the state mines.) There were also factories in private hands, either on private estates or, more often, under the ownership of members of the urban mercantile classes. The landowner had a built-in labor supply, since he could press his serfs into factory labor, which was often light, seasonal work, although mining was a notable exception. Procuring a labor force was much more complicated for representatives of the urban classes. For most of the eighteenth century the government forbade them to buy serfs, largely at the instigation of the nobility, which was eager to preserve its own prerogatives. Instead merchant factory owners had to make do with free labor or "possessional" serfs. The latter were serfs, as well as state peasants, who were assigned to a particular factory or enterprise by the government. They did not belong to the factory owners but, in a sense, to the factory itself. Taken from the land, assigned to strange and unfamiliar work, such workers left much to be desired. The only alternative was the employment of "free workers," a variegated group indeed. The main supply of such workers consisted of peasants on quitrent, but also state peasants and even townspeople.[33] Such a supply was unstable and sporadic at best, and throughout the eighteenth century the urban factory owners fought for the right to acquire a steady and dependable supply of labor, serfs of their own. As the central government became more and more aware of the need to strengthen industry, it grew willing to override the objections of the nobility. Finally in 1798 Paul allowed the procurement of serfs for textile mills by non-nobles. The law of 1798 and a subsequent one of 1808 were so hedged about by conditions, however, as to lose much of their appeal for

THE RUSSIAN EMPIRE AFTER 1815

WHITE
SEA

Helsingfors

BALTIC
SEA

St. Petersburg

Riga

Nizhni-Novgorod   Kazan

Vilna   Moscow°

Warsaw
KINGDOM
OF POLAND

Saratov

Kiev

Kharkov

Ekaterinoslav

Kishinev
Odessa   Rostov   Astrakhan

BESSARABIA

BLACK   SEA   CASPIAN
SEA

Tiflis

Baku

0   100   200   300   400
Miles

factory owners. The 1798 decree was modified by Alexander I in 1802 to forbid the relocation of serfs purchased for factory work, and the 1808 law required that they be given their personal liberty after twenty years of service. The possibility of a free, mobile labor force, exemplified by the Jews, therefore had much to recommend it. The government was ever more willing to assist the emergence of this class because of its own special priorities.

The spate of military actions in which the Russian government found itself involved in the late eighteenth and early nineteenth centuries accentuated the need for reliable sources of military supplies. The government was particularly anxious to secure domestic supplies of the woolen cloth used by the armed forces. Laws of 1797 and 1809, for instance, forbade woolen mills to sell their products to private individuals or to private industry. It is noteworthy that cotton mills, which were of no military use, did not suffer such governmental restriction.[34] It was against this background that Nota Notkin drew up his plan for Jewish factory workers. Derzhavin in turn incorporated the idea into his proposals. These projects inspired those sections of the statute which created the special new class and promised special advantages and aid both to Jews who would set up factories employing Jewish labor and to landowners who permitted and assisted such undertakings on their own land. It was the resettlements of 1805–1807 and 1807–1808 that were supposed to fill the workbenches of these prospective factories.

The basics of the plan emerged in a report by the minister of internal affairs, Prince A. B. Kurakin, which was confirmed as law by the tsar on 30 June 1808.[35] (At this time, the overseeing of industrial development had not yet passed from the authority of the Ministry of Internal Affairs to that of Finance.) The report gave manufacturers who were not nobles the right to purchase serfs, though with the restrictions mentioned above.[36] Kurakin's report was a new approach to the chronic labor shortage, an attempt to create a class of free, factory-working people. This class was to be drawn from the serfs liberated after their twenty years of employment, from the indigent Polish szlachta, whose status had been investigated along with the Jews by the First Jewish Committee, and from the Jews. The creation of this class, as suggested by Kurakin, was clearly designed to correlate with the expulsions and resettlement which were also under the authority of Kurakin's ministry. In theory the Jews were free to enter any profession as long as it was not among those specifically forbidden to them. However, the government was determined to direct them into the classes it was promoting. As Kurakin noted in his text: "It cannot be doubted that the Jews themselves will approve the undertaking of work in the factories; but in the event of their refusal, the governor-general shall induce them to seek shelter in them."[37] Kurakin's proposal to the tsar continually noted that the new manufactories should be located in New

Russia, in other words where the Jews were in theory being resettled, and where Nota Notkin had first suggested that manufacturing colonies be founded.

Any hope of carrying out this ambitious plan was to founder on the same difficulty that had sabotaged the other reforms of the statute, the shortage of capital. In that time of wars and rumors of wars, the Russian treasury was closed to innovative schemes of social reform, especially for the Jews. The theory was different from the practice. Article 21 of the statute had promised:

> In order to establish the most necessary factories, which are cloth-making, linen-making, tanning, and the like, the government, with appropriate certification, can give to the Jews special encouragement by the allotment of necessary land and the loan of money. For this purpose an annual allotment of 20,000 rubles is assigned to every one of the provinces annexed from Poland, so that, from this capital, under the supervision of the governor of the province and through consultation with the Ministry of Internal Affairs, loans may be made to Jews who wish to build especially necessary and useful factories, not demanding a bond for this loan beyond the surety of other reliable Jews.[38]

Kurakin's report of 1808, in contrast, fairly breathed the spirit of economy. There was no mention of the twenty-thousand-ruble loan fund, and precise detail as to how loans should be guaranteed by making the entire kahal responsible for them. This reluctance to commit funds was by no means restricted to governmental activity with the Jews. Kurakin noted elsewhere in the proposal that it would not be wise for the government to offer the same monetary inducements to attract foreign manufacturers that it had given to the agricultural colonists in the past, "since experience has shown that these loans seldom return in full to the treasury." The task of providing workshops for the Jews was thus optimistically abdicated to the occasional ambitious landowner and to the Jews themselves, with one notable exception.

This exception had its genesis in the activities of the ambitious Kurakin. In 1809 he presented to the tsar a proposal for the establishment of two factories in the Ukraine, in the towns of Chernigov and Kremenchug. These factories were to provide employment for Jews while at the same time giving them the expertise necessary to find factory work elsewhere, or even to set up their own establishments. On 11 March 1809, Alexander authorized Kurakin to select one site and to establish a factory there as an experiment. Only if this enterprise was successful would the government expend further funds. Kurakin chose Kremenchug, in southwestern Poltava province, because of its large Jewish population. It was hoped that this "factory-school" would soon furnish a supply of skilled Jewish workers who would afterward be employed in factories constructed by their prosperous coreligionists. Workers were invited to join the factories with their entire family and to live in special housing to be furnished by the state. Besides free housing the workers were to receive tax exemptions, clothing, and a food subsidy. A number of foremen were brought in from state factories to train the Jewish workers. The factory itself was equipped with forty looms, each costing more than eighty-two rubles. Upon completion of their training, and after a year of satisfactory labor in the factory, individual Jews could select any town in the Ukraine for the establishment of their own textile workshop. They would receive a government subsidy while they established themselves in the cloth trade.[39]

The government did not restrict itself to such activist measures alone. In 1811 Alexander sent a member of the Senate, Arshenevskii, on a tour of Belorussia to investigate the various industries there. Arshenevskii was specifically appointed "to examine ways by which, in your opinion, better and more dependable measures can be employed to introduce clothworking among the Jews." Special emphasis was placed on convincing wealthy Jews to establish their own factories and to employ Jewish workers. "They can even be encouraged in this by promises of some assistance from the treasury."[40] Arshenevskii's initial report indicated that a base of sorts already existed for such enterprises. The Jewish community of Vitebsk province, for example, had already created a cloth factory where the tenants of the community poorhouse worked. (This undertaking was really more a workshop than a true factory: it employed only two looms for the weaving of soldiers' cloth.) More important, Arshenevskii was also approached by the owners of a number of existing or proposed woolen mills in Vitebsk and Mogilev provinces who requested loans in order to increase their production.[41] His tour revealed that the government was faced with a responsive group of Jewish entrepreneurs, ready and eager to accept proffered government assistance.

By the end of the 1820s, these Jewish entrepreneurs played a significant role in the textile industry of western Russia. By 1828 there were seventy-five Jewish-owned woolen mills in Russia, and I. U. Iuditskii estimated that Jewish workers constituted 16.95 percent of the textile-mill work force in the western provinces with 2,185 workers out of a total of 12,897.[42] Thus historians have been tempted to assume that this was in large part due to assistance and encouragement of the central government. In fact, a closer inspection of governmental assistance to woolen mills suggests that the significant role of the Jewish woolens entrepreneur cannot be explained by reference to official aid.

To begin with, the activist policy of the government, as represented by the Kremenchug factory experiment, was a disaster. While local Jews at first flocked to the factory, problems arose almost at once.[43] Although

some Jews earned the praise of the authorities by their aptitude and diligence, many more actually fled from the factory. Between 1809 and 1811,
149 workers ran away from the factory. (The largest number of workers
ever employed at one time was 148.) A factory inspector reported how, in
a typical instance, an entire family escaped through a factory window in
the dead of night. The fact that they were compelled to "escape" at all is
suggestive: for all its novel features, the Kremenchug factory was apparently a representative example of an early industrial sweatshop. In the
first months of the operation of the factory, for example, the Jewish kahal
of Kremenchug complained to the authorities about the overcrowded
housing, with several families forced to share a common room. Children
were expected to labor with their parents in the shop, although at reduced
rates of pay. Even some of the promised aid of the government was not
forthcoming: in 1811, at the initiative of the governor-general of Little
Russia, Prince Ia. I. Lobanov-Rostovskii, the subsidies that had been
promised for food supplies were ended. Lobanov-Rostovskii subsequently
became involved with the Kremenchug kahal in a dispute over the length
of time the Jews might leave the factory in order to prepare for and
celebrate the Jewish religious holidays. Later the governor attempted to
change the whole character of the factory-school and to turn it into a
spinning mill to provide thread for weavers in a nearby German colony.
In short, the rigorous organization and conduct of the factory-school recalled the military colonies with which the government was also experi-
menting at this time. The difficulty and unfamiliarity of mill work made
factory labor an employment of last resort for peasants and townspeople
all over Europe, so it is hardly surprising that the Jews viewed the Kremenchug factory with similar disdain. By 1817, there were only nine Jews
left working in the factory, and the government reacted by briefly filling
the workbenches with Gentile convicts. At last, disillusioned by the entire
experiment, the authorities closed the factory in 1817, writing off losses of
ten thousand rubles.[44]

The outcome of the policy of "encouragement," suggested by the Statute of 1804 and represented by Arshenevskii's mission, is also revealing.
However eager the government was to encourage cloth production, the
treasury lacked the necessary capital resources for a comprehensive program of subsidies. There is little evidence that the state was ever able to
provide the money it so glibly promised to Jewish entrepreneurs in the
1804 Statute. This was perhaps to be expected, since the government
showed itself quite distrustful of eager entrepreneurs and fearful that loans
would be wasted. While the government was willing to invite applications
for financial assistance, the treasury proved reluctant to provide the actual
funding.[45]

The only assistance that the government could realistically offer to the
woolen mills was a ready market for their products, and even this incen-

tive disappeared after 1822 when the mills finally began to produce a surplus greater than the needs of army and fleet.[46] Further evidence testifying against the role of the government in the growth of Jewish industry is the fact that the great Jewish textile enterprises of the 1830s were, with few exceptions, establishments that had originally been constructed by landowners with surplus capital. In the unsettled economic conditions which followed the Napoleonic Wars, many of these mills either passed into the hands of Jewish moneylenders in default of loans or were leased or sold to Jewish entrepreneurs. The Russian government played no role in any of these transactions.[47] It was specifically these concerns which were the forerunners of the large Jewish establishments of the late 1820s, for the tiny Jewish workshop-factories generally remained small family endeavors. As more of the Gentile factories passed into Jewish hands, moreover, another phenomenon became apparent. While Jewish owners were willing to employ non-Jewish laborers, the significant trend in such factories was toward the utilization of a predominantly Jewish work force.[48] This fact can be explained in part by the understandable preference of Jewish workers for an employer who understood their own particular social and religious needs. At the same time, the Jewish owner, who was often a community notable, had greater access to the Jewish masses.

Therefore, if Jewish textile manufactories prospered, it was in spite of rather than because of the policies of government. As a consequence, virtually no factories existed sufficient to receive and sustain the newly dispossessed innkeepers and distillers of the Pale.

The decision to halt resettlement that was made at the end of 1808 grew from the government's recognition that the roseate hopes of the framers of the statute were not coming to pass. Officials in the capital received complaints from the provincial authorities which emphasized the impracticality of resettlement and of the proposed economic transformations. These reports pointed out that there were no funds available to expedite resettlement. In addition, there was nowhere to resettle the Jews, since existing towns were unable to accommodate large numbers of refugees. This particular problem was further complicated by the fact that some urban centers, Brest-Litovsk being the most prominent, had recently been badly damaged by fire. The reports emphasized that there were no state factories capable of providing employment for refugees, and no hope that they could be quickly created from private or public funds. When these complaints were transferred to Alexander by Kurakin, the tsar agreed to halt resettlement. At about the same time he appointed yet another committee to examine the Jewish question. The tsar ordered it to examine how obstacles to Jewish resettlement might be removed and how the Jews might be placed in useful work. These deliberations were to be conducted with the participation of another group of Jewish deputies to be sent by the kahals. The committee consisted of Senator V. I. Popov, Senator I. A.

Alekseev, Assistant Minister of Internal Affairs O. P. Kozadavlev, State Councilor Ia. A. Durzhinin, former governor of Minsk province Zakhar Karneev, and Count Potocki. Karneev was a link to the first organized attempt to seek a remedy to the Jewish problem, the Senate survey of the opinions of the marshals of the nobility in 1798. Potocki tied the new committee both to the attempted reforms of the Quadrennial Diet in Poland and the First Jewish Committee in Russia.

In a sense the committee represented a whole new beginning, since it questioned the basic assumptions of past reform efforts. It not only examined and recommended against resettlement in the foreseeable future, but actually proposed that the Pale of Settlement be enlarged by the addition of Kurlandia province (where new Jewish settlement was forbidden) and the districts of Belostok and Tarnopol'. The committee also heard the reports of the Jewish deputies pertaining to the implementation of the other provisions of the statute, chiefly the requirements that rabbis and members of municipal bodies know a language other than Yiddish. More important, the new committee reexamined the fundamental assumptions of the First Jewish Committee, as well as the theoretical justifications for the provisions of the statute itself. This reexamination confronted and rejected some of the most cherished shibboleths of the Russian government regarding the Jews, especially concerning the economic role of the Jews in the countryside. It was in many ways a repudiation of the statute itself.

In the historical overview that was *de rigueur* for any reform proposal, the committee examined the circumstances promoting the concentration of Jews as merchants or leaseholders in the villages and estates. The committee displayed a sympathetic understanding for the manner in which the Jews had come to hold such positions: agriculture had been closed to them in Poland and they were thus forced into economic collaboration with the Polish landowner. In this condition they entered the Russian Empire in the partition of 1772, and became the object of special legislation in 1804. The committee then presented a wholesale justification of Jewish trade and commerce, leasing, and even the liquor trade. Far from being an exploitive group, the committee claimed, the Jews played an important role in the functioning of the rural economy. It would be folly to attempt to replace them, by directing them either into agricultural pursuits for which they were not suited or into nonexistent factories which the government could never hope to establish. In the course of rehabilitating the economic role of rural Jews, the committee tended more and more to implicate the Polish landowner as the party most guilty of rural distress. The committee noted as an example that it was the Polish landowners who encouraged the liquor trade and who benefited most from it, the Jews merely serving as their agents. Should the Jews be resettled, the landowners would simply entrust the trade to Christians, primarily drawn from the peasantry. Russia would not be served by turning farmers into tavern-keepers.

Another striking departure of the committee from the assumptions that dominated earlier policies was a recognition of the positive economic role played by the Jewish merchant and tradesman. The committee acknowledged the usefulness of the Jews as middlemen who could buy up the produce of the peasants in the village and transport it to market, thus saving the peasants time and effort. In addition, the Jews were described as merchandisers of goods necessary for the peasantry, such as scythes, dishes, iron, and salt. Finally, the committee characterized the Jews as a valuable source of loans and aid for the peasants in times of famine or rural distress, since they alone were an easy source of credit. (This latter claim, incidentally, was one of the few expressions of official approval ever lavished upon the hapless Jewish innkeeper/moneylender by an official report in the entire history of the Russian Empire.)

The committee was even indulgent in justifying the continued employment of Jews in the liquor trade. The impossibility of resettlement aside, the committee report denied that the liquor trade was the cause of peasant destitution. The committee cited provinces where there were Jews but no peasant destitution, and argued that the peculiar poverty of the Belorussian peasantry might better be explained by poor soil and inadequate agricultural techniques. The abuses inherent in the liquor trade itself were the responsibility of the landowners, who used the trade in spirits as a reliable source of income. The committee recommended that since the government was unwilling to restrict the nobles' right to distill vodka, it might better allow the Jews to stay where they were, lest 60,000 Jewish families be replaced by 60,000 Gentile peasant families, with the sale of drink continuing as before. For all practical purposes the committee was recommending the suspension of the principal economic provisions of the Statute of 1804.[49]

The willingness of the committee to reject ongoing policies born of the Statute of 1804 and its relative tolerance of the existing economic position of the Jews reflected its disillusionment with the tangible results of past social engineering. Rhetorically the committee members shared the enlightenment values of their predecessors, going so far as to quote extensively from the protocols of the First Jewish Committee. Significantly they chose to cite the warning against reform through constraint, and the exhortation that the government should oversee reform "from afar."[50] Even as they met, the committee members could observe the failure of reform. Neither the resettlement of the Jews from the countryside, nor their transformation into free peasants, nor their metamorphosis into factory workers had proved effective. Until better expedients could be found, a rational response was the maintenance of the status quo.

While the Jews were being excused from their stereotypical role as scapegoats for rural distress, the part was being given to the Polish gentry. As long as the Polish nobles of Belorussia and Poland retained an economy based on the production and sale of alcohol, the committee observed, drunkenness and its consequences would continue unchecked, and neither Christian nor Jew could properly be blamed. Rather than hound tavern-keepers, the government might better seek ways to make the alcohol trade less profitable, as a means of encouraging economic diversification on gentry estates.

The committee's emphasis on the harmful consequences of the szlachta economy was an elaboration of the critical comments of the First Jewish Committee, exemplified by article 35 of the statute, with its admonitions and warnings given to malefactory landlords. The added sharpness in the recommendations of the Third Jewish Committee reflected a less con-strained view of the Poles and their economic practices, perhaps encour-aged by the appearance of a reborn—and hostile—Polish state, the Napo-leonic Grand Duchy of Warsaw, on Russia's doorstep. For the moment, at least, official pressure on the Jews of the Russian Empire was relaxed.

The first scholarly investigator of the legal status of Russian Jewry, I. G. Orshanskii, called the report of the Third Jewish Committee "the most important occurrence in the history of our legal work on the Jews."[51] It was hardly that, however useful it might have been to Orshanskii in the midst of polemics on the Jewish Question in post-reform Russia. The most significant feature of the report was that none of its recommenda-tions were ever implemented. In part this could be attributed to the unfortunate timing of the report, submitted to the tsar on 17 March 1812. Within two months Napoleon had begun his invasion of Russia, and the attention of the government was concentrated on physical survival, not domestic reform. By 1815, however, the French threat was over. The Third Jewish Committee remained in existence, at least on paper, until 1818, yet the government still declined to implement any of its propos-als. It is a plausible conjecture that the report was ignored because its findings ran counter to assumptions and prejudices too firmly ingrained in the bureaucratic consciousness to be lightly abandoned. In general, the Jewish policies of Alexander's govenment began to move in very different directions.

The Russia of 1815 was different from the Russia of 1812, not only territorially, but psychologically as well. These changes had implications for reform as envisioned by either the First or Third Jewish Committee. The most obvious change was the growing receptiveness of Alexander and many of his closest advisers to varieties of Christian mysticism. In the political sphere there was change as well: Alexander's interests had moved from the internal reform of his own realm to arbitration of the fate of Europe. The postwar congress system ensured that the tsar was frequently abroad, leaving domestic oversight to martinets like Count A. Arakcheev. Especially during the last five years of his reign, frightened by the specter of internal and external Jacobinism, Alexander pursued more restrictive policies at home, such as the banning of secret societies in 1823 and the intensification of the censorship. Some interpretations of Alexander's reign, in fact, have attempted to divide it into two halves: a liberal, freethinking, reformist phase up to 1812, followed by a reactionary, obscurantist period. Such a division fails to withstand closer examination. For example, the mystical and authoritarian aspects of Alexander's personality were detectable well before 1812, while many of the reform elements of the first decade carried over into the second. As late as 1818, Alexander commissioned N. N. Novosil'tsev to design a constitutional project for Russia, while constitutional schemes were actually implemented for Finland, Bessarabia, and Poland.[52] The religious mysticism of Alexander's circle was in part a reaction against the sterile formalism of the established church. It included notions of the "brotherhood of all Christian religions" and promoted a general religious toleration.[53] Even the most ill-favored undertaking of the Arakcheev period, the military colonies, began as a reasonable military reform, borrowed from the successful experience of the Austrian Empire.[54]

Alexander's religious awakening, with its contradictory aspects, did not fail to touch the Jews in ways both positive and negative. On the negative side, it resuscitated, to a limited degree, the old Muscovite religious tradition, with its fear of Jewish proselytism and its determination to Christianize Israel. This influence led to the creation by Alexander of the "Society of Israelite Christians" on 25 March 1817. The ostensible purpose of this institution was to provide shelter and sustenance to Jews who wished to accept the truth of Christianity but who were deterred by the intolerance shown converts by the Jewish community. Converts were promised agricultural land from the state and exemption from such imposts as the quartering of troops or the provision of post horses, as well as residence anywhere in the empire and entry into any kind of state service.[55]

Fiscal benefits for converts to Christianity were not new in the Russian Empire, for they had appeared simultaneously with the admission of non-Christians, side by side with promises of religious toleration. Despite her tolerant rhetoric, for example, Catherine II had offered rewards for conversion to both Muslim and Jew. Alexander's plan differed only in the scope and scale of the undertaking. The Society of Israelite Christians enjoyed no greater success than earlier efforts, despite a large staff and an expensive budget. It had failed to convert more than a handful of converts of dubious religiosity when it was abolished by Nicholas I in 1833.[56]

What the government could not accomplish itself it was willing to leave to others. Thus the London Society for Promoting Christianity among the

Jews was permitted to pursue its activities in the Kingdom of Poland. The Russian Bible Society, under the tsar's special protection and sponsorship, had as its chief goal the dissemination of the Christian Scriptures. It nonetheless toyed with mild conversionary efforts by publishing, in 1821, a Hebrew translation of the Gospel of St. Matthew and the Epistle to the Hebrews.[57]

Efforts at conversion reveal an important component of the Russian legal definition of a "Jew." First and foremost a Jew was a member of a religious confession, Judaism. Upon conversion to Christianity, Jews ceased entirely to be Jews and were placed into another estate, depending upon their occupation. Indeed, some legislation actually permitted them to choose their own estate. At most, converts were sometimes characterized as being "of Jewish descent," but the ease with which Jewish converts were assimilated into Russian society suggests that racial elements were almost entirely lacking in Russian attitudes toward the Jews. Such attitudes did not begin to appear until late in the nineteenth century, under a different set of political and social conditions.[58] Until then conversion remained the preferred, if least anticipated, solution to the Jewish Question.

While Russian bureaucrats labored unsuccessfully to attract Jews to Christianity, conversions of a kind less desired by the state were taking place. Beginning in 1814, Orthodox Church officials began to discover communities of "Sabbatarians," who attempted to base their religious life on the Old rather than the New Testament. In 1818 a group of free peasants in Voronezh province actually complained to the tsar that they were being hindered by the local authorities in their attempts to follow the Mosaic Law. Similar "Judaizing" sects were discovered from time to time throughout the eighteenth century. They apparently did not arise from actual Jewish proselytism, since they appeared in areas remote from Jewish settlement. The sectarian groups probably derived their enthusiasm for Judaic Law from an independent reading of the Scriptures. The tendency of the Sabbatarians to selectively choose elements from the Old Testament tradition confirms the suspicion that they were Christian heretics rather than true converts to Judaism. Nevertheless, the government consciously attempted to discredit them in the eyes of other peasants by putting out the claim that they had indeed converted to Judaism (*zhidovstvo*).[59]

Whatever the true source of the conversionary movement, the government responded with panic. The movement was thoroughly investigated wherever it appeared. Individual sectarians were exiled to Siberia, and in 1825 a decree ordered the exclusion of Jews from any district where Sabbatarians appeared. Fears for the integrity of the Christian faith generated by these discoveries also resulted in a ban on the hiring of Christian servants by Jews.[60]

These incidents of intolerance aside, the religious revival in postwar Russia had positive consequences for the Jews as well. Alexander personally was much impressed with the apocalyptic beliefs of the English missionary Lewis Way, who believed that the salvation of the world was to be anticipated by the mass conversion of world Jewry. Until that moment arrived, however, Jews should be treated with complete toleration and even be given full civil rights as a way of attracting them to Christianity. Way was received by Alexander in St. Petersburg, and he submitted a memorandum to the tsar on the need to emancipate European Jewry while he was attending the Congress of Aix-la-Chapelle in 1818. At Alexander's behest, the memorandum was submitted to the congress for discussion.[61]

Alexander's partner in mysticism and trusted adviser was Prince A. N. Golitsyn, who served as ober-procurator of the Holy Synod and, after 1810, as head of the Central Administration of Religious Affairs of Foreign Creeds. These two posts gave him supervision of all religious denominations in the Russian Empire. Golitsyn's power was increased still further when, in a reform reflecting Alexander's religious zeal, his posts were merged with the Ministry of Education to create the "Ministry of Religious Affairs and Public Education" on 24 October 1817. The Third Jewish Committee was abolished, and Jewish affairs were placed specifically under Golitsyn's authority.[62]

Golitsyn took an active interest in the fate of Russian Jewry, and to assist him, he made use of a formal system of Jewish communal representatives. There was nothing new in the use of such "deputies of the Jewish people." Elected representatives of Belorussian Jewry had appeared in the capital in 1785, to petition the Senate against the actions of Governor Passek, and elected deputies had been consulted by the first three Jewish committees. During the War of 1812 two Jews, Zundel Zonnenberg and Leizer Dillon, had served as representatives of Russian Jewry at the headquarters of the Russian army. A delegation of Russian Jews gained an audience with Alexander while he was staying in Bruchsal in Baden in 1814 and received the promise of improved treatment. The delegation was also empowered to elect people to represent them in the capital. In 1818, with Golitsyn's approval, an electoral assembly meeting in Vilna chose three deputies and three alternates to consult directly with Golitsyn on matters of interest to the Jews. On 18 March 1819 the deputy Zonnenberg informed the Jewish communities on behalf of Golitsyn that "in their affairs they were to turn with requests and complaints to such offices and individuals as the rules indicate, directly in the order prescribed by the law. If they do not receive justice from these offices and individuals, then in cases involving communities, and not individual criminal cases or lawsuits regarding their own property, they may seek defense from the Minister of Religious Affairs and Public Education, but not otherwise than through the deputies chosen by their representatives."[63]

Direct representation before the central government initially proved quite expeditious for the Jews. At the very beginning of the deputies' service, in 1816, a rash of ritual murder accusations broke out in the province of Grodno and the Kingdom of Poland. The deputies secured a circular from Golitsyn to local judicial personnel requiring concrete proof before ritual murder charges could be levied against an individual Jew (i.e., the assumption that the Jews required Christian blood was not alone sufficient to begin a criminal case).[64] The deputies also sought, sometimes enlisting Golitsyn's assistance, to circumvent some of the onerous restrictions of the Statute of 1804, such as those prohibiting the use of excommunication, restrictions on traditional dress, and especially those dealing with language instruction in Jewish schools.[65] Golitsyn's sympathy did not prevent renewed attempts to move the Jews from the countryside, nor was Golitsyn always free of anti-Jewish prejudices.[66]

The protection of a high court official like Golitsyn—ironically, almost the "protector" envisioned by Derzhavin—and a permanent, formal system of consultation on Jewish needs were all to the apparent benefit of Russian Jewry. At the same time they had their cost. Such devices served to isolate the Jews still further from the rest of the population and to make them the inevitable "special case." In some respects the system recalled the status of the Jews in pre-partition Poland, with the added disadvantage that their position was dependent upon the caprices of the ruler, instead of the formalized provisions of Polish law. Moreover, Golitsyn eventually lost his position as patron of the Jews. In 1825 he was replaced as minister for public education by A. S. Shiskov, who immediately recommended the cessation of the system of consultation with special Jewish deputies. Despite Golitsyn's opposition, the system was ended in that year.[67]

Events after 1815 ran against the intent of the Statute of 1804 to integrate the Jews more fully into the Russian social system. Increasingly, the lone survival of 1804 was the determination to "render the Jews harmless." This commitment did not result in a conscious campaign, but it was evident in ad hoc responses to local situations. Thus, special measures were undertaken to ascertain the Jewish population accurately, and huge fines were threatened for kahals which hid "souls." In 1816, efforts were made to stop the practice of "*krestsenie*," whereby Jews would purchase crops standing in the field, with the understanding that the landowners' serfs would help to harvest them.[68] The Pale of Settlement was somewhat restricted by the removal of Astrakhan and the Caucasus as areas of Jewish settlement, and by an order that Jews, except those who owned their own real estate, were to be removed from within a zone fifty versts (about thirty-three miles) from the frontiers of the Russian provinces, as a means of discouraging Jewish involvement in the smuggling of contraband goods.[69]

An episode at the end of Alexander's reign demonstrated how completely the government had lost touch with the Jewish Question and its earlier efforts to resolve it. As if there were no experience with the Statute of 1804 and the consequences which accompanied its implementation, the regime set out to rediscover problem and solution. In 1821 crop failures in Belorussia produced yet another famine. A member of the Senate, Baranov, was sent to investigate the area. In his report Baranov joined the local landowners—who now knew well how to play the game—in placing the blame for peasant destitution on the Jews. The tsar responded by establishing another Jewish committee, the fourth of his reign, consisting of the ministers of internal affairs, finance, public education, and religious affairs. The committee was charged with developing a new law code for the Jews, to supersede the Statute of 1804. While the new committee set about its business, the central government forbade Jews in Belorussia to hold leases and began yet another program of resettlement. Only when the order to expel was given did the government give any thought to how the exiles would support themselves, whither they should be sent, and how to pay for the resettlement. Eventually twenty-thousand Jews were expelled from the countryside before the resettlement was halted, largely at the behest of harried local officials. Instead a program was developed calling for the expulsion of one-eighth of the Jewish population each year for the next eight years. This plan too was soon abandoned.[70]

The random, ad hoc nature of Russian legislation concerning the Jews after 1815 is a reminder of the important fact that the Jewish Question was hardly uppermost in the minds of the administrators of the empire. Virtually every edict was a response to a concrete problem, such as the discovery of "Judaizing" peasants, or a new outbreak of famine in Belorussia. Each of these responses took place in a vacuum, far removed from the general principles which past reformers had attempted to follow. This point is underscored through reference to a different context, areas newly added to the empire which had a Jewish population.

As a consequence of wars with Sweden, the Ottoman Empire, and Napoleonic France, Russia acquired Finland, Bessarabia, and the Kingdom of Poland. Alexander attempted to govern these areas through imaginative schemes of local autonomy. The status of the Jews in these annexed areas, excluding Finland, which had no Jews, was invariably subordinated to the grand, constitutionalist scheme.

Bessarabia was a case in point. The Russians resolved to administer this newly won territory—culturally identical to the Ottoman protectorate of Moldavia across the river Prut—through the traditional governmental system which had functioned under Ottoman rule. To achieve this end, Russian officials designed a "constitution" for Bessarabia in 1818. The constitution sought to preserve Bessarabian institutions while at the same time fitting the social system upon which they were based into a Russian framework. Problems which the Russians had encountered when dealing with the lands of partitioned Poland reappeared. How were the social classes of Bessarabia to be made to correspond to the four-tiered Russian model? The Bessarabian boyar (noble) class was fluid and imprecise, while the diverse peasant population possessed few analogies with the Russian serfs.[71]

The Bessarabian constitution of 1818 divided all inhabitants of the province into nine categories, one of which was the Jews. The tension which attended the classification of Russian Jewry reappeared: all Jews were assumed to fit into one of three classes—merchants, townspeople, or farmers. At the same time they were treated as members of a special subgroup, a Jewish merchant or a Jewish farmer, who did not necessarily enjoy all the privileges possessed by the Christian members of that estate. On the other hand, the Jews were promised all the privileges which had been given them before the Russian annexation by the rulers (hospodars) of Moldavia. Thus, Jews in Bessarabia were given important prerogatives which the Statute of 1804 denied their coreligionists in the western provinces of the empire. Bessarabian Jews were permitted to engage in the liquor trade and to hold leases on mills and distilleries, although they were specifically deprived of any control over the peasants who lived on the estates where the leases were located. The only significant disabilities borne by Bessarabian Jewry were prohibitions against buying or leasing private lands and serving in state service. Little effort was made to fit the Jews into the legal mold which had been fashioned for the other Jews of the empire.[72]

Of far greater consequence for the fate of Eastern European Jewry was the Russian grant of significant autonomy to the Kingdom of Poland ("Congress Poland") in 1815. The Kingdom of Poland was not "Russian" from a cultural, institutional, or constitutional point of view. The lands of the kingdom comprised the Polish ethnic heartland of the defunct Polish-Lithuanian Commonwealth. The kingdom was more than a mere adjunct to Russia, as signified in the constitutional arrangement of the new state by which the autocratic tsar of Russia was the king of Poland, a constitutional monarch. While a layer of Russian officials was to be found at the top, led by the tsar's brother, Grand Duke Constantine Pavlovich, the commander-in-chief of the army of the kingdom, and by the tsar's non-constitutional "delegate and plenipotentiary," N. N. Novosil'tsev, the country as a whole was administered directly by Poles until the Revolution of 1830. The legal system of Congress Poland was entirely separate from other regions of the empire. As a result, the status of Polish Jewry was unconnected to that of the Jews in Russia proper. Indeed, the Kingdom of Poland was not included in the Pale of Jewish Settlement to the very end of the empire itself. Despite the occasional yearnings of Russian officialdom to standardize the position of Jews throughout the empire, Polish Jewry always remained juridically distinct from Russian Jewry.

Poland nonetheless proved of great significance for the treatment of Rus-

sian Jewry. The kingdom had a large Jewish population strategically located in both the urban and rural economies. No less than Russian bureaucrats were Poles aware of a "Jewish Question" requiring internal reform.
Indeed, the Poles possessed a longer and richer reform tradition than did
the Russians, who borrowed from the Poles after the partitions. There thus
arose the phenomenon of an autonomous Polish government devising policies for the Jewish population which the Russian state power was continually required to confirm or deny. This situation was muddled by the fact
that the Russian administration in the kingdom, chiefly in the person of
Novosil'tsev, favored a milder approach to the Jews than the Polish authorities, and defended Jewish interests. An emphasis on reform in Congress
Poland, at the very moment that a creative reform impulse was on the wane
in Russia, ensured that Poland once again became the principal conduit into
Russia for ideas, prejudices, and proposals on the Jewish Question.

What held for official circles applied to the Jews as well. Polish Jewry,
while on the whole conservative and traditional, produced ideologues of
the Haskalah and advocates of religious reform in far greater numbers
than their Russian counterparts. Synagogue reform, educational innovation, and a Jewish periodical press all appeared in Congress Poland under
Alexander's rule.[73]

The Kingdom of Poland had not been created from scratch but was the
successor to a series of French protectorates fashioned by Napoleon Bonaparte in Eastern Europe. The most significant of these states was the
Grand Duchy of Warsaw, founded on 22 July 1807 N.S. and ruled by a
French ally, King Frederick August of Saxony. The grand duchy, composed of territory drawn from the Austrian and Prussian shares of the
partitions of Poland, was created to reward the Poles who had swelled the
armies of Revolutionary and Napoleonic France, and to establish a pro-
French outpost on the borders of Russia. The Jews were a significant
presence, a census of the grand duchy in 1810 recording 360,000 Jews out
of a total population of 4,334,280.[74] In theory the grand duchy was a
modern, nonfeudal state in the French mode. The Code Napoléon, employed as the state's civil code, established the theoretical equality of all
citizens before the law.

Despite the progressive rhetoric of the grand duchy's constitution, the
new state retained the contours of Polish Judeophobia. Taking inspiration
from the "Infamous Decree"[75] which Napoleon had directed against the
Jews of France in 1808, the Polish leadership of the grand duchy urged
restrictions on the rights of Polish Jews. In response to these pressures, on
17 October 1808 N.S., King Frederick August surreptitiously signed the
following decree:

> Residents of Our Duchy of Warsaw, professing the religion of
> Moses, are deprived of the political rights, which they have here-

N. N. Novosil'tsev

tofore enjoyed, for ten years. We hope that in the course of this time they will lose those qualities which so differentiate them from other inhabitants.

The aforementioned point does not prevent us from permitting some individual persons, even before the expiration of the ten-year period, from enjoying rights, if they deserve this great benevolence of Ours, and satisfy all the conditions which will be promulgated by

Us in individual statutes regarding persons professing the Mosaic faith.[76]

Although this specific decree spoke only about political rights, it soon became apparent that restrictions were to be placed on civil rights as well. Moreover, the government consistently refused to accede to the requests of individual Jews that it outline the conditions under which Jews might secure full political and civil rights.[77] The grand duchy was in the process of formulating anti-Jewish residential and occupational measures when its independence was swept away by the advancing Russian army in 1813.[78]

After an intense political struggle, the Congress of Vienna created a reconstituted Polish state under Russian hegemony. As noted above, Alexander resolved to employ a constitutional system, featuring extensive autonomy, to rule his new domain. It still remained necessary for the Russians to create the necessary instruments of government. This task was expedited by the retention of elements of previous governmental structures, including those of Austria, Prussia, the grand duchy, and even Prussian decrees promulgated when the grand duchy was briefly under Prussian occupation in 1806. Preparing to design a constitution, officials could not overlook the Jews, who in 1816 constituted 8.7 percent of the population (243,000 out of 2,778,200 inhabitants).[79] Favorable prospects for the Jews appeared ensured when partial direction of the provincial government created by Alexander to administer the Poles during the pre-constitutional period was entrusted to Prince Adam Czartoryski, a veteran of the Jewish reform committee of 1802. On 25 May 1815 this government set forth principles upon which the future constitution was to be based. Paragraph 36 declared that "the Jewish people preserve their civil rights which they have enjoyed until now under the existing laws and rules. A special instruction will establish the conditions under which the Jews are able to enjoy more widely the benefits of civil life."[80]

In July of 1815 a committee was appointed to review the condition of the Polish peasantry and, inescapably, of the Jews as well, because of their vital role in the peasant economy. The chairman of the committee was Czartoryski, who submitted a memorandum characteristic of his thought on the Jewish Question at that time. In some respects, this memorandum was a straightforward précis of the assumptions and principles of the committee of 1802. The source of rights given to the Jews, according to Czartoryski, could only be justice, humanity, the spirit of the age, and the interests of the state. Any shortcomings of the Jews could not be considered innate. Indeed, many of the charges made against them, such as the claim that they were lazy or lacked an aptitude for crafts and agriculture, were largely a reflection of unfounded Christian prejudices. Nothing in the Jewish religion prevented them from becoming good citizens. Czartoryski's conclusion was that the Jews could and should receive full rights

Prince Adam Czartoryski, shortly before his service on the first Jewish committee.

of citizenship as soon as they were capable of fulfilling their civic obligations. The task of the government was to eliminate everything which
degraded the Jews and separated them from the rest of the population, and
to promote everything which brought them closer to the Christian population. The significance of Czartoryski's formula lay in the fact that he
emphasized that the Jews had not yet developed to a sufficient degree to
be awarded full exercise of civil rights. This was a lead eagerly pursued by
the Polish political leadership, then and later.[81]

These general, theoretical precepts echoed the guidelines of 1804, but
when this new committee passed on to practical considerations the tone
shifted much as it had done a decade before. Jewish shortcomings, ascribed by Czartoryski to external conditions, were nonetheless characterized by the committee as an obstacle to the granting of full civil liberties.
The Jews would eventually receive equal rights, but first they had to
abandon the liquor trade and engage in agriculture. Such a *quid pro quo*
ensured that civil emancipation would not soon be forthcoming.[82]

It is not surprising, then, that the constitution for the new Kingdom of
Poland, promulgated on 27 November 1815, said not a word about the
Jews. To be sure, article 11 of the constitution guaranteed freedom of
religion, but the affirmation that "there shall be no distinction in the
enjoyment of civil and political rights" applied only to Christians.[83] Just as
significantly, at the same time as the constitution was being promulgated,
Alexander instructed N. N. Novosil'tsev, as his special representative in
Warsaw (and himself a veteran of the Second Jewish Committee), to
assemble materials relating to the needs of the Jews whereby their lot
might be improved but also so that they "might be more useful for this
area than heretofore."[84] The guiding rule that the Jews needed to be
rendered "harmless" for the rest of the population had easily made the
transition from Poland to Russia and back again.

While Poles shared the Russian conviction that the Jews must be
rendered harmless, they retained a different perspective as to what constituted their harmfulness. As noted above, Poland shared with Russia a
tradition of religious Judeophobia, but the Polish variety was more sophisticated and exotic. (As if to emphasize this fact, a series of ritual murder
accusations suddenly flared up in Poland and in the border province of
Grodno in 1816.) In the reconstituted Polish state, old prejudices began to
revive and to spread into Russia, much as they had done after the first
partition.

A distinctive feature of Polish and medieval European Judeophobia was
fear and suspicion of the Talmud as an anti-Christian codex. This suspicion had been purveyed especially by the Roman Catholic clergy, represented in the modern period by such articulate clerical spokesmen as
Stanisław Staszic, an outstanding Polish intellectual, patriot, and activist.
By 1816, Staszic had lapsed from his religious career and was a member of

the kingdom's Commission on Public Education and Religious Denominations. In that year he published an article in *Pamietnik Warszawski* entitled
"Concerning the Causes of the Harmfulness of the Jews" (*O przyczynakh
szkodliwości Żydów*). Staszic emphasized his belief that the Jews had
wandered far from the teachings of Moses. He placed the blame fully on
the Talmud, which encouraged the Jews to equate Christians with the
idolators of the Old Testament, against whom implacable hatred was
taught. In order to expose the evils of the Talmud, Staszic proposed that it
be translated into Polish.[85]

Staszic's ideas influenced Prince Czartoryski, who had shown no trace
of such prejudices while a member of the reform committee of 1802.
Now, in a special report which he submitted to the government on 6 May
1816, Czartoryski warned that contemporary Jews, by their beliefs and
actions, had completely departed from the principles and morality of the
Old Testament and were inimical to Christian civilization. They could be
reformed only by returning them to the tenets of the Old Testament.[86]
The final seal of approval on such concepts was provided by one of the
most famous desciples of Moses Mendelssohn, David Friedländer of Berlin. Invited by agents of the Polish government to make proposals for
Jewish reform in Poland, he submitted a memorandum in 1817 entitled
"The Correction of the Israelites in the Kingdom of Poland." Friedländer
attacked the backwardness of Polish Jewry in comparison with Jews elsewhere. Their low state he attributed to their Talmudic training, Hasidism, and the system of communal self-government, the kahal.[87] (These
criticisms of Friedländer were typical of "enlightened" Jews, who viewed
the lowly *Ostjuden* of Eastern Europe with scorn and disgust.)[88]

Russians, meanwhile, remained largely unaware of the existence of the
Talmud, much less its alleged harmfulness. Early Russian critics of the
Jews, like Governor Kakhovskii, ignored it, while Derzhavin's under-
standing of the Talmud was vague at best, until instructed by a Jewish
Maskil like Dr. Frank. The First Jewish Committee ignored the possible
significance of the Talmud, and the Statute of 1804 failed to mention it.
Even in the period of Alexandrine religious enthusiasm the Talmud at-
tracted little attention. Russians were finally alerted to the significance of
the Talmud through the efforts of another Roman Catholic clergyman in
Poland, the Abbé Luigi Chiarini.

L. A. Chiarini, an Italian, was Professor of Oriental Languages and
Antiquities at the University of Warsaw, and a member of the Commission on Old Testament Believers, created by the Polish government at the
very end of Alexander's reign. Chiarini received a commission from Tsar
Nicholas I to translate the Babylonian Talmud into French, and two
volumes were completed and issued in Leipzig in 1831. Of greater significance was the publication of a work based upon Chiarini's lectures on Jews
and Judaism at the University of Warsaw entitled *Théorie du Judaïsme* and

published in 1830. The work was a digest of anti-Talmudic lore, especially Eisenmenger's *Judaism Unmasked*.[89]

It took Chiarini's anti-Talmudic warnings over a decade to percolate into Russia. An article in the popular *Biblioteka dlia Chtenii* in 1835 which surveyed Jewish history mentioned the Talmud only in passing, in a neutral fashion.[90] An anonymous discussion of Judaism in the *Journal* of the Ministry of Public Education in 1838 offered a knowledgeable and objective discussion of the Talmud.[91] By 1846, in an article published in the *Journal* of the Ministry of Internal Affairs, a shift had become apparent in official thinking. In a lengthy discussion of the Talmud, the anonymous author complained that all that was moral in the Talmud was lost in the incompatibly greater amount that was immoral. The Talmud was condemned for engendering a spirit of fanaticism, arrogance, and hostility toward all other peoples. Significantly, among the sources which were cited as the basis for the article was Chiarini's *Théorie du Judaïsme*.[92] This was a public admission of the regime's concern with the effects of the Talmud, a concern which dated to about 1840 within the government, and which ushered in a period of new strategies to deal with the Jewish Question.[93]

Chiarini's true moment arrived in 1861, when the government of the reform-minded Alexander II was in the process of dismantling much of the restrictive legislation in place against the Jews. The newspaper *Den'*, edited by the Slavophile publicist I. S. Aksakov, created a sensation by publishing an article by "A. Aleksandrov" on the Talmud, which claimed that no Jew could be a good citizen while he adhered to the antisocial dictates of the Talmud. Aleksandrov's article, based in fact upon Chiarini's work, provided material for anti-Jewish publicists throughout the second half of the nineteenth century in Russia.[94]

Given the prevalence of these ideas in Poland, it is not surprising that the Polish government embarked upon an anti-Jewish legislative program almost from its inception. Under the leadership of the Polish viceroy, General Jósef Zajączek, the Polish State Council attempted a reform on the Russian model by attempting to expel all Polish Jews from the countryside. Ironically, the savior of the Jews was N. N. Novosil'tsev, the tsar's personal agent in the kingdom. He delayed the implementation of the expulsion order and ensured that it was submitted to Alexander for confirmation. Through Novosil'tsev's efforts the expulsion decree was modified to a mild restriction against the Jews selling alcohol to peasants on credit. Later, Novosil'tsev sabotaged an attempt of the police to expel Jews from streets in Warsaw where, under the old strictures of Polish law, they were forbidden to dwell.[95]

Most ambitious of all Novosil'tsev's interventions on behalf of Polish Jewry was his submission to the State Council in 1816 of an extensive reform proposal for the Jews. The plan would have led eventually to full civic equality for Jews in Poland. It called for the abolition of all past privileges and restrictions which had been placed upon the Jews. In return, Jews were to create a reformed school system, featuring instruction in Polish as well as Hebrew and Yiddish. Without schooling, Jews were to be denied the certificates necessary to marry or to carry on trade. Jews were to change the economic shape of their lives by abandoning the liquor trade in favor of agriculture. Jews were also to lose their system of autonomous self-government, and were to carry the most basic of civil obligations, military service. To those Jews who met these conditions, full political and civil rights would be granted.[96]

Contemporaries, as well as later historians, have wondered at Novosil'tsev's interest in the Jewish Question and his active defense of Jewish interests. The most widely accepted assumptions are that Novosil'tsev, renowned for his venality, received compensation from the Jewish community for his endeavors, a charge routinely made against any Russian state official who showed himself sympathetic to the Jews. Others have seen his efforts as an attempt to sow discord between Christians and Jews in Poland, as part of a Russian strategy of divide and rule.[97] While there may well be some truth in both of these assessments, it should also be noted that Novosil'tsev had served on the Second Jewish Committee in Russia, and this in itself could account for his interest in Jewish matters. His projected reform, moreover, displays many affinities with the Statute of 1804, as well as the recommendations of the Third Jewish Committee.

There was never much chance that Novosil'tsev's plan would be adopted, since it ran counter to the hostile attitudes of the Polish members of the State Council. Indeed, whatever its merit, its sponsorship by Novosil'tsev was sufficient to discredit it. Novosil'tsev was, as early as 1816, widely detested for his heavy-handed, irregular intervention in the workings of the Polish constitutional system. Even his dealings with the Jews demonstrated his disdain for procedural niceties. To give but one example, when the Jews of Warsaw considered themselves victimized by the local administration, Novosil'tsev advised them to appeal over its head, directly to St. Petersburg.[98] Consequently, Novosil'tsev's reform was decisively defeated in the State Council. On the other hand, the Jewish Question became so polarized that a rival proposal offered by Novosil'tsev's opponents, and far less sympathetic to the Jews, was also blocked. Political deadlock could not prevent the partial victory of the anti-Jewish policy of the Poles, however. In 1818 the legislative restrictions of the Grand Duchy of Warsaw on the Jews were due to expire. Given the absence of a new code of laws to govern the Jews, the State Council was able to persuade Alexander to reconfirm all the existing legislation.[99]

Nor could the question of Jewish military service be postponed. In the grand duchy the Jews had been exempted from military service in return for a cash payment. Ostensibly this arrangement was implemented because the Jews, not enjoying full civil rights, could not be expected to bear full civic obligations. (In fact, the duchy's minister of finance argued that the exemption payments were necessary for the military budget. In a preamble to the published decree freeing the Jews from service—deleted at the command of the king—it was noted that the Jews were unfit for military service and that the important duty of defending the nation "could not yet be entrusted to them." Whatever the motive, the Jews did not complain.)[100] In the Congress Kingdom the Jews were initially expected to serve with other citizens. The recruitment decree, implemented in 1816, also exempted from service all male citizens under the age of twenty who had married before the decree came into effect. This exemption covered so many Jews, who had a custom of early marriage, that Alexander became concerned and ratified a new decree withdrawing the exemption from married Jews. A greater number of Jewish recruits pleased neither Viceroy Zajączek nor the commander-in-chief of the Polish army, Grand Duke Constantine Pavlovich, both of whom considered large numbers of Jews in the army "not in the interest of national honor."[101] Therefore the pretext which had been employed to exempt Jews from service in the grand duchy was resurrected and the Jews were freed from the army "until such time as they be given the rights of political life."[102] National honor was not insulted by accepting financial compensation from the Jews in lieu of personal service. As in Russia proper, the Jews paid an exemption fee, but while in Russia it was a flat fee of five hundred rubles per exempted recruit, in Poland lengthy negotiations were required to reach a settlement. In the end, Polish Jewry, excepting Warsaw, paid a ransom of 600,000 florins per annum, while the Jews of Warsaw alone paid 700,000 florins.[103] Not until the reign of Alexander's successor, Nicholas I, did policy change and Jewish recruitment begin.

One further arrangement between the Polish state and the Jewish community occurred in this period which had important implications for Russian Jewry. This was the abolition of the kahal system in Poland. Such a measure, as noted in Chapter 5, was the logical, if unaccomplished, conclusion of the investigations of the Jewish Committee of 1802. A variety of considerations, both fiscal and administrative, spared the kahal structure in Russian lands. In Poland, on the other hand, a small constituency for abolition emerged from among the Jews themselves. A small band of "enlightened" Jews waged a vigorous campaign against the kahal. In pamphlets and petitions they decried the abuse of power by the kahal administration, exemplified by the capricious and uncontrolled collection and expenditure of funds, and its tyranny over the Jewish community through the power of excommunication. Poles were willing to do what the Russian government was not. On 20 December 1821/1 January 1822 the kahal structure was abolished and replaced with a system of "Congregational Boards"(*Dozory Bożnice*), headed by the community rabbi and his assistant and three locally elected "overseers." The board was charged with supervising the community's ritual-religious functionaries (such as ritual slaughters), while the civil and fiscal responsibilities of the old kahal were given to Polish officials. After some initial resistance from the Jews, the system of Congregational Boards begin to function tolerably well.[104]

This approach to abolition of the kahal, which did tend to encourage the integration of the Jews into the political life of the nation, should be contrasted with the abolition of the kahal as it was finally accomplished in Russia in 1844. The kahal was "abolished," but a special set of new Jewish functionaries was created in order to carry out the collection of taxes, which were still apportioned by the community, as they had been done by the kahal. Self-rule was abolished, but replaced with self-taxation: it was a system whereby the Jews lost the privileges which were associated with political autonomy, while retaining all the burdens. Unlike the Polish approach, the abolition of the Russian kahal in 1844 did nothing to promote the integration of Jews in the wider Gentile community.[105]

Since the Polish government could not escape the necessity of dealing with the Jews, it is not surprising that nascent Polish public opinion also took an active interest in the Jewish Question. When the first Sejm of the Kingdom of Poland convened in 1818, proposals for the legal reform of Polish Jewry were on its agenda. This provoked a flood of pamphlets and newspaper articles, representing a chorus of conflicting opinions on how to deal with the Jews. Yet the polemics did share one common feature: they addressed the distinctive problems and features of Polish Jewry without a word on the situation of the Jews in Russia.[106] (The reason for the Polish failure to discuss the situation of the Jews in the wider Russian Empire is not as obvious as it might seem. There were large Jewish communities in the Russian provinces created from pre-partition Lithuania, areas which the Poles hoped to rejoin eventually to the kingdom. State officials in the Grand Duchy of Warsaw had discussed limiting the participation of the Jews in the liquor trade, and the minister of police argued that action might most expeditiously be taken before the hoped-for annexation of Lithuania, whose nobility were so dependent upon the alcohol-based economy.)[107]

"Public opinion" in Russia, insofar as it existed, was not invited by the autocracy to pass judgment on any social issue, the Jewish Question included. Since native commentators were missing, the debates and legislative efforts of the kingdom were followed with care by Russian administrators as a useful source of information. The slow penetration of Polish attitudes toward the Talmud has already been noted. Likewise, when Russians embarked yet again on an attempt to regularize the legal status of Russian Jewry, Polish methods were studied with care.

The fact that it was thought necessary to appoint another Jewish committee—the fourth—in 1823 reveals the government's disillusionment with the progress of reform since 1804. The new committee was given two specific tasks: to eliminate or attenuate those special Jewish institutions which enabled the Jews to circumvent governmental measures aimed at the common good; and to move the Jews out of the harmful occupations whereby they despoiled the rest of the population.[108] This mandate testifies to the form which the Jewish Question had by now assumed in Russia: the task of reformers was to "render the Jews harmless" politically, socially, and especially economically.

The Fourth Jewish Committee, whose existence and mandate were confirmed by Alexander's successor, Nicholas I, in 1825, produced a new statute for the Jews in 1835. The preamble to the new law observed that "with the placing into effect of this statute [of 1804], local difficulties were uncovered, indicating from the very beginning the need for several modifications of it."[109] This rhetoric notwithstanding, the new statute, while more detailed and precise than its predecessor, did not depart from its underlying assumptions. It too operated under the guideline that the Jews had to be "rendered harmless." This legal guideline proved to be the most enduring legacy of the Alexandrine period, persisting to the very end of the monarchy itself.[110]

7

Russians and Jews: The Unofficial View

This study has sought to answer three questions fundamental for an understanding of the history of the Jews in the Russian Empire: What was the Jewish Question in Russia? How did Russians become aware of it? How did they propose to remedy it?

Russia acquired a significant Jewish population as a by-product of the partitions of Poland. From the perspective of legal precedent, Russia was totally unequipped to deal with the Jews, having in her most recent past maintained a tradition of religiously motivated exclusion, with deep roots in old Muscovite culture. More concerned with maintaining order in the newly acquired regions, Russian administrators were initially content to retain the status quo in Belorussia. The first Russian administrators to deal with the Jewish Question were the offspring of Peter the Great's administrative reforms. While they might harbor religious prejudice, or even manifest it in their rhetoric, such prejudice never served as either the starting point or the foundation of state policy.

In the Polish-Lithuanian Commonwealth itself, the Jewish Question was a product of the social, economic, and political relationships which existed between Jews and Gentiles. The Russian authorities unthinkingly blundered across this Jewish Question in the course of governing a region of which they had little practical knowledge. The Russian government, declaring itself for the status quo in the annexation decree of 1772, soon gave to the Jews prerogatives which they had not customarily enjoyed in Polish society, and this triggered appeals to the central government from aggrieved elements of the Belorussian population. Faced with protests and dissension, the government, in the person of the Senate, pursued crudely pragmatic policies: it sought to placate the Jews by granting them theoretical rights in response to their own petitions; to placate the szlachta by leaving the disposal of important economic prerogatives, such as distilling, in their hands; to placate the Belorussian townspeople by restricting the electoral rights of Jews where and when necessary. The Russian government, in the capital or in the provinces, pursued no consistent or well-articulated anti-Jewish policy, but its pragmatism did lead to the implementation of policies which were, de facto, discriminatory and restrictive. To appease the merchantry of Moscow, for example, the state restricted the movement of Jews, creating the embryonic Pale of Settlement. To restore health to a shattered exchequer, the government devised a double tax for the Jews. Such pragmatism could work in favor of the Jews as well: seeking revenue and suspicious of the fighting capabilities of Jewish recruits, the government exempted the Jewish *meshchanstvo* from the onerous burden of military service.

Thus, under Catherine, the Jews emerged in the mind of Russian officialdom as a factor that had occasionally to be taken into consideration, especially because of their concentration in the urban centers of Belorussia. Yet despite the negative evaluations made by officials, such as Kakhovskii, other factors, such as the poverty of the two Belorussian provinces and the sparseness of the population, ensured that the Jewish Question was never seen as anything more than an occasional nuisance.

The second and third partitions gave Russia vast new territories and hundreds of thousands of Jews, whom it was impossible for the government to ignore or neglect. Even then the Jewish Question, still not fully developed in Russian minds, came to the fore only because of local peculiarities—the recurrence of famine in the now-unified territory of Belorussia and Lithuania. Russian investigators, charged with investigating the famine-prone local economy, found amid a plethora of complex causes of rural distress one explanation that was simple and direct: blame everything on the Jews. Vested interests, urban and rural, were delighted to encourage the government in this belief and to define and reinforce it with an overlay of their own traditional anti-Jewish prejudices.

Despite assimilating existing prejudices against the Jews, Russians, now intent on the need to reform the status of the Jews, were not necessarily ill disposed to them, for they were also the inheritors of a Western reform tradition which had slowly infiltrated eastward. This tradition operated within a gradualist, rationalist context which held that reform would benefit both the state and the Jews themselves. The Jews need merely permit the cleansing action of rational reform to work on them, and they would become worthy citizens of the wider, religiously neutral community. Attempting to blend these contradictory elements, Russian reform became a tangle of the optimistic rhetoric of the Enlightenment, the prejudice-reinforced complaints of vested economic interests, and sweeping theories of reform which appeared at first glance to be entirely rational but had little basis in existing conditions. Such a combination produced enlightened formulae to justify essentially restrictive, unworkable schemes. Reforms such as the Statute of 1804 encompassed both positive and negative elements, but it was the latter, represented by resettlement and occupational restrictions, which usually won official favor in practice, if only because such expedients appeared to be both cheaper and easier. The government sought to "save the peasants" and to "improve the Jews," but always in that order of priority. Since the proposed reforms were in any case unrealistic, visualizing the instantaneous transformation of tavern-keepers into farmers and factory workers, they were bound to fail. The end result was economic dislocation, bitterness, and disillusionment. What administrators tended to abandon was the rhetoric, sympathetic toward the Jews, while maintaining restrictions which were reinforced and elaborated in later decades. The defeatism of the government when confronting the Jewish Question and its willingness to rely upon discrimination, exclusion, and crude social engineering were the enduring legacy of official Russia's first encounter with the Jews.

There remains one final question upon which this study can only touch, given the paucity of sources. To what extent did the ideas and assumptions prevalent in official circles percolate into the consciousness of the Russian public?

In the case of the Russian peasantry, no satisfactory answer can be given. The failure of proverbs, songs, or other folk literature to touch on Jews and Judaism makes the characterization of peasant attitudes mere speculation. Such a state of affairs has not kept contemporaries or later observers from assuming a strong tradition of religious hatred. Empress Catherine II refused to ratify the readmission of Jews into Russia out of concern for the sensibilities of the devout. Senator Karl-Henrikh Geiking, during the debate over the admissibility of evidence by Jews in civil court cases, argued that Christians were more likely to act prejudicially against Jews, whom they viewed as "deicides, cursed by the Almighty." On the other hand, the spread of Sabbatarianism among Russian peasants indicates a receptiveness to Judaic religious ideas. Against this particular evidence, however, was the decision of the government to accuse the Sabbatarians of apostasy from Christianity to Judaism, a charge which would be effective only if there was strong religious Judeophobia among the peasants.

Educated Russian society, while never as mute as the peasantry, was nonetheless quite unforthcoming. Russian literature, often a useful guide to social values, and very eloquent on the Jewish Question in later times, offered little testimony before 1825. The few literary references that do exist invariably depict the Jews in stereotypical terms borrowed from the West. For example, the renowned satirist N. I. Novikov, writing in 1769, before the passage of Jews under Russian rule, offered a portrait of miserly guile in the person of "Zhidomor," or "Jewish mug."[1] A. S. Pushkin, in poems like "The Covetous Knight" and "The Black Shawl," also failed to rise above the stereotypical, although Pushkin must have been acquainted with Jews as a consequence of his involuntary residence in Kishinev in Bessarabia, where there was a large Jewish population.

The first literary treatment to rise above cliché was N. M. Karamzin's *Letters of a Russian Traveler* (*Pis'ma russkogo puteshestvennika*), published between 1791 and 1801, which contained a description of the Frankfurt ghetto. Richard Pipes has called this account "one of the earliest sympathetic treatments of the Jews in Russian literature."[2] To the extent that Karamzin depicts the Jews as human beings, real flesh-and-blood characters, this is true. At the same time, his account is rife with stereotypical elements and ambivalent sentiments as well. Karamzin notes a pleasant conversation with an intelligent young Jew and his cultured wife, but laments that his enjoyment was dampened by the pervasive stench of their quarters. Similarly, sympathy and condescension are present in equal parts in Karamzin's description of the Jewish synagogue in Frankfurt: "They wished me to see their synagogue. I entered it as if into a gloomy cavern, thinking: 'God of Israel, God of the Chosen People! Should one really worship You here?' Weakly shone the candles in the atmosphere laden with putridness. Despondency, sorrow, fear appeared on the faces of those at prayer; nowhere was there to be seen tenderness; tears of grateful love did not wash their cheeks; their gaze was not directed toward heaven in reverential rapture. I saw some sort of criminals, awaiting the death penalty with trepidation, and hardly daring to beg their judge for clemency."[3] Indeed, Karamzin's account resembles very closely typical travel accounts of Russian visitors to the Pale of Jewish Settlement in the 1850s, accounts which were denounced by Jewish critics as Judeophobic.[4]

As a general rule, the published opinions of educated Russian society followed the lead of the government in the development of attitudes toward the Jews. *Vestnik Evropy*'s commendation of the Statute of 1804 reflected the same facile optimism that moved the members of the reform committee itself. At the same time, the travel notes of Metropolitan Platon indicate that official concerns about the economic harmfulness of the Jews in the western provinces were shared by prominent members of society. It is also interesting to observe that although Platon was a Russian churchman, and no friend of religious toleration, his account was devoid of purely religious prejudices against the Jews. He restricted his observations to the condemnation of Jewish malice, guile, and exploitation of the peasantry.

Indeed, one must look far afield to find any discussion of the Jewish Question from an overtly religious perspective. One of the few examples appeared in the memoirs of the Decembrist F. N. Glinka. When a fellow Decembrist, G. A. Peretts, the son of the prominent contractor in the capital, mentioned his father's dream of bringing all European Jewry together in a state in the Crimea or the Far East, Glinka recalled his reaction: "Well, then, do you want to bring on the end of the world? They say that it is written in the Scriptures (at that time I did not yet know the Scriptures) that when the Jews acquire their freedom, the world will end."[5] To this curious bit of eschatology may be joined the theme of a contemporary poem by V. A. Zhukovskii, "Agasver," which treated the "Wandering Jew," cursed by Christ to wander the earth until the Second Coming.[6] Both these motifs are of obvious Western origin and give little hint of tangible, practical religious prejudice. On the other hand, G. A. Peretts was denied admission to a St. Petersburg Masonic Lodge in 1811, on the grounds that the Christian orientation of Masonry did not permit the recruitment of Jews. Since Peretts had long before converted to Lutheranism, V. I. Semevskii had suggested that this explanation was only a ploy to mask personal antipathies toward Peretts.[7] V. N. and L. N. Peretts, to the contrary, see the rejection as indicative of anti-Semitic sentiments among the Russian aristocrats who made up the Masonic movement.[8]

Whatever their personal feelings, the ideologues of the Decembrist movement included the Jewish Question on the agenda of social ills which their activities were designed to mitigate.[9] N. M. Murav'ev devised a draft constitution for the Decembrist Northern Society which initially envisioned the restriction of Jewish electoral rights in the postrevolutionary government. In subsequent drafts this restriction was dropped altogether.[10]

The most developed Decembrist treatment of the Jews was contained in Pavel Pestel's famous *Russkaia Pravda*, his blueprint for a provisional government which would rule Russia after a revolution and prepare the way for the creation of a progressive and reformed Russian state. One of the obstacles to the attainment of such a progressive state, Pestel believed, was the Jewish community. Pestel's description of the Jews demonstrates how negative perspectives were ascendant in Russian thought on the subject. Pestel's chapter on the Jews could have been written using nothing but Derzhavin's work as a source and shows a number of interesting affinities (although there is no evidence that Pestel in fact was familiar with Derzhavin's original work). As Pestel saw it, the Jewish Question consisted of three main elements: the close ties which bound all Jews together and which were stronger than the loyalty they owed to any state; the power of the rabbis over all Jews, a power which they employed to block enlightenment and integration and to hide from the outside authorities any wrongdoing within the Jewish community; and religious beliefs which set the Jews apart from all other peoples, secure in the belief that their Messiah would grant them domination over all other nations. Such attitudes led inevitably to the fundamental aspects of Jewish life in Russia: dishonesty, exploitation, and alienation.[11]

Only two remedies appeared open to Pestel: a gathering of Jewish rabbis and leaders who would propose to the government measures to remedy the existing condition of the Jews, or expulsion en masse from Russia, preferably into Asia Minor, where they could build an independent state.[12]

The most striking thing about Decembrist proposals for the reformation of the Jews was that they were made at all. The Decembrists were engaged in an attack upon the very foundations of the tsarist autocracy, yet their leading theoreticians still felt the need to consider the Jewish Question, despite the fact that it was on the periphery of Russian politics. Moreover, these activists who sought the destruction of the autocratic state in the name of constitutionalist, liberal principles fully shared the state's concern over the perceived harmfulness of the Jews, as well as its propensity to reorder Jewish life in Russia. As yet this shared concern was a minor phenomenon, but in the next century the alarms of state and society would join into a common chorus.

Notes

CHAPTER I

1. From the community record book of the Minsk kahal for 1802, see chapter 5, n. 25.

2. See Bernard D. Weinryb, "The Beginnings of East-European Jewry in Legend and Historiography," in *Studies and Essays in Honor of Abraham A. Neuman* (Leiden, 1962), 445–502. In 1266, for instance, the Church Council of Wrocław (Breslau) attempted to pass discriminatory legislation against the Jews, with the principal aim of segregating them from Christians, but with little success. Simon M. Dubnow, *History of the Jews in Russia and Poland* (Philadelphia, 1916–1920), 1:48.

3. Majer Bałaban, "Pravovoi stroi Evreev v Pol'she v srednie i novye veka," *ES*, 2 (January–March 1910): 54–55.

4. Ibid., 59–60.

5. David B. Teimanas, *L'autonomie des communautés juives en Pologne aux XVIe et XVIIe siècles* (Paris, 1933), 21.

6. Dubnow, *History*, 1:45–47.

7. An interesting example of such a collection of privileges was preserved in the community archives of Kraków until the Second World War. Confirmed by King Stanisław Augustus on 14 June 1765, it comprised three parts: a group of privileges given to the Jews of all Great Poland by Casimir the Great (1333–1370) and reconfirmed by Casimir IV in 1453 at the request of the Jews of Poznán; privileges of later kings which regulated the social and legal position of Jews in the entire kingdom; and a group of special royal concessions granted at various times to the Jews of Kraków. It is only through such copies that the exact content of the earliest grants in known. M. Schorr, "Krakovskii svod evreiskikh statutov i privilegii," *ES* 1 (April–June 1909): 247–48.

8. Salo W. Baron, *The Jewish Community* (Philadelphia, 1942), 1:22.

9. Bałaban, "Pravovoi stroi" 2 (April–June 1910): 168.

10. Norman Davies, *God's Playground: A History of Poland* (New York, 1982), 1:131, recounts the negotiations between the elders of the Kraków community and treasury officials in 1564.

11. Ibid, 172.

12. By 5 November 1519 the nascent kahal structure was already described in a decree of Sigismund I. Reference was made to the head, called the rabbi or doctor, to two elders, and to a *shkolnik*. Ibid., 172.

13. Teimanas, *L'autonomie*, 38.

14. Bałaban, "Pravovoi stroi" 2 (April–June, 1910): 177. This referred to the community of Kraków and can be extended to the rest of Poland only by inference.

15. Ibid., 174.

16. Ibid., 182; ibid., 3 (July–September, 1910): 324–26.

17. Salo W. Baron, *A Social and Religious History of the Jews* (New York, 1952–1976), 16:291.

18. Isaiah Trunk, "The Council of the Province of White Russia," *YIVO Annual of Jewish Social Science*, vol. 11 (1956–1957), 188.

19. Teimanas, *L'autonomie*, presents a comprehensive examination of the myriad functions of the Va'ad, 35–55. Such bodies were also common among the Jews of Central Europe. See Jacob Katz, *Tradition and Crisis* (Glencoe, Ill., 1961), 122–34.

20. Gershon David Hundert, "An Advantage to Peculiarity? The Case of the Polish Commonwealth," *Association for Jewish Studies Review* 6 (1981): 33. For a

revealing diagram of the organs of Jewish autonomy in Poland, see Davies, *God's Playground*, 1: 442–43. In a recent article, based upon an examination of the institutions of the Scottish and Armenian communities in Poland, Gershon David Hundert suggests that the Jewish kahal, with all its trappings, may not have been the unique institution envisioned by the majority of those who have studied its existence in Poland. He also cites evidence to suggest that the traditional picture of the kahal as in total control of all Jews who were permanent residents within its territorial jurisdiction may be exaggerated. "On the Jewish Community in Poland during the Seventeenth Century: Some Comparative Perspectives," *REJ* 142 (July–December 1983): 349–72.

21. See Wiktor Weintraub, "Tolerance and Intolerance in Old Poland," *Canadian Slavonic Papers* 13 (1971): 21–44.

22. Bernard D. Weinryb, *The Jews of Poland* (Philadelphia, 1973), 46.

23. Controversy still surrounds the case of Katarzyna Weigel Zalaszowska, who was executed in 1539 for rejecting the Catholic doctrine of the Trinity. She has variously been seen as a "Judaizer" and as a proto-Anti-Trinitarian. M. Bałaban, *Dzieje Żydow w Krakówie i na Kazimierzu, 1304–1868* (Kraków, 1912), 1:77–78; Weintraub, "Tolerance and Intolerance," 37. See also Janusz Tazbir, "Die Reformation in Polen und das Judentum," *JGO* 31 (1983): 386–400.

24. Teimanas, *L'autonomie*, 137–38.

25. Ibid., 138–39.

26. Weinryb, *Jews of Poland*, 152–54.

27. Jacob Goldberg, "Poles and Jews in the 17th and 18th Centuries: Rejection or Acceptance," *JGO* 22 (1974): 250–51.

28. Hundert, "An Advantage to Peculiarity?" 32–33.

29. Ibid., 249.

30. Elena Gekker, "Evrei v pol'skikh gorodakh vo vtoroi polovine XVIII veka," *ES* 5 (July–September 1913): 325–26.

31. Ibid., 5 (April–June 1913), 199.

32. Bałaban, "Pravovoi stroi" 3 (January–March 1911): 40–43. For a description of the creation and growth of the Jewish ghetto in Wilno see Israel Cohen, *Vilna* (Philadelphia, 1943), 30–37.

33. Mark Wischnitzer, *A History of Jewish Crafts and Guilds* (New York, 1965), 213–14.

34. Baron, *Social and Religious History*, 16:257.

35. Elena Gekker, "Iudofobiia v Pol'she XVIII veka," *ES* 5 (October–December 1913): 439–40. Such accusations were not restricted to Jews but were also made against Scots, Armenians, and other groups. Hundert, "Advantage to Peculiarity?" 26.

36. The Lithuanian Va'ad had developed the concept of "acquired right" (in Hebrew *ḥazaqah*) in order to keep Jews from continually outbidding one another. It provided that a Jew who held a lease for three years and who met all his obligations was to be free of rival bidders for the rest of his life. Baron, *Social and Religious History*, 16:273.

37. Wischnitzer, *Jewish Crafts*, 227. For an overview of the role of the Jews in the early modern economy of Europe, see Salo W. Baron, Arcadius Kahan, et al., *Economic History of the Jews* (New York, 1975), 55–75.

38. This power of apportionment existed on a hierarchical scale within autonomous Polish Jewry. The national Va'adim assessed regional congresses within Poland and Lithuania, which in turn assessed the local kahals. If the local kahal possessed a satellite community or *przykahal*, it in turn assessed it. Teimanas, *L'autonomie*, 91.

39. Baron, *Jewish Community*, 1:23–24.

40. Teimanas, *L'autonomie*, 45, for Kraków; and Baron, *Jewish Community*, 1:48, for Lwow.

41. The kahal collected considerably more than just state taxes, however, since the community required revenue for its various internal functions. Similar charges of discrimination by the rich against the poor were especially prevalent after 1827 when the regime of Nicholas I required Jewish military conscription. Almost without exception it was the poor who bore the brunt of military service. Levitats, *Jewish Community*, 61–68.

42. Bałaban, "Pravovoi stroi" 2 (July–September 1910): 327.

43. Dubnow, *History*, 1:335–36, provides a detailed description of the destruction of individual Jewish communities.

44. Baron, *Jewish Community*, 2:335–36.

45. I. Galant, "Zadolzhennost' evreiskikh obshchin v XVII veke," *ES* 5 (January–March 1913): 129–32.

46. Cohen, *Vilna*, 171.

47. I. Trunk, "Council of White Russia," 203.

48. Cohen, *Vilna*, 172–75. The contraction of heavy debts in order to repay loans was not a phenomenon restricted to the Jewish communities of Poland. In France such loans proved a serious problem during consideration of Jewish emancipation in the midst of the French Revolution. The revolutionary government ultimately demanded the dissolution of the autonomous Jewish community, since all corporate bodies had been abolished. At the same time the Jews were made responsible as individuals for the debts contracted by the communities of which they had once been a part. See Zosa Szajkowski, *Autonomy and Communal Jewish Debts during the French Revolution* (New York, 1959). The government of the Austrian Empire faced similar problems in 1781 when Galician Jewry began to pile up tax arrears. A rate scale for repayment was set up, but the Jews were 82,131 gulden in arrears after the first year. M. Bałaban, "Perekhod pol'skikh Evreev pod vlast' Avstrii," *ES* 5 (July–September 1913), 293. The Russian government was inclined to write off this confusing welter of debts contracted by the Jews under Polish rule, but at least one reformer, Derzhavin, paid careful attention to the problem. For a wider discussion of Jewish credit operations in Poland, suggesting mercantile motives for large-scale borrowing, see Gershon David Hundert, "Jews, Money, and Society in the Seventeenth-Century Polish Commonwealth: The Case of Krakow," *JCS* 43 (1981): 261–74.

49. Wischnitzer, *Jewish Crafts*, 223.

50. For this motif, see Father Rawita-Gawroński, *Żydzi w historji literaturze ludowej na Rusi* (Warsaw, 1924), 237–66; Vladimir Antonovich and Mikhail Dragomanov, *Istoricheskie pesni malorusskogo naroda*, vol. 2, pt. 1 (Kiev, 1875), 20–32. Information on Jewish leaseholding is contained in Baron, *Economic History*, 125–28, 132–38.

51. Jedrzej Kitowicz complained in the eighteenth century that "whenever the diet convenes to expel the Jews from Warsaw, the Ukrainian and Lithuanian deputies, being educated among the Jews, not knowing any other burghers but Jews, used to being supplied by the Jews with goods and all other necessities of life, from school days fed on Jewish bread and cracknels, made drunk by Jewish drinks . . . others bribed by handsome protection money by the Jews, shout with all their might in their defense." Goldberg, "Poles and Jews," 258.

52. Cohen, *Vilna*, 137–40.

53. Trunk, "Council of White Russia," 196.

54. See Weinryb, *Jews of Poland*, 262–303.

55. Simon Dubnow. "Vmeshatel'stvo russkogo pravitel'stva v antikhasidskuiu bor'bu (1800–1801)," *ES* 2 (January–March 1910): 84–109; and *ES* 2 (April–June 1910): 253–82.

56. W. F. Reddaway et al., eds., *The Cambridge History of Poland* (Cambridge, Eng., 1951), 110–11, 152–53, 175–76; Robert Howard Lord, *The Second Partition of Poland* (Cambridge, Mass., 1915), 54, 390–91.

57. Bałaban, "Perekhod," 291.

58. Arnold Springer, "Enlightened Despotism, and Jewish Reform: Prussia, Austria, and Russia," *California Slavic Studies* 11 (1980): 240.

59. Ibid.

60. I. Kamanin, "Perepisi evreiskogo naseleniia v iugozapadnom krae v 1765–1791 gg.," *Arkhiv Iugo-Zapadnom Rossii*, pt. 5, vol. 2, sects. 1 and 2 (Kiev, 1890), 217.

61. Iulii I. Gessen, *Istoriia evreiskogo naroda v Rossii* (Petrograd, 1925), 1:84–85.

CHAPTER 2

1. S. H. Cross and O. P. Sherbowitz-Wetzor, eds. and trs., *The Russian Primary Chronicle: Laurentian Text* (Cambridge, Mass., 1953), 97.

2. Bernard Weinryb, "The Beginnings of East-European Jewry in Legend and Historiography," in *Studies and Essays in Honor of Abraham A. Neuman* (Leiden, 1962), 499–500.

3. Norman Golb and Omeljan Pritsak, *Khazarian Hebrew Documents of the Tenth Century* (Ithaca and London, 1982), 31–32.

4. See Henrik Birnbaum, "On Some Evidence of Jewish Life and Anti-Jewish Sentiments in Medieval Russia," *Viator* 4 (1973): 232–35, for a discussion of Jewish place names in Kiev. The letter of the Kiev Jewish community found in *Khazarian Hebrew Documents* is evidence of loans and trade as engaged in by Kievan Jews, 6–7.

5. Sergei M. Solov'ev, *Istoriia Rossii s drevneishikh vremen* (Moscow, 1959–1966), 1:401–2.

6. Dubnow, *History*, 1:32; George Vernadsky, *Kievan Russia* (New Haven, 1959), 94.

7. The dramatic episodes of Byzantine persecution of Jews should not obscure the fact that Byzantine Orthodoxy was also capable of lengthy periods of toleration of and accommodation with the Jews. Joshua Starr notes that in the period of Byzantine history from 641 to 1204, 90 percent of the time was free from general and serious persecution. The three emperors who did persecute the Jews did so as part of a program directed against all dissident faiths. *The Jews in the Byzantine Empire, 641–1204* (New York, 1939), 8. Ideology emphasized intolerance, however, especially the segregation of Jews from concourse with Christians.

8. George P. Fedotov, *The Russian Religious Mind* (New York, 1960), 69–93.

9. Dmitro Abramovich, ed., *Kievo-Pechers'kii Paterik* (Kiev, 1930), 106–8. Even here the nature of the Paterikon must be recalled, as well as its possible debt to Greek originals.

10. For a brief analysis of this particular tale, see David K. Prestel, "A Comparative Analysis of Two Patericon Stories," *Russian History*, 7 (1980): 11–20.

11. Birnbaum, "Evidence," 235–38.

12. Fedotov, *Russian Religious Mind*, 92.

13. For St. Hugh of Lincoln, see *New Catholic Encyclopedia* (New York, 1967), 192. It might be noted in passing that the cult of another child martyr done to death by Jews, Simon of Trent (+1475), did not spread to Poland until the late seventeenth century. Baron, *Social and Religious History* 16:101.

14. Dmitri Obolensky, "Russia's Byzantine Heritage," in Michael Cherniavsky, ed., *The Structure of Russian History* (New York, 1970), 17–18.

15. For these motifs see Joshua Tractenberg, *The Devil and the Jews* (London, 1943).

16. "Ecclesia" and "Synagoga" were female figures erected in Gothic cathedrals in the thirteenth century to symbolize the Christian Church triumphant and the Jewish Synagogue rejected and fallen. Wolfgang Seiferth, *Synagogue and Church in the Middle Ages* (New York, 1970), and Henry Kraus, *The Living Theatre of Medieval Art* (Philadelphia, 1967), 139–62.

17. M. Khalanskii, "Bylina o Zhidovine," *Russkii Filologicheskii Vestnik* 23 (1890): 1–23, argues that the tradition of the Jewish bogatyr' was based on a misunderstanding of the "Giant" (*Dzhid*) in the Serbian tradition. Still, whatever the derivation, the tale offered a portrait of the Jew far different from the usual Western stereotypes.

18. Solov'ev, *Istorii*, 2:189 and 527–28.

19. Birnbaum, "Evidence," 243.

20. See the numerous examples in Shemu'el Ettinger, "The Muscovite State and Its Attitudes toward the Jews" (in Hebrew), *Zion* 18 (1953): 136–68.

21. Baron, *Social and Religious History*, 16:175 and 398, n.11.

22. *Pamiatniki diplomaticheskikh snoshenii Moskovskogo gosudarstva s Pol'sko-Litovskim*, II. *Sbornik Imperatorskogo Russkogo Istoricheskogo Obshchestva* (St. Petersburg, 1867–1916): vol. 59, pt. 21, 341–42.

23. Some standard interpretations of the Judaizing Heresy are found in E. E. Golubinskii, *Istoriia russkoi tserkvi* (Moscow, 1900–1917), II; N. A. Kazakova and Ia. S. Lur'e, *Antifeodal'nye ereticheskie dvizheniia na Rusi XIV–nachala XVI veka* (Moscow and Leningrad, 1955); A. I. Klibanov, *Reformatsionnye dvizheniia v Rossii v XIV–pervoi polovine XVI vv* (Moscow, 1960); George Vernadsky, "The Heresy of the Judaizers and the Policies of Ivan III of Moscow," *Speculum* 8 (October 1933): 436–48.

24. For a survey of this debate, especially in the work of Ia. S. Lur'e and John V. A. Fine, see Charles J. Halperin, "Judaizers and the Image of the Jew in Medieval Russia: A Polemic Revisited and a Question Posed," *CASS* 9 (Summer 1975): 141–55. S. Ettinger, "Jewish Influence on the Religious Ferment in Eastern Europe at the End of the Fifteenth Century" (in Hebrew), in *Yitzhak F. Baer Jubilee Volume*, ed. S. W. Baron et al. (Jerusalem, 1960), 228–47, argues forcefully for actual Jewish influence.

25. Joseph L. Wiecznyski, "Archbishop Gennadius and the West: The Impact of Catholic Ideas upon the Church of Novgorod," *CASS* 6 (Fall 1972): 378.

26. Iosif Volotskii, *Prosvetitel' ili oblichenie eresi zhidovstvuiushchikh* (Kazan, 1903), 32, 115–38.

27. Ibid., 85–93, 219–38, 94–114.

28. John L. I. Fennell, "The Attitude of the Josephians and the TransVolga Elders to the Heresy of the Judaizers," *SEER* (June 1951), suggests that Grand Prince Ivan III protected the heretics at first because he approved of their arguments against Church ownership of large landed estates. Ettinger also sees the heresy in the context of foreign-policy debates at court, specifically a struggle between advocates of a Byzantine orientation for Russian policy, aiming at an alliance with the Catholic world for a Crusade against the Turks, and those espousing a policy based upon cooperation with the Tatars, Moldavians, and Wallachians. "Muscovite State," 161–68. The ideological dichotomy drawn by most commentators (i.e., that the Judaizers were de facto enemies of the "Possessors," and that those opposed to clerical estate holding had reason to be sympathetic to them) is challenged by Lur'e, who argues in a recent article that one of the

collaborators in the creation of the *Prosvetitel'* was in fact Nil Sorskii, the leader of the monastic "Non-Possessors." See Ia. S. Lur'e, "Unresolved Issues in the History of the Ideological Movements of the Late Fifteenth Century," in *Medieval Russian Culture*, ed. Henrik Birnbaum and Michael S. Flier (Berkeley, Los Angeles, and London, 1984), 163–71.

29. Golubinskii, *Istoriia russkoi tserkvi*, 2: 583.

30. Wiktor Weintraub, "Tolerance, and Intolerance," 21–44.

31. Dubnow, *History*, 1:95–97.

32. Baron, *Social and Economic History*, 16:296–308.

33. Simon M. Dubnow, "Evrei i reformatsiia v Pol'she v XVI veke," *Voskhod* 5 (May 1895): 43–64, 4–11; see also Tazbir, "Reformation," 386–400.

34. R. G. Lapzhina, "Feodosii Kosoi—ideolog krestianstva XVI v.," *Trudy otdela drevnorusskoi literatury* 9 (Moscow, 1953), 235–50. Lapzhina connects Kosoi with the remnants of the Novgorod (i.e., Judaizer) heresy. D. K. Shelestov, "Svobodomyslie v uchenii Feodosii Kosogo (50-60-e gody XVI v.)," *Voprosy istorii religii i ateizma*, vol. 2 (Moscow, 1954), notes (200–201) that Prince Andrei Kurbskii spoke of the spread of Kosoi's heresy and that it also came to the attention of Ivan IV. Nikolai Kostomarov denies that the movement was "secret Judaism," saying rather that it was an attempt to join the Mosaic view of the unity of God with Arian views on the personality of Jesus Christ. "Velikorusskie religioznye vol'nodumtsy v XVI veke—Matvei Bashkin i ego souchastniki Feodosii Kosoi," *Istoricheskie monografii i issledovaniia* (St. Petersburg, 1872), 1: 419.

35. Halperin, "Judaizers," 154.

36. Ettinger, "Muscovite State," 140.

37. Iulii I. Gessen, "Evrei v moskovskom gosudarstve XV–XVII veka," *ES* 7 (April–June 1915): 153.

38. Ettinger, "Muscovite State," 139–40.

39. Gessen, "Evrei v moskovskom gosudarstve," 157–63.

40. Dubnow, *History*, 1:246–48.

41. *PSZ* 7, no. 5,063 (26 April 1727).

42. The basis for the execution was a provision of the Criminal Code of 1669 which prescribed the death penalty for conversionary activity by non-Christians. See *PSZ* 1 (22 January 1669), art. 109; and 10, no. 7,612 (3 July 1738) for details of the trial.

43. *PSZ* 10, no. 8,169 (11 July 1740).

44. *PSZ* 11, no. 8,673 (2 December 1742).

45. *PSZ* 11, no. 8,840 (16 December 1743).

46. *PSZ* 12, no. 8,867 (25 January 1744).

47. As late as the nineteenth century the metropolitan of Moscow was cautious about permitting the veneration of St. Gavriil Zabludovskii, a ritual murder victim of the late seventeenth century, commemorated by the Orthodox Church in Poland. Simon M. Dubnow, "Tserkovnye legendy ob otroke Gavriile Zabludovskom," *ES* 8 (April–September 1916):309.

48. S. Vaisenberg, "Evrei v velikorusskoi chastushke," *ES* 7 (January–March 1915): 119–20, argues that the Jews are either absent in this oral traditon or are portrayed in a generally favorable light. This observation holds for Great Russian proverbs as well, where negative stereotypes are obviously of West Russian origin. S. Vaisenberg, "Evrei v russkikh poslovitsakh," *ES* 7 (April–June 1915): 228–31. See also Antonovich and Dragomanov, *Istoricheskie pesni*, 2:1 and 20–32, and Rawita-Gawrónski, *Żydzi w historji*, 237–66.

49. *Podrobnyi slovar' russkikh graverov XVI–XIX vv.* (St. Petersburg, 1895), 1:242, 2:454.

50. Salo W. Baron, *The Russian Jew under Tsars and Soviets*, 2d rev. ed. (New York and London, 1976), 6.

51. Gessen, "Evrei v moskovskom gosudarstve," 157.

52. Ibid., 160–61.

53. *PSZ* 1, no. 398, n. 11 (30 January 1667). K. V. Kharlampovich, *Zapadno-russkie pravoslavnye shkoly XVI i nachala XVII veka* (Kazan, 1898), 137, 165.

54. Ettinger, "Muscovite State," 146. For a description of the mutiny of 1682 and the fate of von Gaden, who was accused of having poisoned Tsar Fedor, see John Keep, "Mutiny in Moscow, 1682," *Canadian Slavonic Papers* 23 (1981): 410–42. Keep suggests that "although not evident from the sources, anti-Semitic prejudice as well as monarchist legitimism may explain the persistence with which the strel'tsy searched for him and his gruesome death (17 May) after lengthy torture" (427, n. 21).

55. V. Stoklitskaia-Tereshkovich, "Pervyi ritual'nyi protsess v Rossii (1702 g.)," *ES* 10 (1918): 7–26.

56. Ibid., 16.

57. *PSZ* 7, no. 5,032 (14 March 1727); and 7, no. 5,063 (26 April 1727).

58. *PSZ* 8, no. 5,324, n. 14 (22 August 1728).

59. *PSZ* 8, no. 5,852 (10 September 1731); 9, no. 6,610, n.21 (31 July 1734); and 9, no. 6,614 (8 August 1734).

60. *PSZ* 11, no. 8,169 (11 July 1740).

61. *PSZ*, no. 8,840 (16 December 1743).

62. *PSZ* 12, no. 8,867 (25 January 1744).

63. Roger Bartlett, *Human Capital: The Settlement of Foreigners in Russia, 1762–1804* (Cambridge, Eng., 1979), 37.

64. "Eschche rasskaz Ekateriny II-i o svoem tsarstovanii," *Russkii arkhiv* 3 (1880), 3.

65. See the definition in *Encyclopédie ou Dictionnaire raisonné des sciences, des arts et des métiers* (Geneva, 1777), 10: 884–85: "Dévotion: f. n. (Morale) piété, culte de Dieu avec ardeur et sincérité. La dévotion se peut définir un attendrissement de coeur et une consolation intérieure que sent l'âme du fidèle dans les exercices de piété. On appelle practiques de dévotion, certaines practiques religieuses dont on se fait une loi de s'acquitter régulièrement: si cette exactitude est soutenue d'une solide piété, elle est louable et méritoire; autrement elle n'est d'aucun mérite, et peut-être quelquefois désagréable à Dieu." An example of Catherine's use of the latter connotation may be found in her "Réflexions sur Pétersbourg et sur Moscow," in *Sochinenie* (St. Petersburg, 1907), XII, 642.

66. Nikolai N. Golitsyn, *Istoriia russkogo zakonodatel'stra o Evreiakh* (St. Petersburg, 1886), 61.

67. Iu. I Gessen, "Stremlenie Ekateriny II vodvorit' Evreev v Rossii (1764 g.)," *ES* 7 (July–December 1915): 339–40.

68. Bartlett, *Human Capital*, 119.

69. Ibid., 62.

70. Gessen, "Stremlenie," 338–46.

71. Bartlett, *Human Capital*, 62.

72. John Locke, *A Letter Concerning Toleration* (Indianapolis and New York, 1955), 56.

73. Jacob Katz, *Out of the Ghetto* (Cambridge, Mass., 1973), 70.

74. Christian Wilhelm Dohm, *De la réforme politique des Juifs* (Halle, 1782), 5–8.

75. Ibid., 27–28.

76. Ibid., 43–44.

77. Ibid., 115.

78. Ibid, 146–69.

79. Marc Raeff, "The Well-Ordered Police State and the Development of Modernity in Seventeenth- and Eighteenth-Century Europe: An Attempt at a Comparative Approach," *American Historical Review* 80 (December 1975): 1222.

80. Ibid., 1239.

81. Arthur Hertzberg sees this duality of Enlightenment thought represented by Montesquieu and Voltaire. The former, he argues, initiated the belief that the Jews were ultimately capable of reform. Voltaire, on the other hand, believed that the Jews were far too depraved for there to be a realistic hope of their moral improvement. They were a menace from whom the unwary required protection. *The French Enlightenment and the Jews* (New York, 1970).

82. Springer, "Enlightened Despotism," 237–67.

83. Marc Raeff, *The Well-Ordered Police State: Social and Institutional Change Through Law in the Germanies and Russia, 1600–1800* (New Haven and London, 1983), 96.

84. Raphael Mahler, *A History of Modern Jewry, 1780–1815* (London, 1971), 326–29.

85. Bałaban, "Perekhod," 299–301.

86. For a description of the Galician Patent see ibid., 302–5.

87. Kurt Stillschweig, "Jewish Assimilation as an Object of Legislation," *HJ* 8 (April 1946): 8. Some German states had already banned the use of Yiddish for business bookkeeping. Katz, *Out of the Ghetto*, 65.

88. Bałaban, "Perekhod," 298–99.

89. Mahler, *History*, 344.

90. Ludwig von Rönne and Heinrich Simon, *Die früheren und gegenwärtigen Verhältnisse der Juden in den sämmtlichen Landestheilen des Preussischen Staates* (Breslau, 1843), 291–302. See articles 2, 3, and 13.

91. Hertzberg, *French Enlightenment*, 314–68.

92. This subject is examined in detail in Szajkowski, *Autonomy*.

93. Elena Gekker, "Proekty reformy evreiskogo byta v Pol'she v kontse XVIII veka," *ES* 6 (April–June 1914): 207–9.

94. M. Vishnitser, "Obshchii ocherk politicheskoi i sotsial'noi istorii Evreev v Pol'she i Litve," in *Istoriia evreiskogo naroda* (Moscow, 1914), 97.

95. Gekker, "Proekty," 209. Compare Dohm: "The moral character of the Jews, like that of all other men, is equally susceptible to accept culture and the most perfect purity, or to descend to the lowest brutalization, all depending, as I have observed, on exterior circumstances." *Réforme*, 122.

96. Gekker, "Proekty," 210.

97. Ibid., 3–4 (July–December 1914), 329–30.

98. Ibid.

99. Czacki failed to give a source for his figures, but they were apparently accepted uncritically by his contemporaries. Another example was his estimate for the Second Russian Jewish Committee under Alexander I that sixty thousand Jewish families would be left indigent by the implementation of new laws restricting Jews from trading in alcohol. See below.

100. Tadeusz Czacki, *Rozprawa o Żydach i Karaitach* (Vilna, 1807), 215–20.

101. Ibid., 220–44.

102. Moses Mendelssohn, *Jerusalem and Other Writings* (New York, 1969), 90–91.

103. For a discussion of the ideal of the "neutral society," see Katz, *Tradition and Crisis*, 245–59.

104. Mendelssohn, *Jerusalem*, 104.

CHAPTER 3

1. Isabel de Madariaga, *Russia in the Age of Catherine the Great* (New Haven and London, 1981), 310, 324.

2. Ibid., 308–24.

3. Victor Kamendrowsky and David M. Griffiths, "The Fate of the Trading Nobility Controversy in Russia: A Chapter in the Relationship between Catherine II and the Russian Nobility," *JGO* 26 (1978): 198–221.

4. The *Landsassen* were Livonian landowners, often serving as officers in the Russian army, who were nonetheless not recognized as nobles under the *Matricula* (genealogical book) then in use in Livonia. Consequently they were denied positions in local government open to matriculated nobles. Madariaga, *Russia*, 322. The *mirzas* were Tatar nobles who owned land in the Crimea. Catherine's administrators sought to integrate them into the broader estate of the Russian nobility. Alan Fisher, *The Crimean Tatars* (Stanford, 1978), 75.

5. Madariaga, *Russia*, 74. The annual disbursement for the Ukraine under Hetman Kyrill Razumovsky (1750–1764) was 48,000 rubles.

6. Edward C. Thaden, *Russia's Western Borderlands, 1710–1870* (Princeton, 1984), 44–45.

7. Dubnow, *History*, 1:307.

8. Louis Greenberg, *The Jews in Russia*, ed. Mark Wischnitzer (New Haven, 1965), 8, follows Dubnow. Richard Pipes, "Catherine II and the Jews," *SJA* 5 (1975) sets the number at 100,000, also too high.

9. V. M. Kabuzan, *Narodonaselenie Rossii v XVIII–pervoi polovine XIX v.* (Moscow, 1963), 161. The census of Belorussia was taken in 1772 to supplement the figures of the Third Census. There were 289,877 males listed for Vitebsk province and 325,116 for Mogilev.

10. Raphael Mahler, *Yidn in amolikn Poiln in likht fun tsifern* (Warsaw, 1958). Mahler's estimates are based on the statistics contained in "Perepisi evreiskogo naseleniia v iugo-zapadnom krae v 1765–1791," *Arkhiv Iugo-Zapadnoi Rossii*, part 5, II, 1 and 2 (Kiev, 1890). See also the review of this work by Artur Eisenbach, "Żydzi w dawnej Polsce w swietle liczb," *Kwartalnik Historyczny* 66 (1959): 511–20.

11. Kh. Korobkhov, "Perepis' evreiskogo naseleniia vitebskoi gubernii v 1772 g.," *ES* 4 (April–June 1912): 164–77.

12. Taken from official data published in Gavriil R. Derzhavin, *Sochineniia Derzhavina*, ed. Ia. Grot (St. Petersburg, 1864–83), 7:313.

13. Bałaban, "Perekhod," 290–91.

14. Wischnitzer, *Jewish Crafts*, 223.

15. Sergei A. Bershadskii, "Polozhenie o Evreiakh 1804 goda," *Voskhod* 15 XV (January 1895): 89–90; Wischnitzer, *Jewish Crafts*, 223–24. Baron, *Economic History*, 75–78. Compare the statistics on the Jewish population in the district of Zhitomir in 1789 (when the area was still under Polish rule). Of the 10,526 Jews counted, 54 percent lived in 13 different towns, 10.6 percent lived in 15 different hamlets, and 35.3 percent lived in 421 villages. Occupationally, 73.7 percent were engaged in liquor trade. Sucher Berek Weinryb (Bernard D. Weinryb), *Neueste Wirtschaftsgeschichte der Juden in Russland und Polen* (Breslau, 1934), 219–23.

16. P. I. Liashchenko, *History of the National Economy of Russia to the 1917 Revolution* (New York, 1970), 341–42.

17. *PSZ* 19, no. 13,865 (September 13, 1772).

18. Ibid.

19. Golitsyn, *Istoriia*, 104–8; *Slovar' Akademii Rossiiskoi* (St. Petersburg, 1809), 2:822.

20. Gessen, *Istoriia*, 1:47.

21. See the discussion in Matthias Rest, *Die Russische Judengesetzgebung von der Ersten Polnischen Teilung bis zum "Položenie dlja Evreev"* (1804) (Wiesbaden, 1975), 251, n. 148.

22. This was not the first time that the Russian state gave a blank check for privileges it did not understand. While confirming the traditional rights of the Livonian nobility in December 1762, Catherine wrote to a correspondent: "Il faut cependant en confidence que je vous dise qu'en honneur ni moi ni personne ne sais ce que je confirmerai, si cela est utile au pais, si ce sont des moeurs ou des coutumes ou des loix, mais j'ai cru que le repos d'une province entière étoit préférable à tout le teste" (Madariaga, *Russia*, 61–62).

23. Golitsyn, *Istoriia*, 329, n. 182.

24. Not only Chernyshev but the Senate routinely used the terms *Zhid* and *zhidovskii* in decrees until about 1783.

25. Pipes, "Catherine II and the Jews," 7.

26. See my article *"Zhid:* The Biography of a Russian Epithet," *SEER* 50 (January 1982): 1–15.

27. In her voluminous instructions to the two governors of Belorussia, Catherine emphasized that the Russian administration was to conduct itself so that all the inhabitants would see the superiority and advantage of Russian citizenship over the previous rule of the Poles. See the entry for Kakhovskii in *Russkii biograficheskii, slovar'* (St. Petersburg, 1896–1918), s. v. "Kakhovskii," 8:565–72.

28. Kakhovskii's report is found in Derzhavin, *Sochineniia*, 7:308–14.

29. Ibid., 308–9.

30. See J. Kaunitz, *Russian Literature and the Jew* (New York, 1929); Shlomo Breman, "Toward the Image of Jews in Russian Literature of the Nineteenth Century" (in Hebrew), *He-Avar* 20 (1973): 135–75.

31. Kakhovskii, "Kopiia," in Derzhavin, *Sochineniia, VII,* 309.

32. Ibid., 311.

33. Ibid., 309–12.

34. Ibid., 312.

35. Ibid., 313.

36. *PSZ* 21, no. 15,436 (16 June 1782).

37. *PSZ* 19, no. 13,865 (13 September 1772).

38. *PSZ* 20, no. 14,522 (17 October 1776).

39. An examination of this phenomenon in the area of local self-government through the provincial reform of 1775 is found in Robert E. Jones, *The Emancipation of the Russian Nobility, 1762–1785* (Princeton, 1973), 220–72.

40. See Dawid Fajnhauz, "Konflikty społeczne wśród ludności Żydowskiej na Litwie i Białorusi w pierwszej połowie XIX wieku," *BZIH* 52 (October–December 1964), 3–15; Israel Klausner, "The Inner Struggle in Jewish Communities in Russia and Lithuania at the End of the XVIII Century" (in Hebrew), *He-Avar* 19 (1972): 54–73.

41. *PSZ* 19, no. 13,865 (13 September 1772). The Jewish head tax was apparently assessed on all male Jews, since the census report for Polotsk (or Vitebsk, as it was then called) province taken for tax-collecting purposes listed only the adult male population. Korobkov, "Perepis'," 164–77.

42. *PSZ* 20, no. 14,522 (17 October 1776); and 20, no. 14,892 (3 July 1779). The decree of 17 October 1776 granted special privileges to Jews who would convert to any Christian faith. Such converts were promised the right to enroll in any merchant guild or artisan trade that they desired and were to be administered by the courts and administration of such estates, rather than by the kahal. The

wording seemed to imply that unconverted Jews were forbidden at that time to enroll in the urban estates, although the decree also ordered all Jews to register in the towns.

43. *PSZ* 20, no. 14,392 (17 November 1775); and no. 14,522 (17 October 1776). The latter decree, offering special prerogatives to Jews who converted to Christianity, at first glance would seem to violate Catherine's repeated assurances that, in her realm, all peoples and religions were equal before the law. Policies of proselytism were not new, however, nor were they restricted to the Jews. As Roger Bartlett summarizes Catherine's treatment of non-Christians in the borderlands of the empire: "Russian policy towards non-Christian subjects held traditionally to the dual principles of toleration and proselytism. The latter in particular was approved, since adoption of Orthodoxy implied acceptance of Russian hegemony and the Russian way of life," *Human Capital*, 11. Suspicion toward the validity of conversion, evident in the future treatment of Jewish converts to Orthodoxy, was to be found in dealings with other peoples as well.

44. *PSZ* 20, no. 14,962 (7 January 1780).

45. *PSZ* 21, no. 15,130 (10 March 1781).

46. Iulii I. Gessen, *Evrei v Rossii* (St. Petersburg, 1906), 206.

47. Gessen quotes a report of the Polotsk magistracy to the Senate that "they [the Jews] were all enrolled in the *kupechestvo* and the *meshchanstvo*." Ibid., 203.

48. Ibid., 289–90.

49. The rules governing distillation illustrate again the divergence in law between the Russian heartland and the non-Russian areas. A completely different system operated in the Great Russian provinces, described in John P. LeDonne, "Indirect Taxes in Catherine's Russia. II. The Liquor Monopoly," *JGO* 24 (1976): 173–207.

50. Gessen, *Evrei v Rossii*, 208.

51. See Marc Raeff, *Origins of the Russian Intelligentsia* (New York, 1966), 103.

52. *PSZ* 22, no. 16,188 (April 21, 1785).

53. Ibid.

54. *PSZ* 22, no. 16,391 (7 May 1786).

55. Aleksandr A. Kizevetter, *Gorodovoe polozhenie Ekateriny II 1785 g.* (Moscow, 1909). See, for example, the confusion surrounding the terms *meshchanin* and *meshchanstvo*, 35–38, 87. Kizevetter notes (321) that in a number of cases the statutes were so ambiguous and unclear that further legislation was necessary in order to interpret them.

56. Bershadskii, "Polozhenie" (June 1895): 45–55.

57. M. Kulisher notes that foreigners who became Russian citizens without converting to Orthodoxy always seem to have had the option to leave the country in the eighteenth century after making some sort of payment, on the basis of the statutes of 1763 and 1784. In essence, then, they retained a quasi-foreign status. Kurlandian Jews were briefly permitted to leave the province under these conditions in the 1790s, but this right was soon rescinded. M. I. Kulisher, "Istoriia russkogo zakonodatel'stva o Evreiakh v sviazi s sistemoi vziamaniia nalogov i otbyvaniia povinnostei," *ES* 2 (October–December 1910): 475.

58. Gradovskii argues that this was an incorrect interpretation of the law by the Senate, "an arbitrary and a dangerous precedent." N. D. Gradovskii, *Torgovye i drugie prava Evreev v Rossii* (St. Petersburg, 1886), 80.

59. Pipes, "Catherine II and the Jews," 14; Madariaga, *Russia*, 79.

60. Gessen, *Istoriia*, 1:56–57.

61. This trend continued into the next century, with Jewish representation being reduced to one-third the total number of Christians. In the reign of Nicholas

I, Jews were sometimes forced by local officials to vote in the curiae of foreigners in order to reduce their representation. Gessen, *Istoriia*, 2:50.

62. *PSZ* 23, no. 17,006 (23 December 1791).

63. See Yakov Lestchinsky, "The Economic Background of the Jewish Pale of Settlement" (in Hebrew), *He-Avar* 1 (1952): 31–44; Yitshak Maor, "The Pale of Jewish Settlement" (in Hebrew), *He-Avar* 19 (1972): 35–53.

64. Just as Catherine had deferred to the merchants of Riga when they requested a Jewish presence in 1763, so now she acted to bar Jews from areas where they would be inconvenient. *Arkhiv gosudarstvennogo soveta*, vol. 1, pt. 2 (St. Petersburg, 1869), 365–68.

65. Kulisher, "Istoriia," 477–78.

66. *PSZ* 24, no. 17,605 (3 December 1796).

67. The decree of 23 June 1794 permitted the Jews to reside in the provinces of Chernigov, Novgorod-Seversk, and Kiev, which had been entirely or partially outside the area allotted for Jewish settlement in 1791. *PSZ* 23, no. 17,224.

68. *PSZ* 23, no. 17,224 (23 June 1794). This decree again treated the Jews somewhat like foreigners (see note 57). On the other hand, the very fact that they were living in Russia indicated that they were *not* foreigners: Catherine, in her growing xenophobia after the outbreak of the French Revolution had ordered all foreign Jews expelled from the country in 1792. Golitsyn, *Istoriia*, 168.

69. *PSZ* 5, no. 2,991 (8 February 1716); no. 2,996 (18 February 1716); and no. 3,232 (9 October 1718). The Polish diets had upon occasion levied a double tax on Jews. Kh. Korobkov, "Ekonomicheskaia rol' Evreev v Pol'she v kontse XVIII v.," *ES* 2 (July–September 1910): 346–77. Property taxes for Polish burghers were sometimes doubled for Jews and Armenians. Weinryb, *Jews of Poland*, 53–54.

70. *PSZ* 23, no. 17,340 (8 June 1795).

71. Nikolai N. Varadinov, *Istoriia Ministerstva Vnutrennikh Del* (St. Petersburg, 1858–62), 3:343.

72. Gessen, *Evrei v. Rossii*, 365.

73. *PSZ* 23, no. 17,327 (3 May 1795).

74. Gessen, *Istoriia*, 1:83–86. Golitsyn, it will be recalled, argued that this legislation sprang from Catherine's realization that the Jews were exploitive and were ruining the well-being of the peasantry. *Istoriia*, 140. This charge, formulated at a time when the argument was closely tied to contemporary polemics, remains without documentary proof.

75. Rest, *Judengesetzgebung*, 123.

76. See *PSZ* 23, nos. 17,221, 17,222, 17,223, 17,224, 17,225, 17,226, and 17,227 (all 23 June 1794).

77. Mikhail T. Shugurov, "Doklad o Evreiakh imperatoru Aleksandrv Pavlovichu," *Russkii arkhiv* 41 (February 1903): 272.

78. Golitsyn is in the minority when he argues that the advantages the Jews received from their status as free people with full property rights and special privileges outweighed the inconvenience of the tax. *Istoriia*, 161–68.

79. *PSZ* 39, no. 30,004 (29 July 1824).

80. Gradovskii, *Torgovye i drugie prava*, 129–31.

81. Katz, *Out of the Ghetto*, 165. In the reign of Francis I (1793) Jews were obliged to serve in the regular army unless they had sufficient capital to buy an exemption. In Congress Poland, Jews were one of the few social categories permitted to buy an exemption from military service. The army here was under the command of Alexander's brother, the Grand Duke Constantine Pavlovich. Frank W. Thackeray, *Antecedents of Revolution: Alexander I and the Polish Kingdom* (Boulder, Colo., 1980), 36.

82. According to Gessen's statistics from 1797–1800, in the areas of Jewish settlement there were 2,309 Jewish merchants and 148,968 Jewish townspeople. In the same areas there lived 11,637 and 166,713 Christian merchants and townspeople, respectively. *Istoriia*, 84–85.

83. *PSZ* 23, no. 17,249 (7 September 1794).

84. *PSZ* 23, no. 17,432 (21 January 1796).

85. It would perhaps be useful here to note Alan W. Fisher's synopsis of the activities of Catherine's government toward the Muslim minority, which provides interesting parallels. Fisher observes that Catherine did not aim at Russification of these peoples so much as to "fit peoples and areas into 'normal' Russian administrative categories." Alan W. Fisher, "Enlightened Despotism and Islam under Catherine II," *SR* 27 (December 1968): 552.

CHAPTER 4

1. Gessen, *Istoriia*, 1:84–85.

2. *PSZ* 24, no. 17,694 (29 December 1796); and 24, no. 18,015 (23 June 1797). Gessen argues that this latter decree, apparently a verbatim restatement of the decree of 23 June 1794, never existed and is actually the earlier decree miscatalogued. *Evrei v Rossii*, 364.

3. *PSZ* 24, no. 17,605 (3 December 1796).

4. *PSZ* 24, no. 18,132 (8 September 1797).

5. Gessen, *Istoriia*, 1:92.

6. Iu. I. Gessen, "Evrei v Kurliandii (XVI–XVIII v.)," *ES* 6 (July–December 1914): 382.

7. *PSZ* 25, no. 18,889 (14 March 1799).

8. Ibid.

9. Ibid.

10. P. G. Kozlovskii, a Soviet historian of rural Belorussia, claims that the more pessimistic evaluations of contemporaries, as well as the subsequent historiography, have tended to generalize the conditions for all of Belorussia from the experience of those villages found in the worst condition and have failed to differentiate among the various strata of the peasantry. Still, he does not dispute that contemporaries almost unanimously emphasized the poor conditions of the countryside. *Krest'iane Belorussii vo vtoroi polovine XVII–XVIII v.* (Minsk, 1969), 137–41.

11. Ibid., 64.

12. Bershadskii, "Polozhenie," 87.

13. See I. D. Koval'chenko, "K voprosu o sostoianii pomeshchich'ego khoziaistva pered otmenoi krepostnogo prava v Rossii," *Ezhegodnik po agrarnoi istorii Vostochnoi Evropy: 1959 g.* (Moscow, 1961), 192–227.

14. Kozlovskii, *Krest'iane*, 112.

15. Ibid., 120–21.

16. Bershadskii, "Polozhenie," 87–88.

17. The reports of the noble electors and deputies to Catherine's Legislative Commission of 1767 are quite similar in nature and variety to those of the Minsk marshals. See Paul Dukes, *Catherine the Great and the Russian Nobility* (Cambridge, Eng., 1967), 110–44. It is understandable that the central government might take an interest in a new variable.

18. Gessen, *Evrei v Rossii*, 20.

19. Bershadskii, "Polozhenie," 92–93. The 31 March 1755 decree forbade the

distillation of spirits under another's name by those who did not have the right to engage in distillation. *PSZ*, no. 10,384.

20. Bershadskii was able to locate in the archives the complete reports of the marshals of Minsk, Lithuania, and Podolia, while the views of the Volynia marshals were gleaned from the extract of the report written by the military governor of Kamenets-Podolsk, Count I. V. Gudovich.

21. Bershadskii, "Polozhenie," 94–95.

22. Lithuania province was created in 1796 and comprised nineteen districts, with its administrative capital at Vilna. In 1802 the territory was divided between Vilna and Grodno provinces.

23. Bershadskii, "Polozhenie," 70–71.

24. Kozlovskii, *Krest'iane*, 36–37.

25. Bershadskii, "Polozhenie," 75–77.

26. Ibid., 72–73.

27. Ibid., 85.

28. Ibid.

29. Ibid., 88–91.

30. Ibid., 91–92.

31. Ibid., 93.

32. Ibid.

33. Ibid., 93–94.

34. Ibid., 94–96.

35. Gavriil R. Derzhavin, *Zapiski* (Moscow, 1860), 133.

36. Ibid., 719–20. Iulii I. Gessen, "K istorii 'srednevekovykh' obvinenii," *Knizhki Voskhoda* 22 (April 1902): 55–56.

37. Ibid., 749.

38. Ibid., 800–801.

39. Paul I to Derzhavin in *Sochineniia*, 6, no. 1,201 (16 June 1800), 385.

40. Obol"ianinov to Derzhavin, in ibid., no. 1,202 (16 June 1800), 385–86.

41. Derzhavin's final judgment on the famine of 1800 in Belorussia was that it was caused not only by the lack of grain but also by poor distribution of the existing grain reserves. Obol"ianinov to Paul I, ibid., no. 1,204, n.d., 387–89.

42. Derzhavin, *Zapiski*, 408–9.

43. Derzhavin, "Mnenie," in *Sochineniia*, 7, 306–29.

44. Ibid., 259.

45. I. Frank in Gessen, *Evrei v Rossii*, 447.

46. Ibid., 448.

47. Russian Maskilim may have been few in number, but they were energetic in submitting proposals for educational reform, in the style of Moses Mendelssohn, to the Russian government. Frank's efforts to influence Derzhavin were anticipated seventeen years earlier by the submission to the Russian government of a similar proposal for the Jews of Belorussia authored by the Mogilev merchant Iakov Hirsh. On this occasion the intervention attracted no official attention or interest. See Yehuda Slutsky and M. Bobe, "To the History of the Jews in Russia at the End of the Eighteenth Century (Three Documents)" (in Hebrew), *He-Avar* 19 (1972): 78–80.

48. Derzhavin, *Zapiski*, 409.

49. See Arnold R. Springer, "The Public Career and Political Views of G. R. Derzhavin," (Ph.D. diss., University of California at Los Angeles, 1971).

50. Derzhavin, "Mnenie," in *Sochineniia*, 7:231–32.

51. Ibid., 235.

52. Ibid., 235–42.

53. Ibid., 245–46.
54. Ibid., 251.
55. Ibid., 298.
56. Ibid., 250, 254.
57. Ibid., 314–17. As noted, this material was connected with the Sennensk ritual murder trial of 1799.
58. Ibid., 254.
59. See Jacob Katz, "A State within a State: The History of an Anti-Semitic Slogan," in *Emancipation and Assimilation* (Richmond, Eng., 1972), 47–76.
60. Derzhavin, "Mnenie," in *Sochineniia*, 7:252–58.
61. Ibid., 292–93.
62. Ibid., 294–96. This was a use of the terminology for Jewish places of worship and study, the *shul* and the synagogue, as administrative terms.
63. Fisher, "Enlightened Despotism," 500–501.
64. Derzhavin, "Mnenie," in *Sochineniia*, 7:293–98.
65. Bartlett, *Human Capital*, 135–36.
66. The ober-procurator was a lay official, created by Peter the Great, charged with overseeing the work of the clerical governing board of the Russian Orthodox Church, the Holy Synod.
67. Gessen, *Evrei v Rossii*, 68.
68. Springer, "Derzhavin," 214–76.
69. Ibid., 259.
70. Nota Khaimovich Notkin in Gessen, *Evrei v Rossii*, 443–45.
71. See Szajkowski, *Autonomy and Communal Jewish Debts*.
72. Derzhavin, "Mnenie," in *Sochineniia*, 7:270.
73. Ibid., 274.
74. Ibid., 275–76.
75. Ibid., 276–77.
76. Ibid. Springer, for instance, suggests that the Jews who settled on private estates in Belorussia would have been enserfed by Derzhavin's plan. "Derzhavin," 304. In the "Mnenie," however, Derzhavin explicitly stated (281) that the agriculturalists "should be considered free men and not serfs."
77. Derzhavin, "Mnenie," in *Sochineniia* 7:278–81.
78. Ibid., 300–305.
79. Compare the analyses of Simon Dubnow and Arnold Springer. Dubnow emphasizes Derzhavin's project as "a medley of hereditary Jew-hatred, vague appreciation of the historic tragedy of Judaism, and the desire to 'render the Jews useful to the state,' " *History* 1:333–34. Springer emphasizes Derzhavin's role as an agent of enlightened absolutism, operating within a utilitarian and statist context. He suggests that Derzhavin "intended his project as a vehicle to force Russian Jews to be free." See Arnold Springer, "Gavriil Derzhavin's Jewish Reform Project of 1800," *CASS* 10 (Spring 1976): 1–2.
80. Shemu'el Ettinger, "The Statute of 1804" (in Hebrew), *He-Avar* 22 (1977): 87.
81. See Hans Rogger, "Government, Jews, Peasants, and Land in Post-Emancipation Russia," *CMRS* 17 (January–March 1976): 5–25; and 2–3 (April–September): 171–211.
82. Bershadskii, "Polozhenie," 34–36.
83. Platon, Metropolitan of Moscow, *Polnoe sobranie sochinenii* (St. Petersburg, n.d.), 2:327–28.
84. There was one slight indication under Paul that the government was beginning to see that Jews might serve in capacities other than those of tradesmen and

merchants. In a decree of 1 May 1800, the crown ordered that Jews in Kurland who were unable to pay their taxes should be sent to work in the local state mines. *PSZ* 26, no. 19,409.

CHAPTER 5

1. Bershadskii, "Polozhenie," 54.
2. Ibid.
3. Ibid., 55. Or, as the Senate declared, to these provinces "where such magistracies exist, and where the Jews do not lack the rights of citizenship."
4. Ibid., 45–49.
5. Ibid., 55–56.
6. Ibid.
7. Ibid., 50–54.
8. Ibid., 58–59.
9. L. Trotskii, "Evrei v kievskoi gubernii v 1802 g.," *ES* 13 (1930):131–34.
10. Bershadskii, "Polozhenie," 61–63.
11. *PSZ* 28, no. 21,547 (9 December 1804).
12. Derzhavin, *Zapiski*, 799.
13. Ibid., 802–3. The fate of this group was curiously tied to that of the Jews. In 1808, when the Ministry of Interior attempted to engage the Jews in factory labor, it included the *chinshevye* nobles in the same project. See below.
14. Richard S. Wortman, *The Development of a Russian Legal Consciousness* (Chicago and London, 1976), 114–17.
15. Derzhavin, *Zapiski*, 800.
16. The affair was a rather complicated one. After initial approval by the Senate, a decree was promulgated on 5 December 1802 which specified that all members of the gentry in the armed forces should either reach non-commissioned officer status or serve twelve years before being allowed to retire. A similar provision had been contained in earlier legislation, but Potocki, as a member of the Senate, pointed out that it had been invoked only in wartime. The enforcement of such a regulation in peacetime, he argued, would be a violation of the prerogatives of the nobility. He exhorted the Senate to exercise the right of remonstrance recently granted to the Senate by Alexander. The right of remonstrance permitted the Senate to advise the tsar of the apparent illegality of proposed decrees. When the Senate attempted to vote a remonstrance on the question, Derzhavin opposed it rather heavy-handedly in the belief that it was another trick of the Poles and the "magnates" to weaken the state. On several occasions he openly attacked Potocki in the Senate. The result was a bitter feud, humiliating for both men. Springer, "Derzhavin," 477–79.
17. Derzhavin's relations with the tsar had become strained, and his stubborn opposition to the Law on Free Agriculturists was probably the last straw in convincing Alexander to dismiss him. Wortman, *Russian Legal Consciousness*, 177–78.
18. *RBS* 9:366–82.
19. Czartoryski was also a friend and patron of the Jewish Maskil Mendel Lefin of Satanów, who served as a tutor for his son, and who was presumably a source of information on the Jews. Mahler, *History*, 306.
20. While Czartoryski's own evaluation of Derzhavin does not discuss the latter's enmity toward him, he does describe the poet with thinly veiled sarcasm: "a worthy man, and a writer of some much-admired lyrics which were full of swing

and passion, he was imperfectly educated and knew no language but Russian. The emperor had been attracted to him by his ardent sentiments and poetic dreams, not being able to resist fine phrases. . . ." *Memoirs of Prince Adam Czartoryski and His Correspondence with Alexander I*, ed. Adam Gielgud (London, 1888), 1:301. In fact, Derzhavin did know German.

21. *RBS*, 14:699–704.

22. Czartoryski, *Memoirs*, 1:307–8.

23. See Iulii I. Gessen, " 'Deputaty evreiskogo naroda' pri Aleksandre I," *ES* 1 (July–September, 1909): 17–29; and 4 (October–December 1909): 196–206.

24. Derzhavin, *Zapiski*, 799.

25. Iakov Brafman, *Kniga kagala* (Vilna, 1869), 152. Brafman's book is useful because it purports to be the communal "Minute Book" of the Minsk kahal and thus a valuable source for the day-to-day operations of the kahal. The documents were tendentiously edited and occasional mistranslated, however, in order to support Brafman's claim that the kahal still existed as an anti-Russian "state within the state." See I. Levitats, "The Authenticity of Brafman's 'Book of the Kahal' " (in Hebrew), *Zion* 3 (January 1938): 170–78.

26. Shugurov, "Doklad," 255. Material from the First Jewish Committee, which otherwise would have been lost, can be extracted from this report of the Third Jewish Committee, which was created in 1809 and submitted its report to the tsar in 1812.

27. *EJ* 13:279.

28. Leiba Nevakhovich, *Vopl' dshcheri iudeiskoi* (St. Petersburg, 1803), 12–14.

29. Ibid., 18–31.

30. Ibid., 34–38.

31. Ibid., 42–46.

32. Ibid., 48–49. The volume containing the *Vopl'* also carried an apostrophe, "Feeling of a True Citizen on the Occasion of the Establishment by Alexander of a Committee for the Organization of the Jews for the Advantage of the State and Themselves," and a dialogue between (Religious) Intolerance, Truth, and Tolerance, which concluded with "mad" Intolerance being put to flight.

33. Ironically, it was Notkin who was accused by Derzhavin of being the Jewish agent who attempted to bribe members of the committee not to make any changes in the prerogatives of Belorussian Jewry. Derzhavin, *Zapiski*, 800–801.

34. Golitsyn, *Istoriia*, 434–35.

35. Ibid., 464–70. Golitsyn points to wording in the statute which suggests virtual transcription from Czacki's earlier project.

36. Gessen, *Istoriia*, 1:46.

37. Ibid., 146–49.

38. Hertzberg, *French Enlightenment and the Jews*, 273–80.

39. Shugurov, "Doklad," 254–55. Dubnow, *History*, 1:340, saw this entry as penned under the influence of Speranskii. Ettinger sees it rather as a virtual paraphrase of Montesquieu's *L'Esprit des Lois*, book 19, chapter 14. Ettinger, "Statute," 101. Ironically, Montesquieu was offering a critique of Peter the Great's civilizing of Muscovy.

40. Golitsyn, *Istoriia*, 440.

41. "Ob uzakonenii dlia blaga Evreev, obitaiushchikh v Imperii Vserossiiskoi," *Vestnik Evropy* 10 (May 1805): 139.

42. Ibid., 139–40.

43. Gessen argues the point at length in *Evrei v Rossii*, 3–4 ff.

44. Golitsyn, *Istoriia*, 432. Golitsyn attributes the covering report to Speranskii.

45. Ibid., 435–37. Italics mine.

46. *PSZ* 28, no.21,547 (9 December 1804). All other references to the statute are cited from this source.

47. Bershadskii, "Polozhenie" (June 1895), 63.

48. Golitsyn argues this in *Istoriia*, 477.

49. For the Tatar merchants see Chantal Lemercier-Quelquejay, "Les missions orthodoxes en pays musulmans de Moyenne-et Basse-Volga, 1552–1865," *CMRS* 8 (July–September 1967): 393.

50. See Michael Stanislawski, *Tsar Nicholas I and the Jews: The Transformation of Jewish Society in Russia, 1825–1855* (Philadelphia, 1983), 123–54.

51. See Patrick L. Alston, *Education and the State in Tsarist Russia* (Stanford, 1969), 20–30.

52. Orshanskii, *RZE*, 305.

53. *PSZ* 29, no. 22,678 (8 November 1807). In the course of enumerating tax rates this decree notes that Jews no longer pay the double tax.

54. In articles 16, 27, 34, 36, 37, 38, 39, 40, and 41.

55. Gradovskii claimed that the stringent punishments were aimed at the petty szlachta, from whom the government expected stiff opposition to the reform. *Torgovye i drugie prava*, 181.

56. In articles 42, 44, 45, 46, and 49, respectively.

CHAPTER 6

1. This is notable in the committee's journal entry for 20 September 1803, Shugurov, "Doklad," 254–55, which is quoted in chapter 5.

2. Solomon V. Pozner, *Evrei v obshchei shkole* (St. Petersburg, 1914), 5. These figures are all the more striking when one recalls that these were the areas that had been part of the empire for the longest time.

3. This campaign was typified, and named, by a famous article, "Zhid idet" ("The Jew Is Coming"), which appeared in *Novoe vremia*, no. 1461 (23 March 1880), detailing the fears of the overseer of the Odessa school district that Jews were displacing Christians in the public school system.

4. *VPSZ* 30, no. 29,276 (3 May 1855), requiring all *heder* teachers to receive a diploma from a Russian school (where they would be forced to learn Russian).

5. Gessen, *Istoriia*, 1:191.

6. See the dissatisfaction of Alexander II while on a state visit to Poland in Dubnow, *History*, 2:190. See also "Iz letopisi minuvshogo: 'Bor'ba pravitel'stva s' evreiskoi odezhdoi v Imperii i Tsarstve Pol'skom,' " *Perezhitoe* 1 (1909): 10–18.

7. This permission was granted in response to the appeals of deputies from the kahals. Gessen conjectures that the kahal leadership hoped in this way to eventually gain wider, governmentally sanctioned use of the ban. Gessen, *Istoriia*, 1:188.

8. *VPSZ* 32, no. 31,831 (13 May 1857), requiring rabbis to receive instruction in state schools.

9. *PSZ* 28, no. 21,967 (21 December 1805).

10. Gradovskii argues for this interpretation, specifying that the law was directed against the petty szlachta. *Torgovye i drugie prava*, 181.

11. In testimony before the Third Jewish Committee of 1809, kahal representatives appealed to the government against article 46, by which a Jew wishing to change residence was obliged to submit evidence from the local landowner that he had fulfilled his financial obligations on the estate. The petition claimed that the landowners were withholding this evidence in order to keep Jews from leaving

their estates. Shugurov, "Doklad," 271. This report contains résumés of petitions submitted to the Third Jewish Committee, which met from 1809 to 1812.

12. Golitsyn, *Istoriia*, 544–55.

13. Mahler, *History*, 423–29.

14. Shugurov, "Doklad," 257–58.

15. Ibid., 258.

16. Gessen suggests, without advancing proof, that the issue of the French threat to Russian Jews was merely a device to disguise the true motives of the government, which were to halt resettlement because of the demonstrated impossibility of carrying it out as originally planned. This interpretation fails to explain why resettlement should have begun so soon after the Tilsit Treaty. Gessen, *Istoriia*, 1:162–63.

17. Shugurov, "Doklad," 258.

18. *PSZ* 29, no. 22,651 (19 October 1807). In this way, incidently, the two provinces of Astrakhan and the Caucasus were temporarily added to the Pale of Settlement, to be withdrawn again in 1825.

19. *PSZ* 30, no. 23,424 (29 December 1808).

20. A detailed examination of the "resettlement theme" in Russian legislation is found in Iulii I. Gessen, *Zakon i zhizn'* (St. Petersburg, 1911).

21. Gessen, *Istoriia*, 1:154–55.

22. Gessen, *Istoriia*, 1:199–200.

23. Iulii I. Gessen, "Istoricheskie miniatiury," *Novyi Voskhod*, no. 25, 20 June 1913, 29–30.

24. Iulii. I. Gessen, "Iz proshlogo: Kol Nidre," *Voskhod*, no. 38, 19 September 1903, 42.

25. Iulii I. Gessen, "Istoricheskie miniatiury," *Novyi Voskhod*, no. 27, 4 July 1913, 31–32.

26. *PSZ* 32, no. 25,649 (21 August 1814).

27. Shugurov, "Doklad," 272; S. Pen, "Deputatsiia evreiskogo naroda," *Knizhki Voskhoda* 35 (February 1905): 61–66.

28. Pen, "Deputatsiia," 25, no. 3 (March 1905): 61–63.

29. N., "Evreiskie zemledel'cheskie kolonii," *Voskhod* 1 (January 1881): 88–89.

30. *PSZ* 31, no. 24,185 (6 April 1810).

31. For a complete record of Jewish colonization schemes and their outcome through the 1880s, see V. N. Nikitin, *Evrei-zemledel'tsy* (St. Petersburg, 1887).

32. M. I. Tugan-Baranovsky, *The Russian Factory in the Nineteenth Century*, translation of 3d Russ. ed. by Arthur and Claora S. Levin (Homewood, Ill., 1970), 89.

33. A. G. Rashin, *Formirovanie promyshlennogo proletariata v Rossii* (Moscow, 1940), 79–82.

34. Tugan-Baranovsky, *Russian Factory*, 58–60.

35. *PSZ* 30, no. 23,132 (30 June 1808).

36. The provision in the 1808 decree that factory workers should receive their freedom after twenty years of service was not a humanitarian gesture. Rather, it was designed to help to create a group of native Russians with manufacturing skills. This would have allowed Russia to escape gradually from a dependence on imported, and expensive, foreign specialists.

37. The uncompromising tone of this statement and of the entire decree led Gradovskii to conclude that it was aimed at making the Jews into enserfed workingmen. In my opinion this is an exaggerated reading of the decree. *Torgovye i drugie prava*, 186–77. It might be noted as well that this treatment of the Jews was not anomalous: at the same time the Ministry of Interior endeavored to discourage

the mobility of Gypsies by enrolling them in towns as craftsmen and workers. Varadinov, *Istoriia MVD*, pt. 1, 234–35.

38. *PSZ* 28, no. 21,547 (9 December 1804).

39. I. F. Pavlovskii, "Kremenchugskaia fabrika suknodeliia dlia Evreev v nachale XIX veka," *Golos minuvshogo* 1 (October 1913): 175–77.

40. A. D. Iuditskii, "Evreiskaia burzhauziia i evreiskie rabochie v tekstil'noi promyshlennosti pervoi poloviny XIX v.," *Istoricheskii sbornik* (1935): 107–8.

41. Ibid., 109–10.

42. Ibid., 119–33.

43. I. Krashinskii points out that almost one-fourth of the Jewish population of the town of Kremenchug was initially employed in the factory. "Kazennaia fabrika dlia Evreev pri Aleksandre I," *ES* 8 (April–September 1916): 347. The Jewish population of Kremenchug numbered 530 persons.

44. Pavlovskii, "Kremenchugskaia fabrika," 178–79.

45. The career of the Jewish Maskil Giler Markevich is illustrative of this situation. He submitted numerous proposals for Jewish factories and craft enterprises of exactly the type that the government was supposedly encouraging. His requests for financial aid were rejected with the summary judgment that "Markevich has in view, not the common good, but personal advantage." Iuditskii, "Evreiskaia burzhuaziia," 112–13.

46. Ibid., 114.

47. Ibid., 117.

48. Ibid., 126.

49. Shugurov, "Doklad," 259–66. In general the committee approved the continuation of the cultural and societal reforms of the statute.

50. See above, p. 202.

51. Il'ia G. Orshanskii, *Russkoe zakonodatel'stvo o Evreiakh* (St. Petersburg, 1877), 280.

52. For Novosil'tsev's "Constitutional Charter," see Marc Raeff, *Plans for Political Reform in Imperial Russia, 1730–1905* (Englewood Cliffs, N.J., 1966), 110–20. See also Leonid I. Strakhovsky, "Constitutional Aspects of the Imperial Russian Government's Policy toward National Minorities," *JMH* 13 (December 1941): 467–92.

53. Judith Cohen Zacek, "The Russian Bible Society and the Russian Orthodox Church," *Church History* 35 (December 1966): 421–23.

54. Richard Pipes, "The Russian Military Colonies, 1810–1831," *JMH* 22 (September 1950): 205–19.

55. *PSZ* 34, no. 26,752 (25 March 1817).

56. Stefan Schreimer, "Alexander I. und Die Bekehrung der Juden: Der Ukas vom 25. marz 1817," *Judaica* 33 (1977): 59–67; M. M., "Obshchestvo Izrail'skikh Khristian," *Rassvet*, no. 17, 23 March 1881.

57. The activities of the London Society for Promoting Christianity among the Jews may be followed in the documents contained in "Papers of the Church's Ministry among the Jews," in the Bodleian Library in Oxford, England. For the efforts of the Russian Bible Society among the Jews, see William Canton, *A History of the British and Foreign Bible Society* (London, 1904), 1:414.

58. John D. Klier, "The Jewish Question in the Reform Era Russian Press, 1855–1865," *Russian Review* 39 (July 1980): 301–19.

59. *PSZ* 40, no. 30,436 (29 July 1825).

60. *PSZ* 35, no. 27,352 (22 April 1818); and 37, no. 28,249 (22 April 1820). The requirement that all Jews be removed from districts where Sabbatarians were found lay dormant until 1880, when it was used as a pretext for the resettlement of

Jews from the countryside. See *Times of London*, no. 29,878 (11 May 1880). The governmental response to Sabbatarianism under Alexander I is traced in Antoine Scheikevitch, "Alexandre Ier et L'Hérésie Sabbatiste," *Revue d'Histoire Moderne et Contemporaine* 3 (1956): 223–35.

61. For Way, see Dubnow, *History*, 1:397–98; Max J. Kohler, "Jewish Rights at the Congresses of Vienna (1814–1815) and Aix-La-Chapelle (1818)," *Publications of the American Jewish Historical Society* 26 (1918): 116–25; and James Parkes, "Lewis Way and His Times," *Transactions of the Jewish Society of England* 20 (London, 1964): 189–201.

62. *PSZ* 34, no. 26,624 (18 January 1817); and no. 27,106 (24 October 1817).

63. Pen, "Deputatsiia," 2:54–55; and 3:51.

64. Gessen, "K istorii," 58.

65. Gessen, " 'Deputaty,' " 1, no. 3 (July–September 1909): 17–29; and no. 4 (October–December): 196–206.

66. It was Golitsyn, for example, who proposed that peasant Sabbatarians be accused of converting to Judaism; he was also skeptical of the reliability of Jewish oaths.

67. Gessen, *Istoriia*, 1:209.

68. *PSZ* 34, no. 26,805 (19 April 1817); and 37, no. 28,501 (20 December 1820). Harsh punishment of Jews who had violated the regulations against "*krestsentsiia*" was averted through the personal intervention of Golitsyn.

69. *PSZ* 40, no. 30,404 (30 June 1825); and no. 30,402 (30 June 1825).

70. Gessen, *Istoriia*, 1:207–8.

71. George F. Jewsbury, *The Russian Annexation of Bessarabia, 1774–1828* (New York and Guildford, Eng., 1976), 60–63.

72. *PSZ* 35, no. 27,357 (29 April 1818).

73. For the internal life of Polish Jewry, see Dubnow, *History*, 2:100–104; for the Polish Jewish press see S. L. Tsinberg, *Istoriia evreiskoi pechati v Rossii* (Petrograd, 1915).

74. The grand duchy, as originally constituted, comprised 102,744 square kilometers and almost 2.6 million inhabitants, under the hereditary rule of Frederick August, the king of Saxony. The duchy was born out of the Prussian debacle at Jena and comprised the Prussian share of the last two partitions, excluding Danzig and Białystok district. After a victorious war with Austria in 1809, the duchy received New Galicia, increasing her territory to 155,430 square kilometers and her population to 4.3 million persons. Piotr S. Wandycz, *The Lands of Partitioned Poland, 1795–1818* (Seattle, 1974), 43. Congress Poland included these lands, minus a small territory returned to Prussia and the city of Kraków.

75. *Le Decret Infâme* was a reflection of Napoleon's disenchantment with the alleged misuse by the Jews of the civic equality they had received in the aftermath of the French Revolution. It placed severe restrictions and limitations upon Jewish credit activities, trade, and settlement. The term of the decree was set at ten years, within which time, it was hoped, "there will no longer exist any difference between them and the other citizens of our Empire" (Mahler, *History*, 72–74).

76. Gessen, *Istoriia*, 1:216. Significantly, the decree was not promulgated openly and was not published in the official register of laws but was listed among acts connected with the calling of a new Sejm.

77. John Stanley, "The Politics of the Jewish Question in the Duchy of Warsaw, 1807–1813," *JSS* 44 (1982): 53.

78. Ibid., 53–57.

79. Arthur Eisenbach, *Kwestia równouprawnienia Żydów w Królestwie Polskim* (Warsaw, 1972).

80. Gessen, *Istoriia*, 1:219–20.

81. M. L. Vishnitser, "Proekty reformy evreiskogo byta v Gertsogstve Varshavskom i Tsarstve Pol'skim (po neizdannym materialam)," *Perezhitoe* 1 (1909): 174–75; Artur Eisenbach, "Les droits civiques des Juifs dans le Royaume de Pologne," *REJ* 123 (January–June 1964):39 ff.

82. Ibid., 175–77.

83. Thackeray, *Antecedents*, 16.

84. Gessen, *Istoriia*, 1:220.

85. Ibid., 226.

86. Ibid., 227.

87. Friedländer's work was published as *Die Verbesserung der Israeliten im Königreich Polen* (Berlin, 1819). Dubnow, *History*, 2:90–91.

88. See Steven E. Aschheim, *Brothers and Strangers: The East European Jew in German and German Jewish Consciousness, 1800–1923* (Madison, Wis., 1982).

89. L. A. Chiarini, *Théorie du Judaïsme, appliquée à la réforme des Israélites*, 2 vols. (Paris, 1830). Chiarini acknowledges his use of Eisenmenger in vol. 1, 8.

90. T. N. Granovskii, "Sud'by evreiskogo naroda," *Biblioteka dlia Chtenii* 13, pt. 1 (1835), reprinted in *Sochinenie*, 4th ed. (Moscow, 1900), 110–133.

91. "Ob Iudeistve," *Zhurnal ministerstva narodnogo prosveshcheniia* 19 (1838): 503–28.

92. "Evreiskie religioznye sekty v Rossii," *Zhurnal ministerstva vnutrennikh del* 15 (September 1846): 3–49; (August 1846): 282–309; (November 1846): 211–73; and (December 1846): 500–580. The debt to Chiarini is acknowledged in September, 8–10. The Talmud is most extensively discussed in the November issue.

93. See Stanislawski, *Tsar Nicholas I and the Jews*, 43–48. In citing an official memorandum on the pernicious effect of the Talmud, Stanislawski laments that "all the sources of these spurious, and often curious, views cannot be traced" (197, n. 26). I believe that the works cited provide important clues in this regard.

94. Klier, "Jewish Question in the Reform Era Russian Press," 314. The author was, in fact, A. N. Aksakov, Ivan Aksakov's cousin and a future specialist on spiritualism in Russia.

95. Gessen, *Istoriia*, 1:222–23.

96. Ibid., 225.

97. See N. M. Gelber, "The Jewish Problem in Poland in the Years 1815 to 1830" (in Hebrew), *Zion* 13–14 (1948–1949): 123–43.

98. Gessen, *Istoriia*, 1:22–23.

99. Eisenbach, *Kwestia*, 30.

100. Gessen, *Istoriia*, 1:218; Stanley, "Politics of the Jewish Question," 56.

101. Gessen, *Istoriia*, 1:231.

102. Eisenbach, *Kwestia*, 36. The Jews were not the only group exempted from military service. Teachers and clergymen were also freed.

103. Gessen, *Istoriia*, 1:232.

104. Dubnow, *History*, 1:100–103; Isaac Levitats, *The Jewish Community in Russia, 1844–1917* (Jerusalem, 1981), 16–18.

105. Stanislawski, *Nicholas I and the Jews*, 123–27.

106. Golitsyn, *Istoriia*, 600–607.

107. Thackeray, *Antecedents*, 42–47; Stanley, "Politics of the Jewish Question," 57.

108. The Fourth Jewish Committee, to be discussed below, carefully studied contemporary Polish legislation on the Jews in the course of its own deliberations. See Ministerstvo Narodnogo Prosveshcheniia, *Arkhiv kazennye evreiskie uchilishcha* (Petrograd, 1920), 6.

109. Ibid., 6.
110. *VPSZ*, no. 8,054 (13 April 1835).

CHAPTER 7

1. Gregory L. Freeze, "Nuns, Jews and Religion in Russia: A Comment," forthcoming in *Proceedings of the Third International Conference of the Study Group on Eighteenth-Century Russia*. The word itself is cited in the dictionary of the Russian Academy of Sciences (1806), with the meanings "miser, skinflint, usurer." *Slovar' Akademii Rossiiskoi* 2:450.

2. Richard Pipes, *Karamzin's Memoir on Ancient and Modern Russia* (New York, 1969), 31.

3. N. M. Karamzin, *Pis'ma russkogo puteshestvennika* (St. Petersburg, 1884), 163.

4. See the account of S. Gromeka, "Pol'skie Evrei," *Sovremennik* 70, otd. 1 (1858); and the response of Kh. Rozenblat in *Otechestvennye Zapiski*, 120, otd. 3 (1858): 69–80.

5. V. N. Peretts and L. N. Peretts, *Dekabrist Grigorii Abramovich Peretts* (Leningrad, 1926), 26.

6. Aleksandr Donat, ed., *Neopalimaia Kupina* (New York, 1973), 49.

7. V. I. Semevskii, *Politicheskie i obshchestvennye idei Dekabristov* (St. Petersburg, 1909), 343.

8. Peretts and Peretts, *Dekabrist*, 25.

9. The Decembrists addressed the Jewish Question artistically as well. A leader of the Northern Society, the well-known civic poet K. F. Ryleev, mentioned the Jews in his famous historical poem "Nalivaiko," published in 1825. Concerning the economic role played by the Jews in the past in the Ukraine, Ryleev classed them with the Uniates, Poles, and Lithuanians as "bloodthirsty enemies" preying on the Cossacks and the peasants. Donat, *Neopalimaia Kupina*, 59.

10. Semevskii, *Idei Dekabristov*, 522.

11. *Vosstanie Dekabristov. Materialy/Dokumenty po istorii vosstaniia Dekabristov* (Moscow, 1925–1958), 7:146–47.

12. Ibid., 148.

BIBLIOGRAPHY

The bibliography lists material cited in the text, as well as other sources consulted in order to answer specific questions encountered in the preparation of this work.

ARCHIVAL MATERIALS

Oxford. Bodleian Library.
Papers of the Church's Ministry among the Jews, formerly the London Society for Promoting Christianity among the Jews, 1808–1970.

PUBLISHED MATERIALS

Abramovich, Dmitro. *Kievo-Pechers'kii Paterik*. Kiev, 1930.
Alston, Patrick L. *Education and the State in Tsarist Russia*. Stanford, 1969.
Antonovich, Vladimir, and Dragomanov, Mikhail. *Istoricheskie pesni malorusskogo naroda*. Kiev, 1875.
Arendt, Hannah. *The Origins of Totalitarianism*. 2d rev. ed. New York, 1960.
Arkhiv gosudarstvennogo soveta. Vol. 1, pt. 2. St. Petersburg, 1869.
Aronson, I. Michael. "The Attitudes of Russian Officials in the 1880s toward Jewish Assimilation and Emigration." *SR* 34 (March 1975): 1–18.
———. "The Prospects for the Emancipation of Russian Jewry during the 1880s." *SEER* 55 (July 1977): 348–69.
Aschheim, Steven E. *Brothers and Strangers: The East European Jew in German and German Jewish Consciousness, 1800–1923*. Madison, Wis., 1982.
Bałaban, Majer. *Dzieje Żydów w Krakówie i na Kazimierzu, 1304–1868*. 2 vols. Kraków, 1912–1936.
———. "Perekhod pol'skikh Evreev pod vlast' Avstrii." *ES* 5 (July–September 1913): 289–307.
———. "Pravovoi stroi Evreev v Pol'she v srednie i novye veka." *ES* 2, no. 1

(January–March 1910): 39–60; no. 2 (April–June): 161–91; no. 3 (July–September): 324–45; and 3, no. 1 (January–March, 1911): 40–54; no. 2 (April–June): 180–96.

Baron, Salo Wittmayer. *History and Jewish Historians*. Philadelphia, 1964.

———. *The Jewish Community*. 3 vols. Philadelphia, 1942.

———. *The Russian Jew under Tsars and Soviets*. 2d rev. ed. New York and London, 1976.

———. *A Social and Religious History of the Jews*. 16 vols. 2d rev. ed. New York, 1952–1976.

Baron, Salo W., Kahan, Arcadius, et al. *Economic History of the Jews*. New York, 1975.

Bartlett, Roger. *Human Capital: The Settlement of Foreigners in Russia, 1762–1804*. Cambridge, Eng., 1979.

Bernard, Paul P. "Joseph II and the Jews: The Origins of the Toleration Patent of 1782." *Austrian History Yearbook* 4–5 (1968–1969): 101–19.

Bershadskii, Sergei A. "K istorii Evreev v Litve i Pol'she." *EB* 7 (1879): 1–35.

———. *Litovskie Evrei*. St. Petersburg, 1883.

———. "Materialy dlia istorii Evreev v Iugo-Zapadnoi Rossii i Litve." *EB* 8 (1880): 1–32.

———. "Opyt novoi postanovki nekotorykh voprosov po istorii Evreev v Litve i Pol'she." *EB* 7 (1879): 1–34.

———. "Polozhenie o Evreiakh 1804 goda." *Voskhod* 15 (January 1895): 82–104; (March): 69–96; (April): 86–109; (June): 33–63.

Birnbaum, Henrik. "On Some Evidence of Jewish Life and Anti-Jewish Sentiments in Medieval Russia." *Viator* 4 (1973): 225–55.

Black, Cyril E. *The Dynamics of Modernization*. New York, 1966.

Bloch, Philipp. *Die General-Privilegien der polnischen Judenschaft*. Posen, 1892.

Blum, Jerome. *Lord and Peasant in Russia*. Princeton, 1971.

Brafman, Iakov. *Kniga kagala*. Vilna, 1869.

———. *Kniga kagala*. Pt. I. St. Petersburg, 1888.

Breman, Shlomo. "Toward the Image of the Jews in Russian Literature of the Nineteenth Century." In Hebrew. *He-Avar* 20 (1973): 135–75.

Canton, William. *A History of the British and Foreign Bible Society*. 5 vols. London, 1904.

Cassirer, Ernst. *The Philosophy of the Enlightenment*. Boston, 1960.

Catherine II. *Sochinenie Imperatritsy Ekateriny II*. Vol. 12, Edited by A. N. Pypin. St. Petersburg, 1907.

Chiarini, Luigi A. *Théorie du Judaïsme, appliquée à la réforme des Israélites*. 2 vols. Paris, 1830.

Cohen, Israel. *Vilna*. Philadelphia, 1943.

Cohn, Norman. *Warrant for Genocide*. New York and Evanston, Ill., 1969.

Cohn, Willy. "Christian Wilhelm von Dohm." *HJ* 13 (October 1951): 101–8.

Cross, Samuel H., and Sherbowitz-Wetzor, Olgerd P., eds. *The Russian Primary Chronicle: Laurentian Text*. Cambridge, Mass., 1953.

Czacki, Tadeusz. *Rosprawa o Żydach i Karaitach*. Vilna, 1807.

Czartoryski, Adam. *Memoirs of Prince Adam Czartoryski and His Correspondence with Alexander I*. 2 vols. Edited by Adam Gielgud. London, 1888.

Davies, Norman. *God's Playground. A History of Poland*. 2 vols. New York, 1982.

Dawidowicz, Lucy S. *The Golden Tradition: Jewish Life and Thought in Eastern Europe*. New York and Chicago, 1967.

Derzhavin, Gavriil R. *Sochineniia Derzhavina*. 9 vols. Edited by Ia. Grot. St. Petersburg, 1864–1883.

————. *Zapiski*. Moscow, 1860.
Ditiatin, I. *Ustroistvo i upravlenie gorodov Rossii*. 2 vols. St. Petersburg, 1875–1877.
Dohm, Christian Wilhelm von. *De la réforme politique des Juifs*. Halle, 1782.
Donat, Aleksandr. *Neopalimaia Kupina*. New York, 1973.
Druzhinin, N. M. "Prosveshchennyi absoliutizm v Rossii." In *Absoliutizm v Rossii (XVII–XVIII)*. Edited by N. Druzhinin, N. Pavlenko, and L. Cherepnin. Moscow, 1964.
Dubnow, Simon M. "Evrei i reformatsiia v Pol'she v XVI veke." *Voskhod* 5 (May 1895): 4–11, 43–64.
————. "Evreiskaia Pol'sha v epokhu poslednikh razdelov." *ES* 3 (October–December 1911): 441–63.
————. "Evreiskaia Pol'sha v epokhu razdelov." *ES* 1 (January–March 1909): 3–16.
————. *History of the Jews in Russia and Poland*. 3 vols. Philadelphia, 1916–1920.
————. "Tserkovnye legendy ob otroke Gavriile Zabludovskom." *ES* 8 (April–September 1916): 309–16.
————. "Vmeshatel'stvo russkogo pravitel'stva v antikhasidskuiu bor'bu (1800–1801)." *ES* 2 (January–March 1910): 84–109; (April–June): 253–82.
Duker, Abraham. "Bibliography of *Evreiskaia starina*." *Hebrew Union College Annual*, 8–9 (1931–1932): 525–603.
Dukes, Paul. *Catherine the Great and the Russian Nobility*. Cambridge, Eng., 1967.
Dunlop, Douglas M. "H. M. Baratz and His View of Khazar Influence on the Earliest Russian Literature, Juridical and Historical." In *Salo Wittmayer Baron Jubilee Volume*. 3 vols., 1:345–67. New York, 1974.
Dziewanowski, M. K. "Czartoryski and His *Essai sur la diplomatie*." *SR* 30 (September 1971): 589–605.
Eisenbach, Artur. "Les droits civiques des Juifs dans la Royaume de Pologne." *REJ* 123 (January–June 1964): 19–84.
————. *Kwestia równoprawnienia Żydów w Królestwie Polskim*. Warsaw, 1972.
————. "Rozprzestrzenienie i Warunki Mieszkaniowe Ludności Żydowskiej w Warszawie w Swietle Spisu w 1815 r.," *BZIH* 25 (January–April 1958): 50–86.
————. "Wokół problematyki emancypacji Żydow w Królestwie Polskim," *BZIH* 4 (October–December 1974): 71–89.
————. "Żydzi w dawnej Polsce w świetle liczb (na inarginesie pracy R. Mahlera na ten temat)," *Kwartalnik Historyczny*, 66 (1959): 511–20.
Encyclopedia Judaica. 16 vols. New York, 1971–1972.
Encyclopédie ou Dictionnaire raisonné des sciènces, des arts et des métiers. Vol. 10. Geneva, 1777.
Eroshkin, N. P. *Ocherki istorii gosudarstvennykh uchrezhdenii dorevoliutsionnoi Rossii*. Moscow, 1960.
"Eshche rasskaz Ekateriny II-i o svoem tsarstvovanii." *Russkii arkhiv* 3 (1880): 3.
Ettinger, Shemu'el. "The Grounds and Tendencies in the Shaping of Russian Policy in Regard to the Jews on the Partition of Poland." In Hebrew. *He-Avar* 19 (1972): 20–34.
————. "Jewish Influence on the Religious Ferment in Eastern Europe at the End of the Fifteenth Century." In Hebrew. In *Yitzhak F. Baer Jubilee Volume*, 228–47. Edited by W. Baron et al. Jerusalem, 1960.
————. "The Muscovite State and Its Attitudes toward the Jews." In Hebrew. *Zion* 18 (1953): 136–68.
————. "Russian Society and the Jews." *Bulletin on Soviet and East European Jewish Affairs* 5 (1970): 36–42.

————. "The Statute of 1804." In Hebrew. *He-Avar* 22 (1977): 87–110.
"Evreiskie religioznye sekty v Rossii." *Zhurnal ministerstva vnutrennikh del* 15 (September 1846): 3–49; (August): 282–309; (November): 211–73; (December): 500–580.
Fajnhauz, Dawid. "Konflikty społeczne wśród ludności Żydowskiej na Litwie i Białorusi w pierwszej połowie XIX wieku." *BZIH* 52 (October–December 1964): 3–15.
Fedotov, George P. *The Russian Religious Mind.* New York, 1960.
Fennell, John L. I. "The Attitude of the Josephians and the Trans-Volga Elders to the Heresy of the Judaizers." *SEER* (June 1951), 486–509.
————. *The Correspondence between Prince A. M. Kurbskii and Tsar Ivan IV of Russia, 1564–1579.* Cambridge, 1963.
Fisher, Alan. *The Crimean Tatars.* Stanford, 1978.
————. "Enlightened Despotism and Islam Under Catherine II." *SR* 27 (December 1968): 542–43.
Frankel, Jonathan. *Prophecy and Politics: Socialism, Nationalism, and the Russian Jews, 1862–1917.* Cambridge, Eng., 1981.
Freeze, Gregory L. "Nuns, Jews and Religion in Russia: A Comment." Forthcoming in *Proceedings of the Third International Conference of the Study Group on Eighteenth-Century Russia.*
————. *The Russian Levites. Parish Clergy in the Eighteenth Century.* Cambridge, Mass., 1977.
Freund, I. *Die Emanzipation der Juden in Preussen unter besonderer Berucksichtigung des Gesetzes vom 11. März 1812.* 2 vols. Berlin, 1912.
Friedländer, David. *Die Verbesserung der Israeliten in Königreich Polen.* Berlin, 1819.
Gattsuk, Aleksandr. "Evrei v russkoi istorii i poezii." *Sion,* nos. 1 (7 July 1861); 5 (4 August 1861); 10 (10 September 1861); 11 (17 September 1861); 38 (23 March 1861); 39 (30 March 1861).
Galant, I. "Zadolzhennost' evreiskikh obshchin v XVII veke." *ES* 5 (January–March 1913): 129–32.
Gay, Peter. *The Party of Humanity.* New York, 1964.
Gekker, Elena. "Evrei v pol'skikh gorodakh vo vtoroi polovine XVIII veka." *ES* 5 (January–March 1913): 184–200; 3 (July–September): 325–32.
————. "Iudofobiia v Pol'she XVIII veka." *ES* 5 (October–December 1913): 439–54.
————. "Proekty reformy evreiskogo byta v Pol'she kontse XVIII veka." *ES* 6 (April–June 1914): 206–18; (July–December): 328–40.
Gelber, N. M. "The Jewish Problem in Poland in the Years 1815 to 1830." In Hebrew. *Zion* 13–14 (1948–1949): 106–43.
Gessen, Iulii I. " 'Deputaty evreiskogo naroda' pri Aleksandre I." *ES* 1 (July–September 1909): 17–29; (October–December): 196–206.
————. "Evrei v Kurliandii (XVI–XVIII v.)." *ES* 6 (January–March 1914): 145–62; (July–December): 365–84.
————. "Evrei v moskovskom gosudarstve XV–XVII veka." *ES* 7 (January–March 1915): 1–19; (April–June): 3–19; (April–June): 153–72.
————. *Evrei v Rossii.* St. Petersburg, 1906.
————. "Istoricheskie miniatury." *Novyi Voskhod* 25 (20 June 1913): 29–31; 27 (4 July 1913): 30–32.
————. *Istoriia evreiskogo naroda v Rossii.* 2 vols. Leningrad, 1925–1927.
————. "Iz proshlogo: Kol Nidre." *Voskhod* 38 (19 September 1903): 41–44.
————. "K istorii 'srednevekovykh' obvinenii." *Knizhki Voskhoda* 22 (April 1902): 54–62.

————. "Moskovskoe getto." *Perezhitoe*. Vol. 1. (St. Petersburg, 1908), 51–65.
————. "Stremlenie Ekateriny II vodvorit' Evreev v Rossii (1764 g.)." *ES* 7 (July–December 1915): 338–46.
————. *Zakon i Zhizn'*. St. Petersburg, 1911.
Ginsberg, Morris. "On Dubnow's Conception of Jewish History." In *Simon Dubnow: The Man and His Work*. Edited by Aaron Steinberg. Paris, 1963.
Ginsburg, Shaul M. *Historical Works*. In Yiddish. 3 vols. New York, 1937.
Golb, Norman, and Pritsak, Omeljan. *Khazarian Hebrew Documents of the Tenth Century*. Ithaca, N.Y., and London, 1982.
Goldberg, Jacob. "Poles and Jews in the 17th and 18th Centuries: Rejection or Acceptance." *JGO* 22 (1974), 248–82.
Golitsyn, Nikolai N. *Istoriia russkogo zakonodatel'stva o Evreiakh*. St. Petersburg, 1886.
Golubinskii, E. E. *Istoriia russkoi tserkvi*. 2 vols. Moscow, 1900–1917.
Gradovskii, Nikolai D. *Otnosheniia k Evreiam v drevnei i sovremennoi Rusi*. St. Petersburg, 1891.
————. *Torgovye i drugie prava Evreev v Rossii*. St. Petersburg, 1886.
Graetz, Heinrich. *History of the Jews*. 6 vols. Philadelphia, 1891–1898.
Granovskii, T. N. "Sud'by evreiskogo naroda." *Biblioteka dlia Chtenii*. Vol. 13, pt. 1 (1835). Reprinted in *Sochinenie*, 4th ed. (Moscow, 1900): 110–33.
Greenberg, Louis. *The Jews in Russia*. 2 vols. in 1. Edited by Mark Wischnitzer. New Haven, 1965.
Gromyka, S. "Polskie Evrei." *Sovremennik* 70 (1858).
Halperin, Charles J. "Judaizers and the Image of the Jew in Medieval Russia: A Polemic Revisited and a Question Posed." *CASS* 9 (Summer 1975): 141–55.
Handelsman, Marceli. *Adam Czartoryski*. 3 vols. in 4. Warsaw, 1948–1950.
Hertzberg, Arthur. *The French Enlightenment and the Jews*. New York, 1970.
Hundert, Gershon David. "An Advantage to Peculiarity? The Case of the Polish Commonwealth." *Association for Jewish Studies Review* 6 (1981): 21–38.
————. "Jews, Money and Society in the Seventeenth-Century Polish Commonwealth: The Case of Krakow." *JSS* 43 (1981): 261–74.
————. "On the Jewish Community in Poland during the Seventeenth Century: Some Comparative Perspectives." *REJ* 142 (July–December 1983): 349–72.
Iosif Volotskii. *Prosvetitel' ili oblichenie eresi zhidovstvuiushchikh*. Kazan, 1903; reprint, Westmead, Eng., 1972.
Iuditskii, A. D. "Evreiskaia burzhuaziia i evreiskie rabochie v tekstil'noi promyshlennosti pervoi poloviny XIX v." *Istoricheskii sbornik* (1935): 107–8.
"Iz letopisi minuvshogo: 'Bor'ba pravitel'stva s" evreiskoi odezhdoi v Imperii i Tsarstve Pol'skom.' " *Perezhitoe* 1 (1909): 10–18.
Jewish Encyclopedia. 12 vols. Reprint of 1901 ed. New York, 1964.
Jewsbury, George F. *The Russian Annexation of Bessarabia, 1774–1828*. New York and Guildford, Eng., 1976.
Jones, Robert E. *The Emancipation of the Russian Nobility, 1762–1785*. Princeton, 1973.
Juszczyk, Jan. "O Badaniach nad Judaizantyzmem." *Kwartalnik Historyczny* 76 (1969): 141–51.
Kabuzan, V. M. *Narodonaselenie Rossii v XVIII-pervoi polovine XIX v*. Moscow, 1963.
Kamanin, I. "Perepisi evreiskogo naseleniia v iugo-zapadnom krae v 1765–1791 gg." *Arkhiv Iugo-Zapednoi Rossii*. Part 5, vol. 2, sects. 1 and 2. Kiev, 1890.
Kamendrowsky, Victor, and Griffiths, David M., "The Fate of the Trading Nobility Controversy in Russia: A Chapter in the Relationship between Catherine II and the Russian Nobility." *JGO* 26 (1978): 198–221.

Karamzin, N. M. *Pis'ma russkogo puteshestvennika*. St. Petersburg, 1884.
Katz, Jacob. "A State within a State: The History of an Anti-Semitic Slogan."
    Emancipation and Assimilation. Richmond, Eng., 1972.
————. *Out of the Ghetto*. Cambridge, Mass., 1973.
————. *Tradition and Crisis*. Glencoe, Ill., 1961.
Kaunitz, J. *Russian Literature and the Jew*. New York, 1929.
Kazakova, N. A., and Lur'e, Ia. S. *Antifeodal'nye ereticheskie dvizheniia na Rusi XIV–
    nachala XVI veka*. Moscow and Leningrad, 1955.
Keep, John. "Light and Shade in the History of the Russian Administration."
    CASS 6 (Spring 1972): 1–9.
————. "Mutiny in Moscow, 1682." *Canadian Slavonic Papers* 23 (1981): 410–42.
Khalanskii, M. "Bylina o Zhidovine." *Russkii Filologicheskii Vestnik* 23 (1890): 1–23.
Kharlampovich, K. V. *Malorossiiskoe vliianie na velikorusskuiu tserkovnuiu zhizn'*.
    Vol. 1. Kazan, 1914.
————. *Zapadnorusskie pravoslavnye shkoly XVI i nachala XVII veka*. Kazan, 1898.
Kizevetter, Aleksandr A. *Gorodovoe polozhenie Ekateriny II 1785 g*. Moscow, 1909.
————. *Posadskaia obshchina v Rossii XVIII st*. Moscow, 1903.
Klausner, Israel. "The Inner Struggle in Jewish Communities in Russia and Lith-
    uania at the End of the Eighteenth Century." In Hebrew. *He-Avar* 19 (1972):
    54–73.
Kleinman, I. A. "Karaimskii 'ritual'nyi protsess' v XVII veke." *ES* 11 (1924): 228–
    33.
Klibanov, A. I. *Reformatsionnye dvizheniia v Rossii v XIV–pervoi polovine XVI vv*.
    Moscow, 1960.
Klier, John D. "The Jewish Question in the Reform Era Russian Press, 1855–
    1865." *Russian Review* 39 (July 1980): 301–20.
————. "*Zhid*: The Biography of a Russian Epithet." *SEER* 60 (January 1982).
Kohler, Max J. "Jewish Rights at the Congresses of Vienna (1814–1815), and
    Aix-La-Chapelle (1818)." *Publications of the American Jewish Historical Society* 26
    (1918): 33–125.
Korf, M. *Zhizn' Grafa Speranskogo*. St. Petersburg, 1861.
Korobkov, Kh. "Ekonomicheskaia rol' Evreev v Pol'she v kontse XVIII v." *ES* 2
    (July–September 1910): 346–77.
————. "Perepis' evreiskogo naseleniia vitebskoi gubernii v 1772 g." *ES* 4 (April–
    June 1912): 164–77.
————. "Statistika evreiskogo naseleniia Pol'shi i Litvy vo vtoroi polovine XVIII
    veka." *ES* 3 (October–December 1911): 541–62.
Kostomarov, Nikolai. "Velikorusskie religioznye vol'nodumtsy v XVI veke.—
    Matvei Bashkin i ego souchastniki Feodosii Kosoi." *Istoricheskie monografii i
    issledovanii*. Vol. 1, 385–428. St. Petersburg, 1872.
Koval'chenko, I. D. "K voprosu o sostoianii pomeshchich'ego khoziaistva pered
    otmenoi krepostnogo prava v Rosii." *Ezhegodnik po agrarnoi istorii Vostochnoi
    Evropy: 1959 g*. Moscow, 1961.
Kozlovskii, P. G. *Krest'iane Belorussii vo vtoroi polovine XVII–XVIII v*. Minsk, 1969.
Krashinskii, I. "Kazennaia fabrika dlia Evreev pri Aleksandre I." *ES* 8 (October–
    December 1916): 345–51.
Kraus, Henry. *The Living Theatre of Medieval Art*. Philadelphia, 1967.
Kukiel, Marian. *Czartoryski and European Unity, 1770–1861*. Princeton, 1955.
Kulisher, M. I. "Ekaterina II i Evrei." *Voskhod* 16 (November 1896): 133–48.
————. "Evrei v Kieve." *ES* 5 (October–December 1913): 417–38.
————. "Istoriia russkogo zakonodatel'stva o Evreiakh v sviazi s sistemoi vzimaniia
    nalogov i otbyvaniia povinnostei." *ES* 2 (October–December 1910): 467–503.

Kunitz, Joshua. *Russian Literature and the Jew.* New York, 1929.
Kurin, I. "Evrei v Moskve vo vtoroi polovine XVII v." *ES* 5 (January–March 1913): 96–101.
L., A. "K istorii zapadno-russkikh Evreev." *EB* 4 (1873): 7–15.
Lapzhina, R. G. "Feodosii Kosoi—ideolog krestianstva XVI v." In *Trudy otdela drevnorusskoi literatury.* Vol. 9, 235–50. Moscow, 1953.
LeDonne, John P. "Indirect Taxes in Catherine's Russia. II. The Liquor Monopoly." *JGO* 24 (1976): 173–207.
———. "The Territorial Reform of the Russian Empire, 1775–1796." *CMRS* 23 (April–June 1982): 147–86; 24 (October–December 1983): 411–58.
Lehtonen, Uno Ludvig. *Die polnischen Provinzen Russlands unter Katerina II in den Jahren 1772–1782.* Berlin, 1907.
Lemercier-Quelquejay, Chantal. "Les missions orthodoxes en pays musulmans de Moyenne-et Basse-Volga, 1552–1865." *CMRS* 8 (July–September 1967): 369–403.
Lestchinsky, Yakov. "The Economic Background of the Jewish Pale of Settlement." In Hebrew. *He-Avar* 1 (1952): 31–44.
Levanda, V. O. *Polnyi khronologicheskii sbornik zakonov i polozhenii kasaiushchikhsia Evreev.* St. Petersburg, 1874.
Levenberg, S. "The Historian of Russian Jewry." In *Simon Dubnow: The Man and His Work.* Edited by Aaron Steinberg. Paris, 1963.
Levitats, Isaac. "The Authenticity of Brafman's 'Book of the Kahal.' " In Hebrew. *Zion* 3 (January 1938): 170–78.
———. *The Jewish Community in Russia, 1772–1844.* New York, 1943.
———. *The Jewish Community in Russia, 1844–1917.* Jerusalem, 1981.
Lewin, I. "Nachalo emansipatsii Evreev v pobezhdennoi Prussii (1808–1812 g.)." *ES* 7 (July–September 1915): 241–66.
Liashchenko, P. I. *History of the National Economy of Russia to the 1917 Revolution.* New York, 1970.
Lord, Robert H. *The Second Partition of Poland.* Cambridge, Mass., 1915.
Lur'e, Ia. S. "Unresolved Issues in the History of the Ideological Movements of the Late Fifteenth Century." In *Medieval Russian Culture*, 163–71. Edited by Henrik Birnbaum and Michael S. Flier. Berkeley, Los Angeles, and London, 1984.
M., M. "Obshchestvo Izrail'skikh Khristian." *Rassvet*, no. 17. 23 March 1881.
M., M. "Svoeobraznaia ob"ektivnost'. (Istoriia russkogo zakonodatel'stava o Evreiakh, sochinenie kniazia N. N. Golitsyna)." *Voskhod* 7 (March 1877): 29–50.
Madariaga, Isabel de. *Russia in the Age of Catherine the Great.* New Haven and London, 1981.
Mahler, Raphael. *A History of Modern Jewry, 1780–1815.* London, 1971.
———. *Yidn in amolikn Poiln in likht fun tsifern.* Warsaw, 1958.
Maor, Yitshak. "The Pale of Jewish Settlement." In Hebrew. *He-Avar* 19 (1972): 35–53.
Mendelssohn, Moses. *Jerusalem and Other Writings.* New York, 1969.
Meshalin, I. V. *Tekstil'naia promyshlennost krest'ian moskovskoi gubernii v XVIII i pervoi polovine XIX veka.* Moscow and Leningrad, 1950.
Meyer, Michael A. *The Origins of the Modern Jew.* Detroit, 1967.
Mezhov, V. M. "Bibliografiia evreiskogo voprosa." *EB* 4 (1873): 1–36 (after 301); 5 (1875): 37–77 (after 198).
Ministerstvo Narodnogo Prosveshcheniia. *Arkhiv kazennye evreiske uchilishcha.* Petrograd, 1920.
Minor, Z. "Predstavleniia i rezoliutsii o kurliandskikh Evreiakh pri Pavle I." *EB* 4 (1873): 114–24.

Mirabeau, Honoré G. R. *Sur Moses Mendelssohn, sur la réforme politique des Juifs.* Paris, 1968.

Montesquieu, Baron de (Charles de Secondat). *The Spirit of Laws.* Translated by Thomas Nugent. 2 vols. New York and London, 1900.

Morley, Charles. "Czartoryski as a Polish Statesman." *SR* 30 (September 1971): 606–14.

Mysh, M. I. "Bor'ba pravitel'stva s piteinym promyshlom Evreev v selakh i derev- niakh." *Voskhod* 1 (August 1881): 15–47.

N. "Evreiskie zemledel'cheskie kolonii." *Voskhod* 1 (January 1881): 85–131; (Febru- ary): 92–119; (March): 87–115; (May): 37–70; (June): 76–106. Reprinted as Nikitin, V. N., *Evrei-zemledel'tsy,* St. Petersburg, 1887.

Nevakhovich, Leiba. *Vopl' dshcheri iudeiskoi.* St. Petersburg, 1803.

New Catholic Encyclopedia. 16 vols. New York, 1967.

Nikitin, V. I. "Eshche o knige N. N. Golitsyna." *Voskhod* 7 (April 1887): 15–27.

Nolte, Hans-Heinrich. *Religiöse Toleranz in Russland, 1600–1725.* Gottingen, 1970.

"Ob Iudeistve." *Zhurnal ministerstva narodnogo prosveshcheniia* 19 (1838): 503–28.

Obolensky, Dmitri. "Russia's Byzantine Heritage." In *The Structure of Russian History.* Edited by Michael Cherniavsky. New York, 1970.

O'Brien, Charles H. "Ideas of Religious Toleration at the Time of Joseph II." *Transactions of the American Philosophical Society.* Vol. 15, pt. 7, 1969.

"Ob uzakonenii dlia blaga Evreev, obitaiushchikh v Imperii Vserossiiskoi." *Vestnik Evropy* 10 (May 1805): 139–40.

Orbach, Alexander. "The Saul Ginsburg Archival Collection: A Major Source for the Study of Russian Jewish Life and Letters." *SJA* 11 (May 1981): 39–52.

Orshanskii, Il'ia G. *Evrei v Rossii.* St. Petersburg, 1872.

———. *Russkoe zakonodatel'stvo o Evreiakh.* St. Petersburg, 1877.

———. "Russkoe zakonodatel'stvo o Evreiakh." *EB* 2 (1872): 97–158.

———. "Vzgliad na ekonomicheskii byt' russkikh Evreev." *Den',* no. 14. August 1869.

Parkes, James. *The Conflict of the Church and the Synagogue.* London, 1934.

———. "Lewis Way and His Times." *Transactions of the Jewish Historical Society of England.* Vol. 20, 189–201. London, 1964.

Pavlovskii, I. F. "Kremenchugskaia fabrika suknodeliia dlia Evreev v nachale XIX veka." *Golos minuvshogo.* October 1913, 175–80.

Pen, S. "Deputatsiia evreiskogo naroda." *Knizhki Voskhoda* 25, no. 1 (January 1905): 62–84; no. 2 (February 1905): 50–65; no. 3 (March 1905): 50–71.

Peretts, V. N., and Peretts, L. N. *Dekabrist Grigorii Abramovich Peretts.* Leningrad, 1926.

Pinkus, B., and Greenbaum, A. A. *Russian Publications on Jews and Judaism in the Soviet Union, 1917–1967.* Jerusalem, 1970.

Pipes, Richard. "Catherine II and the Jews." *SJA* 5 (1975).

———. *Karamzin's Memoir on Ancient and Modern Russia.* New York, 1969.

———. "The Russian Military Colonies, 1810–1831." *JMH* 22 (September 1950): 205–219.

Platon, Metropolitan of Moscow. *Polnoe sobranie sochinenii.* 2 vols. St. Petersburg, n.d.

Polnoe sobranie zakonov rossiiskoi imperii. Sobranie pervoe. 46 vols. St. Petersburg, 1830–1843.

Polnoe sobranie zakonov rossiiskoi imperii. Sobranie vtoroe. 30 vols. St. Petersburg, 1830–1856.

Portal, Roger. "Manufactures et classes sociales en Russie au XVIIIᵉ siècle." *Revue historique* 201 (April–June 1949): 1–23.

Pozner, Solomon V. *Evrei v obshchei shkole.* St. Petersburg, 1914.

Prestel, David K. "A Comparative Analysis of Two Patericon Stories." *Russian History* 7 (1980): 11–20.

Rabinovich, G. "Brafmanskie vidy evreiskoi eksploatatsii." *EB* 3 (1892): 373–91.

Raeff, Marc. *Michael Speransky, Statesman of Imperial Russia.* The Hague, 1957.

———. *Plans for Political Reform in Imperial Russia, 1730–1905.* Englewood Cliffs, N.J., 1966.

———. "Seventeenth-Century Europe in Eighteenth Century Russia?" *SR* 41 (Winter 1982): 611–19.

———. "The Well-Ordered Police State and the Development of Modernity in Seventeenth- and Eighteenth-Century Europe: An Attempt at a Comparative Approach." *American Historical Review* 80 (December 1975): 1221–43.

———. *The Well-Ordered Police State: Social and Institutional Change through Law in the Germanies and Russia, 1600–1800.* New Haven and London, 1983.

———. *Origins of the Russian Intelligentsia.* New York, 1966.

———. "Patterns of Russian Imperial Policy toward the Nationalities." In *Soviet Nationality Problems.* Edited by Edward Allworth. New York, 1971.

Rashin, A. G. *Formirovanie promyshlennogo proletariata v Rossii.* Moscow, 1940.

Rawita-Gawroński, Fr. *Żydzi w historji literaturze ludowej na Rusi.* Warsaw, n.d. [1924].

Reddaway, W. F. *Documents of Catherine the Great.* Cambridge, England, 1931.

Reddaway, W. F., et al., eds. *The Cambridge History of Poland.* Cambridge, England, 1951.

Rest, Matthias. *Die Russische Judengesetzgebung von der Ersten Polnischen Teilung bis zum "Položenie dlja Evreev" (1804).* Wiesbaden, 1975.

"Ritual'nye protsessy 1816 g." *ES* 4 (April–June 1912), 144–63.

Rogger, Hans. "Government, Jews, Peasants, and Land in Post-Emancipation Russia." *CMRS* 17 (January–March 1976): 5–25; (April–September): 171–211.

———. "The Jewish Policy of Late Tsarism: A Reappraisal." *Wiener Library Bulletin*, 25, nos. 1 and 2 (n.s. 22 and 23, 1971): 42–51.

———. "Russian Ministers and the Jewish Question, 1881–1917." *California Slavic Studies* 8 (1975): 15–76.

———. "Tsarist Policy on Jewish Emigration." *SJA* 3 (1973): 26–36.

Rönne, Ludwig von, and Simon, Heinrich. *Die früheren und gegenwärtigen Verhältnisse der Juden in den sämmtlichen Landestheilen des Preussischen Staates.* Breslau, 1843.

Rovinskii, D. *Russkie narodnye kartinki.* 5 vols. St. Petersburg, 1881–1893.

———. *Podrobnyi slovar' russkikh graverov XVI–XIX vv.* 2 vols. St. Petersburg, 1895.

Rozenblat, Ia. "O stat'e g-na Gromeki 'Pol'skie Evrei." *Otechestvennye Zapiski* 120 (September 1858): 69–80.

Russia. Academiia Nauk. *Slovar' Akademii Rossiiskoi.* 6 vols. St. Petersburg, 1806–1822. Reprinted by Odense University Press: Odense, Denmark, 1970.

Russia. Imperatorskoe Russkoe Istoricheskoe Obshchestvo. *Pamiatniki diplomaticheskikh snoshenii moskovskogo gosudarstva s Pol'sko-Litovskim.* In *Sbornik Imperatorskogog Russkogo Istoricheskogo Obshchestva.* Vol. 59, pt. 21. 341–42. St. Petersburg, 1867–1916.

Russia. Ministerstvo Narodnogo Prosveshcheniia. *Arkhiv kazennye evreiskie uchilishcha.* St. Petersburg, Petrograd, 1920.

Russkii biograficheskii slovar'. 25 vols. St. Petersburg, 1896–1918.

Ryvkin, Kh. D. "Eshche ob otroke Gavriile Zabludovskom." *ES* 8 (October–December 1916): 465–68.

Scheikevitch, Antoine. "Alexandre Ier et L'Hérésie Sabbatiste." *Revue d'Histoire Moderne et Contemporaine* 3 (1956): 223–35.

Schorr, M. "Krakovskii svod evreiskikh statutov i privilegii." *ES* 1 (April–June 1909): 247–64.

Schreimer, Stefan. "Alexander I. und Die Bekehrung der Juden: Der Ukas vom 25. märz 1817." *Judaica* 33 (1977): 59–67.

Selzer, Michael. *The Wineskin and the Wizard.* New York, 1970.

Seiferth, Wolfgang. *Synagogue and Church in the Middle Ages.* New York, 1970.

Semevskii, V. I. *Politicheskie i obshchestvennye idei Dekabristov.* St. Petersburg, 1909.

Shatzky, Jacob. "An Attempt at Jewish Colonialization in the Kingdom of Poland." *YIVO Annual of Jewish Social Science* 1 (1946): 44–63.

Shelestov, D. K. "Svobodomyslie v uchenii Feodosiia Kosogo (50–60e gody XVI v.)." In *Voprosy istorii religii i ateizma.* Vol. 2. Moscow, 1954.

Shugurov, Mikhail T., ed. "Doklad o Evreiakh imperatoru Aleksandru Pavlovichu." *Russkii arkhiv* 41 (February 1903): 253–74.

———. "Istoriia Evreev v Rossii." *Russkii arkhiv* 32 (1894): 55–93, 129–81, 289–349, 465–500, and 45–102.

Shulvass, Moses A. *Jewish Culture in Eastern Europe. The Classical Period.* New York, 1975.

Slutsky, Yehuda, and Bobe, M. "To the History of the Jews in Russia at the End of the Eighteenth Century (Three Documents)." In Hebrew. *He-Avar* 19 (1972): 74–82.

Soifer, Paul Eric. "The Bespectacled Cossack: S. A. Bershadskii (1850–1896) and the Development of Russo-Jewish Historiography." Ph.D. diss. Pennsylvania State University, 1975.

Solov'ev, Sergei M. *Istoriia Rossii s drevneishikh vremen.* 15 vols. Moscow, 1959–1966.

Sombart, Werner. *The Jews and Modern Capitalism.* Glencoe, Ill., 1951.

Springer, Arnold. "Enlightened Despotism and Jewish Reform: Prussia, Austria, and Russia." *California Slavic Studies* 11 (1980), 237–67.

———. "Gavriil Derzhavin's Jewish Reform Project of 1800." *CASS* 10 (Spring 1976): 1–24.

———. "The Public Career and Political Views of G. R. Derzhavin." Ph.D. diss. University of California at Los Angeles, 1971.

Stanislawski, Michael. *Tsar Nicholas I and the Jews: The Transformation of Jewish Society in Russia, 1825–1855.* Philadelphia, 1983.

Stanley, John. "The Politics of the Jewish Question in the Duchy of Warsaw, 1807–1813." *JSS* 44 (1982): 47–62.

Starr, Joshua. *The Jews in the Byzantine Empire, 641–1204.* New York, 1939.

Steinberg, Aaron, ed. *Simon Dubnow: The Man and His Work.* Paris, 1963.

Stillschweig, Kurt. "Jewish Assimilation as an Object of Legislation." *HJ* 8 (April 1946): 1–18.

———. "Nationalism and Autonomy among Eastern European Jewry." *HJ* 6 (April 1944): 28–68.

Stoklitskaia-Tereshkovich, V. "Pervyi ritual'nyi protsess v Rossii (1702 g.)." *ES* 10 (1918): 7–26.

Strakhovsky, Leonid I. "Constitutional Aspects of the Imperial Russian Government's Policy toward National Minorities." *JMH* 13 (December 1941): 467–92.

Szajkowski, Zosa. *Autonomy and Communal Jewish Debts during the French Revolution.* New York, 1959.

Tazbir, Janusz. "Die Reformation in Polen und das Judentum." *JGO* 31 (1983): 386–400.

Teimanas, David B. *L'autonomie des communautés Juives en Pologne aux XVIe et XVIIe siècles*. Paris, 1933.

Thackeray, Frank W. *Antecedents of Revolution: Alexander I and the Polish Kingdom*. Boulder, Colo., 1980.

Thaden, Edward C. *Russia's Western Borderlands, 1710–1870*. Princeton, 1984.

Tikhonravov, N.S. "Slovo o vere khristiianskoi i zhidovoskoi." *Letopisi russkoi literatury i drevnosti* 3 (Moscow, 1861): 66–77.

Torke, Hans J. "Continuity and Change in the Relations between Bureaucracy and Society in Russia, 1613–1861." *CASS* 5 (Winter 1971): 457–76.

Tractenberg, Joshua. *The Devil and the Jews*. London, 1943.

Trotskii, L. "Evrei v kievskoi gubernii v 1802 g." *ES* 13 (1930): 131–34.

Trunk, Isaiah. "The Council of the Province of White Russia." *YIVO Annual of Jewish Social Science* 11 (1956–1957): 188–210.

Tsinberg, S. L. *Istoriia evreiskoi pechati v Rossii*. Petrograd, 1915.

Tugan-Baranovsky, Mikhail I. *The Russian Factory in the 19th Century*. 3d Russ. ed. Translated by Arthur and Claora S. Levin. Homewood, Ill., 1970.

Universal Jewish Encyclopedia. 10 vols. New York, 1939–1943.

Vaisenberg, S. "Evrei v russkikh poslovitsakh." *ES* 8 (April–June 1915): 228–31.

———. "Evrei v velikorusskoi chastushke." *ES* 7 (January–March 1915): 119–20.

Varadinov, Nikolai N. *Istoriia Ministerstva Vnutrennikh Del*. 7 vols. St. Petersburg, 1858–1862.

Vernadsky, George. "The Heresy of the Judaizers and the Policies of Ivan III of Moscow." *Speculum* 8 (October 1933): 436–48.

———. *Kievan Russia*. New Haven, 1959.

Vishnitser, M. "Obshchii ocherk politicheskoi i sotsial'noi istorii Evreev v Pol'she i Litve." *Istoriia evreiskogo naroda*. Moscow, 1914.

———. "Proekty reformy evreiskogo byta v Gertsogstve Varshavskom i Tsarstve Pol'skim (po neizdannym materialam)." *Perezhitoe* 1 (1909): 164–222.

Vosstanie Dekabristov. (Materialy/Dokumenty po istorii vosstaniia Dekabristov.) 11 vols. Moscow, 1925–1958.

Walter, Hermann. *Moses Mendelssohn, Critic and Philosopher*. New York, 1930.

Wandycz, Piotr S. *The Lands of Partitioned Poland, 1795–1918*. Seattle, 1974.

Warner, Elizabeth A. *The Russian Folk Theatre*. The Hague and Paris, 1977.

Weinryb, Bernard D. (Weinryb, Sucher Berek). "The Beginnings of East-European Jewry in Legend and Historiography." In *Studies and Essays in Honor of Abraham A. Neuman*, 445–502. Leiden, 1962.

———. *The Jews of Poland*. Philadelphia, 1973.

———. *Neueste Wirtschaftgeschichte der Juden in Russland und Polen*. Breslau, 1934.

Weintraub, Wiktor. "Tolerance and Intolerance in Old Poland." *Canadian Slavonic Papers* 13 (1971): 21–44.

Wieczynski, Joseph L. "Archbishop Gennadius and the West: The Impact of Catholic Ideas upon the Church of Novgorod." *CASS* 6 (Fall 1972): 374–89.

Wischnitzer, Mark. *A History of Jewish Crafts and Guilds*. New York, 1965.

Wortman, Richard S. *The Development of a Russian Legal Consciousness*. Chicago and London, 1976.

Yaney, George L. *The Systematization of Russian Government*. Urbana, Chicago, and London, 1973.

Zacek, Judith Cohen. "The Russian Bible Society and the Russian Orthodox Church." *Church History* 35 (December 1966): 411–37.

"Zhid idet." *Novoe vremia*, no. 1,461. 23 March 1880.

Zlotnikov, M. F. "Ot manufaktury k fabrike." *Voprosy istorii* 11–12 (1946): 31–48.

Index

M

De Madariaga, Isabel, xvii
Magdeburg Law, 118
Magistrat, 72
Magnates, 11, 13
Mahler, Raphael, 43, 56
Maimonides, Moses, 49
Maria Theresa (Empress of Austria), 42
Markevich, Giler, 209n.45
Marriage, Jewish customs of, 93, 179
Maskilim, 51, 203n.47
Masonic lodges, 186
Massalski (Bishop of Wilno), 16
Matricula, 198n.4
Me'asef (Collector; journal), 51
Mel'gunov, A. P., 37
Mendel Lefin of Satanów, 205n.19
Mendelssohn, Moses: in Berlin, 20, 42; disciples of, 176; influence of, 92, 99; works, 49–51
Merchantry, 37, 67
Meshchane, 57, 67
Mestechko. See Shtetl
Military colonies, 165
Military service: in Austria, 42, 201n.81; Derzhavin's attitudes to, 112; exemption of Jews from, 80, 183; in Grand Duchy of Warsaw, 178; in Kingdom of Poland, 178–79, 201n.81; and Russian Jews, 79
Mills, woollen, 157; Jewish role in, 159–61
Mines, 155
Ministry of Internal Affairs, 157; *Journal* of, 177
Ministry of Finance, 152
Ministry of Public Education, 123; *Journal* of, 177
Ministry of Religious Affairs and Public Education, 167
Minsk province: agricultural settlement in, 138, 154; and double tax, 79; elections in, 118; Jews in, 85–87; marshals of nobility and Jews in, 85–87; organization of, 152; resettlement of Jews from, 78
Minute Book (of Minsk kahal), 124
Mirzas, 198n.4
Mitnaggedim, 17, 51, 65, 142
Mitzvot, 51

Kozlovskii, P. G., 202n.10
Kraków, 7, 10, 26, 190n.7
Kremenchug, 158–60
Krestsenie, 168
Kuptsy. See Merchantry
Kurakin, A. B., 87, 157, 158
Kurbskii, Andrei, 195n.34
Kurlandia province, 82, 84, 205n.84

L

Lament of the Daughter of Judea (Nevakhovich), 125
Landowners, 207n.11
Landsassen, 198n.4
Leaseholding: in Belorussia, 86; Derzhavin's attitude toward, 102; restrictions on, 146, 169; and Statute of 1804, 146
Legislative Commission of 1767, 55, 202n.17
A Letter Concerning Toleration (John Locke), 38
Letters of a Russian Traveler (N. M. Karamzin), 185
Levitats, Isaac, xvii
Literacy, of Jews, 136
Lithuania, 19, 183; alcohol trade in, 180; attitudes toward Jews in, 9; elections in, 136; Hasidism in, 17; Jews in, 24; legal system in, 118; municipal government in, 151; privileges of Poles in, 135; search for Judaizers in, 27; settlement of Jews in, 138; taxation in, 153. *See also* Grand Duchy of Warsaw; Kingdom of Poland; Poland (post-partition state); and Polish-Lithuanian Commonwealth
Lithuania province, 88–90, 118, 203n.22
Lithuanian Statute, 151
Livonia, 53–55, 198n.4
Livonian War, 25
Lobanov-Rostovskii, Ia. I., 160
Locke, John, 38
London Society for Promoting Christianity among the Jews, 165–66
Lopukhin, P. V., 121, 149
Łuck, 13
Lumière, 38, 40, 115
Lur'e, Ia. S., 194–95n.28
Lwów, 10